BAKUNIN

Other books by Anthony Masters

A POCKETFUL OF RYE

THE SEA HORSE

A LITERARY LION

CONQUERING HEROES

THE SYNDICATE

THE NATURAL HISTORY OF THE VAMPIRE

THE SUMMER THAT BLED: THE BIOGRAPHY OF

HANNAH SENESH

As Richard Tate:

THE DONOR

THE DEAD TRAVEL FAST

THE EMPEROR ON ICE

BIRDS OF A BLOODIED FEATHER

BAKUNIN

THE FATHER OF ANARCHISM

Anthony Masters

Saturday Review Press/E. P. Dutton & Co., Inc.
New York 1974

ISBN: 0-8415-0295-1
Library of Congress Catalog Number: 74-7892

To Michael Sissons,
who inspired this new study of Bakunin

The people, the poor class, which without doubt constitutes the greatest part of humanity; the class whose rights have already been recognized in theory but which is nevertheless still despised for its birth, for its ties with poverty and ignorance, as well as indeed with actual slavery – this class, which constitutes the true people, is everywhere assuming a threatening attitude and is beginning to count the ranks of its enemy, far weaker in numbers than itself, and to demand the actualization of the right already conceded to it by everyone . . . Even in Russia, the boundless snow-covered kingdom so little known, and which perhaps also has a great future in store, even in Russia dark clouds are gathering, heralding storms . . . Let us therefore trust the eternal Spirit which destroys and annihilates only because it is the unfathomable and eternal source of all life. The passion for destruction is a creative passion, too!

Michael Bakunin, 'The Reaction in Germany'
(*Bakunin on Anarchy*, tr. Dolgoff, pp. 56–7)

Acknowledgements

First, I should like to thank my friend Sam Dolgoff for his continuous encouragement, for providing me with new material, for allowing me to quote from his book *Bakunin On Anarchy*, for the use of further material and for checking my manuscript. However, I take full responsibility for the conclusions drawn in this book.

Thanks are also due to the following, who are listed alphabetically: Chimen Abramsky; the Archives Nationales, Paris; Paul Avrich; the Bodleian Library; the British Museum Department of Printed Books; Professor E. H. Carr; Centre International de Recherches Sur L'Anarchisme; Noam Chomsky; Stuart Christie; Christie and Moore; Professor Michael Confino; Freedom Press; Madame Violette Gaffiot; Nan Green; Daniel Guérin; Jim Huggon; International Institute for Social History, Amsterdam; Eve Johansson; Roderick Kedward; Professor E. Lampert; Jean Maitron; Michael Mansfield; Vladimir Muñoz; James Nash; K. Pearson, Cultural Attaché at the British Council, Paris; Jenny Quinn; Professor William O. Reichert; Raphael Samuels; Lyman Tower Sargent; Eugene Schulkind; Swiss Federal Archives; Philip Venning; Sam Wolf; Lillian Wolfe.

The author and publishers are grateful to the following for permission to quote from copyright material: George Allen & Unwin and Sam Dolgoff (*Bakunin On Anarchy* by Sam Dolgoff); Jonathan Cape (*The Paris Commune of 1871* by Eugene Schulkind); Chatto & Windus (*My Past and Thoughts* by Alexander Herzen); Lawrence & Wishart (*Documents of the First International*, Volume IV, 1870–1871; *Documents of the First International*, Volume V, 1871–1872; *Anarchism and Anarcho-Syndicalism*); Routledge & Kegan Paul (*Studies in Rebellion* by E. Lampert); Schocken Books (*In Russian and French Prisons* by Peter Kropotkin); Anthony Sheil Associates (*Anarchism* by George Woodcock); Dover Publications (*Memoirs of a Revolutionist* by Kropotkin); Macmillan (*Michael Bakunin* by E. H. Carr); Jim

Huggon of Freedom Press (*The Catechism of the Revolutionist Sergei Nechayev*); Monthly Review Press (*Anarchism* by Daniel Guérin); Oxford University Press (*Karl Marx* by Isaiah Berlin); Pelican Books (*Anarchism* by George Woodcock); Mrs Sonia Brownell Orwell and Secker & Warburg (*Homage to Catalonia* by George Orwell); and Allen & Unwin (*The Unmentionable Nechaev* by Michael Prawdin).

The quotations from Natalie Herzen's Diary and from Bakunin's letters to Nechaev appear in full in *Daughter of a Revolutionary: Natalie Herzen and the Bakunin-Nechaev Circle*. Alcove Press (U.K.), Library Press (U.S.).

Finally I should like to thank my wife Robina for her invaluable editorial help, and my assistant Julie Higgins for typing this manuscript in all its drafts.

Contents

Foreword

It is often claimed that Michael Bakunin is a dated figure whose life has a romantic and nostalgic appeal but whose revolutionary activities and writings are mainly irrelevant to the social and political problems of the modern world. In the 1920s, fifty years after Bakunin's death, there were few who would have quarrelled with this opinion. Today, almost a hundred years since Bakunin died, apparently by-passed by events, there is a growing respect for the tireless Russian revolutionary and a serious interest in his anarchist theories. This exciting biography by Anthony Masters is a product of this new interest and a substantial contribution to the reappraisal of Bakunin as a man of ideas as well as a man of action.

The author does not underestimate or deny the egocentric bravura of Bakunin's life; on the contrary, his portrait of an individual who was a kind of revolutionary prima donna is a colourful and vigorous one. But his careful treatment of Bakunin's developing insight into mid-nineteenth century Europe leading to a rejection of both traditional authority and the new authority of Karl Marx shows an intellectual quality in Bakunin which has too often been ignored. As a result the reader can well understand why Bakunin is treated with mounting respect, and still more can draw imaginative parallels between Bakunin and the revolutionary activists of the 1960s and 1970s, between the Europe of Bakunin's failed revolutions and the world of today.

Without wishing to overstate the similarities, for inevitably the differences are equally marked, I felt on finishing the book that there are three major ways in which we are closer to Bakunin than we were fifty years ago. In the first place, Bakunin's incredible capacity for moving across Europe, from Russia to Paris, from Scandinavia to Italy, from urban centre to rural commune, and from industrialized economies to backward agricultural societies makes his Europe appear like a microcosm of the wider world of the mid-twentieth century. His concern to create a practice and theory of revolution to embrace all these disparate situations and to apply with equal force to both town and country, shows all the tenacious optimism of those on the contemporary political left who encompass the United States and South East Asia, France and South America, the universities of the West and the Bantustans of South Africa in one revolutionary ideal. In particular, Bakunin's driving determination to liberate the people of backward nations has a significance today which was less apparent in the decades when Marxism concentrated revolutionary hopes and theories on the proletariat of industrialized Europe.

Secondly, the aspect of Bakunin best known to critics and followers alike is his belief that the revolution would be made by all the disinherited, underprivileged and victimized elements of society, regardless of class. He attacked the Marxist notion of class as being exclusive: 'Class, power, state,' he wrote, 'are three terms of which each presupposes the two others and which are to be summed up by the words: *the political subjection and the economic exploitation of the masses.*' This attitude can perhaps be explained by his own aristocratic origins and by his unselfconscious friendship for other aristocratic rebels, bourgeois intellectuals, artisans, workers and peasants without distinction of origin or precise economic function. In his own words he was classless or *déclassé*, and it is just this that recommends itself to many young radicals and socialists today who feel uneasy but not disqualified by their middle-class origins and who claim, like Bakunin, that backward peasants, dissident students, exploited workers and the victims of any social or political system, can form a fraternity of protest to override the divisions of class. For these middle-class rebels Bakunin is more attuned to the ambiguities of their position than the more astringent followers of Marx.

Thirdly, the very failure of Bakunin and his revolutionary movement gave him a kind of ideological purity, the most vaunted possession of those who find themselves always in opposition, of those who are, in a sense, natural opponents of any kind of power structure. Throughout his life Bakunin was an ingrained opponent, as Anthony Masters documents in great detail. He was a rebel within his family, within Russia, within Europe and within international socialism, and he placed great emphasis in his writings on the purity of his libertarian position. It is the core of his anarchist theory. 'Freedom can only be created by freedom' were the words he used in his conflict with Marx whose intellect he had much admired but whose methods he regarded as authoritarian and therefore only capable of producing an authoritarian regime after the revolution.

For all his elaborate scheming and flamboyant self-projection Bakunin never posed as an infallible authority. He deeply distrusted the *savants*, the specialists in any field, though he was far from opposed to the acquisition of knowledge or the process of reason. He saw the *savant* as a man crowned by an academic laureate and immobilized in his thinking by status and success. With authority comes sluggishness and a loss of spontaneity, a loss, he wrote, of 'that troublesome and savage energy characteristic of the greatest geniuses, ever called to destroy old tottering worlds and lay the foundations of new'. In terms of knowledge and behaviour this implies an incessant questioning of things established, and in terms of politics it suggests unmitigated opposition, even within the process of revolution itself. The paradox of an impressive and militant thinker who believes he is right yet who believes that others will and should contradict him is the paradox of anarchism and, arguably, its major contribution to modern revolutionary practice.

In the contemporary world where protest and opposition have developed a life-style of their own this paradox is located in the notion of an 'alternative society', which both attempts to undermine orthodox society and yet also lives alongside it in permanent opposition. There is a kind of resolution here to the anguish of failure felt by Bakunin: to be a successful revolutionary one does not have to destroy the system which exists, one can create an alternative one outside it. Undoubtedly Bakunin would find this attitude too passive, but the purity of opposition which it enshrines, its hostility to the specialist, the academician, the ranks of authority and to the established values of whatever society, gives it an affinity to the code of intellectual and political behaviour which Bakunin identified with freedom.

Spontaneity, creativity, freedom, the people, instinctive rebellion, the values of rural life, individual violence and destruction – these are some of the concepts which seem to make Bakunin a loose and abstract thinker compared with Marx, and allow him to be easily listed as utopian and idealistic. They are also the concepts by which he is currently being re-established in a period when socialist traditions other than Marxism are being rediscovered and developed, when Third-World revolutionary situations have turned attention away from European communism, when ecological arguments are accentuating the appeal of rural life and when in many circles permissiveness is extended not just to alternative morality but to individual acts of violence to combat the organized violence of the state, whether capitalist, Marxist, liberal or conservative.

All this suggests that Anthony Masters is here presenting a figure of persuasive relevance to certain trends in modern society. But even more so the author is scrupulously concerned to set Bakunin in his own context, and whatever we may think of the permanence or significance of his thought we cannot deny the dynamic effect which this relentless individual, with his weaknesses of jealousy, anti-semitism, pathological anti-Germanism and periods of great gullibility, had on his contemporaries. To this extent we can be sure that the Bakunin increasingly discussed in modern political debate is no mere cypher, but rather the outstanding individual who energized and provoked a closely interconnected society of émigré revolutionaries and sustained the scattered impulse of rebellion across nineteenth-century Europe. It is surely what Bakunin himself would have wanted.

August 1973

RODERICK KEDWARD
Lecturer in History
University of Sussex

PREFACE

by the Author

Anarchy is one of the most abused and most misunderstood words in common usage. It is immediately associated with the dark-caped villain, a bomb in one hand and a gun in the other, with assassination, chaos and unconstructive demolition of the entire fabric of society. Anarchy is a word used against erring children by blinkered parents, dissenting students by worried reactionaries, restless minority groups by guilty oppressors and rebellious social elements by devious politicians. It is a highly emotive word and when used by the Establishment is calculated to win support from those in ignorance of its proper meaning.

The original Greek word *anarchia* meant non-rule and therefore anarchism came to be defined as 'a political doctrine advocating the abolition of organized authority'.[1] Unfortunately this meaning is extremely broad and can have either positive or negative implications, for while its adherents would define anarchism as an anti-authoritarian and communal way of life its detractors would describe it as a state of wilful disorder.

The great scientific philosopher of anarchism, Peter Kropotkin, gave a definition that was generally speaking broad enough to cover the belief in all its varying forms. He said that it was

> the name given to a principle or theory of life and conduct under which society is conceived without government – harmony in such a society being obtained, not by submission to law, or by obedience to any authority, but by free agreements concluded between the various groups, territorial and professional, freely constituted for the sake of production and consumption, as also

xvii

for the satisfaction of the infinite variety of needs and aspirations of a civilized being.[2]

This then is anarchism, to which anarchy, the activity necessary to create such a utopian society, is a stepping-stone. The anarchist, the planner or performer of this activity, is therefore rather more philosophically and politically committed than the generalizers would make out.

David E. Apter, writing in *Anarchism Today*, rightly pointed out that 'the virtue of anarchism as a doctrine is that it employs a socialist critique of capitalism and a liberal critique of socialism',[3] and it is certainly one of the most idealistic, utopian and vulnerable of all social doctrines. The conditions for such a future society are love, companionship, federalism, non-competitiveness and total mutual tolerance – very close to the original conception of Christian society.

It is, and always would be, the ideal form of life, but it is possible that only somebody of Michael's optimism could ever truly believe that mankind was capable of bringing it about and, having brought it about, selfless enough to maintain it.

Philosophically anarchism is thousands of years old. Ovid, in the first book of *Metamorphoses*,

> writes about the golden age which was without law and in which, with no one to use compulsion, everyone of his own will kept faith and did the right. There was no fear of punishment, no legal sanctions were engraved on bronze tablets, no mass of supplicants looked, full of fear, upon its avenger, but without judges everyone lived in security. The only difference between the vision of the Roman poet and that of modern philosophical anarchists is that he placed the golden age at the beginning of human history, whereas they put it at the end.[4]

During the sixteenth and seventeenth centuries some highly utopian anarchist works appeared, largely in France but also in England. However, it was during the late eighteenth century that writings on an anarchist theme became more practical, one of the most constructive being William Godwin's work of philosophical anarchism, *Enquiry Concerning Political Justice*, which was published in 1793. This was followed by one of the most controversial: Pierre-Joseph Proudhon's *What is Property?*, which was published in 1840. Both Godwin and Proudhon, however, represented the political aspirations of the radical bourgeoisie which by the French Revolution of 1789 had in fact broken the circle of power originally wielded by the aristocracy and the crown. Unfortunately the bourgeoisie soon became the *haute* bourgeoisie by marrying into aristocratic circles and left the masses, unprivileged and unsupported, to fend for themselves. As a result the moderates concentrated on lobbying for parliamentary reform, the radicals turned towards Paine and chartism and the super-radicals turned towards anarchism.

Because of mutual revolutionary aims anarchism and socialism became linked in nineteenth-century Europe, but as the advantages of capitalism increased anarchism became more and more the theoretical exercise of a very small group of intellectuals. A catalyst was required – somebody of stature, of vitality and of action – and it was this function that Michael Bakunin filled so admirably.

As a person Bakunin was full of contradictions. Alexander Herzen described him as 'born not under an ordinary star but a comet' whilst another contemporary, less flatteringly, described him as 'a great and rudderless ship'. His fragmentary writings, his illogical thought-process, his deviousness, his naivety, his domination, his magnetic personality and his incurable optimism were reflected in his life-style which was one of feverish intensity. Unfulfilled, lonely and cut off from the Russian homeland he loved so dearly, Bakunin channelled all his energies into the pursuit of global liberty. This crusade earned him immense loyalty, immense distrust and immense dislike.

Unlike Marx, Michael was an activist and as such he threw himself wholeheartedly into the revolutionary movement. This type of work brought out the best in him, demonstrating qualities of courage and tenacity that were far more admirable than the fantasy and ambiguity which characterized his long periods of political scheming.

Michael expressed the profound belief that the ideal revolutionary must be a man with nothing to lose and accordingly he diverted his recruitment of revolutionary material from the petty bourgeoisie to the workers, the *déclassé* and Marx's much despised *Lumpenproletariat*. As a result he turned theoretical anarchism into practical anarchism, and can certainly be termed the father of anarchism as we know it today. Bakunin was concerned, above all, with the immediate practical problems of social revolution and he never attempted to describe an anarchist Utopia. It was left to James Guillaume, one of Bakunin's followers, to supply an approximation of what this might have been like. Extracts from this essay are reproduced towards the end of this book, on pages 256–60.

In fact Michael Bakunin's doctrine is if anything more relevant to our time than it was to his own and some of his opinions have a

curiously contemporary ring. 'There will be a qualitative transformation, a new living, life-giving revolution, a new heaven and a
new earth, a young and mighty world,' he wrote. Later he said,
'Let us therefore trust the eternal spirit which destroys and annihilates only because it is the unfathomable and eternal source of all
life.' In a world that is increasingly re-examining Marxism,
Bakuninism is resurgent. There are the same *déclassé* elements as
there were in his time – probably there are more – and the qualities
of another Bakunin have been long awaited.

Without doubt, anarchism is a goal for the unselfish and for the
genuine humanist, yet its ideology is so demanding that it is
doubtful whether sophisticated and politically contaminated mankind could possibly achieve, let alone maintain, such an ideal state.

ANTHONY MASTERS

PROLOGUE

The Homecoming

The family caught the first glimpse of him as the sleigh, a black and heaving mass, came dimly into sight amidst the snow-laden woodlands. Beyond these the Osuga could just be discerned, flowing sluggishly, a band of molten silver, threading its way through the undulating countryside that surrounded Premukhino. From the sleigh Michael Bakunin, his feelings numbed and insubstantial, gradually saw the familiar eighteenth-century shape of the long, one-storey Italianate house appear. Premukhino – the spiritual focus of so many dreams. Dreams in prison, dreams in loneliness, dreams in suffering. Now, seventeen years after he had left, he was home again. And yet he felt nothing. He was, at last, penetrating the dream, and as in all dreams he was undecided whether he was a shadow amongst substance or the house and its occupants were the shadows against his substance. Slowly his mind filled with sharpening recollection: recollection that had grown stylized over the years, memories that had been over-preserved, over-recalled and eventually exploded. But now, as he neared the portico and as the sleigh glided over the packed snow as if it were ice, he caught a fleeting glimpse of the garden at Premukhino early on a spring morning, dusted by cobwebs, glistening with dew. He smelt the heavy scent of cherry blossom at night and hazily saw his sister Lyubov bury her pet sparrow while the German tutor intoned an epitaph over the tiny grave. Faintly he heard again the familiar evening music-making of a family that he had now ceased to believe in as tangible beings. But they *were* real, real strangers as they stood in the portico waiting silently for Michael to greet them, wondering what kind of human wreckage was returning to them.

Suddenly, as the sleigh drew towards the door, a new and miserable reality gripped him, for this was not the grand return he had dreamt of – it was not the reuniting of a hero with a wondering and awe-struck family. Instead he was returning as a broken and prideless failure. How could he face them? How could he face any one of them? The numbing blanket crept further over his mind while the pallid memories of childhood mocked him. He looked towards the guard sitting next to him and thought of begging him to turn the sleigh round and to continue on towards Siberia. But as he turned to the guard, light from Premukhino flooded Michael's pale features and he found himself staring abstractedly at his family. They stared back in bewilderment at the old man in the sleigh. Was this Michael? This toothless, prematurely aged wreck? His mother, Tatyana, Paul and Alexis, despite the visits they had made to him in prison, were still shocked by the contrast between the Michael that had left Premukhino and Russia seventeen years ago and what now returned; the horror of the others, Varvara, Alexandra, Nicholas, Ilya and Alexander, who had not seen him during those long years, was even more pitifully apparent.

As Michael greeted them and walked into the Spartan hallway he might have remembered the yearning homesickness contained in the letter that he had written to Premukhino fifteen years ago.

Do you remember how once, late on an autumn evening, we imagined pictures in the hedgerow between Lopatino and Mytnits wood?

Michael walked through the bare rooms, past the familiar and beloved objects of the past that were now the same irrelevant ghosts as himself. The grandfather clock, the portrait of Catherine the Great, the tapestry-covered chairs. The Bakunin family followed silently, with nothing to say. Silently, with the alien being that had once been their brother.

Do you remember how a flock of cranes flew over? Now I am in the country to which the cranes fly from you.

And now the twenty-four hours of Michael's farewell began to drag by. He looked upon them with lethargy and indifference. He ate his meals silently, and made little response to the tentative questions about his past imprisonment and impending Siberian exile.

What has happened to my trees in the little wood? We lighted a fire there one spring, in Holy Week. Lyubov was ill then and near to death, and she came in a carriage to join us . . . Then I went away.

And now, briefly, he was back. Sitting in silence, playing draughts with his old nurse, while around him the others uneasily gathered, hoping that somehow the fire and vitality would return and once again the old dominating, forceful and rebellious Michael would emerge. But nothing happened, and he continued to sit in morose abstraction until next morning it was time for his guard to take him away. The Bakunins gathered at the front door of Premukhino to watch Michael's vast bulk settle in the sleigh. Still his apathy covered him like a shroud and as his family's bewilderment increased the sleigh began to move over the snow. They watched it disappear into the woods and down towards the Osuga. It was as if the ghost of Michael Bakunin had paid a brief visit home, and for years afterwards none of them could ever link the silence of their blank-eyed visitor with the dominating ebullience of a Michael that belonged totally to the past and now, as far as Premukhino was concerned, was dead.

PART ONE

Premukhino: 1814–40

I

The Premukhino estate was bought by Michael Bakunin's grand-father, Michael Vasilevich Bakunin, in 1779. Approximately five hundred male serfs were employed on the estate and its new owner was an undistinguished aristocrat who had attained the position of State Counsellor at the Court of Catherine II. Apolitical, unintellectual Michael Vasilevich Bakunin had only one claim to being colourful: he was a huge man with a filthy temper. This temper earned him a legendary reputation amongst future generations of the Bakunin family. Michael Bakunin had five daughters and three sons. The youngest of these sons, Alexander, was a delicate, intellectual child – a complete contrast to his robust, rather uninteresting father. Alexander spent most of his childhood and adolescence in Italy, which was considered to be better for his health than Russia. There he attended the University of Padua, from which he graduated as a Doctor of Philosophy. Having gained his degree, Alexander then travelled in a Europe where liberal ideas were prevalent. In fact the French Revolution was imminent and indeed it was rumoured that Alexander witnessed the storming of the Bastille. After a short period in the Russian Legations in Tunis and Florence, he returned to Russia at the age of thirty to manage the family estate. He brought with him to Premukhino a whiff of European liberalism.

Shortly after his return Michael Vasilevich died and it was now Alexander's responsibility to care for his widowed mother and his three remaining unmarried sisters. These three sisters were fanatically religious and created about them an atmosphere of somewhat hysterical piety. This heady religious romanticism seemed to act as an emotional charge to the next generation and somehow give Premukhino a permanent aura of passion and intensity.

For the next ten years Alexander devoted himself to the estate. He was a tolerant, gentle and kindly overlord, and in this he was considerably different from the mainstream of Russian landowners. He was not a reformer, however, and was content to live in a safe and conventional world, of which Premukhino was the core and indeed his all-consuming interest.

In 1810 the pastoral existence of Alexander Bakunin was shattered: at the age of forty he fell in love with a girl of eighteen. Varvara Muraviev belonged to one of the oldest and most distinguished families in Russia. Her widowed mother had married a man named Poltoratsky who owned a nearby estate and in this way Alexander met Varvara and fell instantly and blindingly in love with her. Varvara, despite the age-gap, idolized Alexander to such an extent that she became the model of a perfect wife – and the epitome of a bad mother. Whilst Alexander dented his liberalism by leaning towards Varvara's reactionary immaturity, Varvara lost her youth and its attendant elasticity by leaning towards Alexander's maturity. As a result they both became too engrossed by their own relationship, and as far as Varvara was concerned it meant that she had little time for her children's needs or sensibilities.

Years later Michael Bakunin wrote of Varvara as 'a vain and egotistical woman'. He added that none of her children loved her and later still, just before he died, he blamed his own need for ultimate destruction on Varvara, whose 'despotic character inspired him with an insensate hatred of every restriction on liberty'. Certainly Michael's apathy towards women throughout his life might partially be blamed on the unloving Varvara, but there is also his deep and passionate relationship with his sisters to take into account. Varvara's main faults appeared to be her indiscriminate agreement with her husband's highly conventional principles and the fact that she could find no room in her heart for anyone except him. However, it is quite possible that Michael was looking not only for an excuse for his sexual inadequacy but also for a justification for some of his more openly condemned political mistakes.

The first few weeks of their marriage were spent at the minuscule but fashionable court of the Grand-Duchess Catherine, who had the unimpeachable social position of being the Tsar's sister. Later, however, Alexander brought his young bride back to Premukhino, which had now been vacated by his mother and sisters, who had been forced to find a new sanctuary for their devotions. Almost at once the dutiful Varvara settled down to the task of giving the middle-aged Alexander what he had been deprived of for so many years – children. Over the next fifteen years Varvara produced eleven children: Lyubov, Varvara, Michael, Tatyana, Alexandra, Nicholas, Ilya, Paul, Alexander, Alexis, and a daughter who died at the age of two. Varvara had a breathing-space between Alexandra and Nicholas, which meant that the family was divided into two sets of five. Michael was the only boy in the elder of the two sets, and as a result he commanded a superbly dominating position – as the only boy amongst a set of girls and as the elder brother to a set of younger brothers.

The atmosphere of Michael's childhood was divided into two phases of parental influence: the phase that existed before the Decembrist Uprising, and the one that followed it, when Alexander abandoned his European liberalism and hurriedly became extremely pro-Tsarist.

Until 1825, the year of the Decembrist Uprising, when Michael was eleven years old, Alexander Bakunin's enlightened education made him a very different figure from the average unrefined Russian landowner, most of whom were brutish and self-indulgent, and this liberal outlook was at its height during the birth and childhood of his first five children. It had always been locally rumoured that Alexander Bakunin had been sympathetic to the European revolutions he had witnessed, but Napoleon's invasion of Russia in 1812 stirred within him such strong nationalistic feelings that any idea of revolution against the Tsar filled him with horror. Basically Alexander Bakunin's sympathies were with the advanced circles of humane and philosophical aristocratic thought that had been engendered by Catherine II, but he was a cautious man and despite the fact that between 1815 and 1825 he was a member of an esoteric organization called the Secret Society of North Russia, time after time he declined its presidency. At this time he was a sharp contrast to his baby son, to whom secret societies and their domination were to be so dear. In short, Deism was basically the limit of Alexander Bakunin's philosophy, although he was much drawn to the European Age of Reason and its attendant Rights of Man – despite the fact that as a result he should have taken positive steps to liberate the serfs on the Bakunin estate. To be fair, Alexander Bakunin gave theoretical opportunities of freedom to his serfs, but never actually master-minded such a major social revolution. Somehow he managed to justify the retention of this feudal system and in a long autobiographical poem named after the river Osuga he reacts strongly against the radicals he met in Europe, becomes eulogistic over the pastoral delights of

Premukhino and compromises over the uneasy subject of serfdom by guilty references to the landowner being a paternalistic figure, stating that master and servant are two entirely different and quite unmergeable breeds. Sheltered by the delights of Premukhino, Alexander Bakunin found that his liberalism could be effectively blinkered and that certain uneasy questions of realism could go unanswered, at least until Michael became adolescent.

However, Alexander Bakunin's refinement and love of culture were to find expression in the upbringing and education of his children. Michael's younger brother Paul later wrote that 'we were born and grew up in Russia but under a clear Italian sky'. Amid the loving pastorality of Premukhino Michael grew up in this uniquely European atmosphere and thus acquired early the habit of extensive reading and analytical discussion that was to play such an important part in his life. Alexander taught his children history, natural science and geography, and Michael learnt to play the violin while his sisters played the piano. Religious instruction was divided between Alexander, who read them the gospels and explained the ceremony and ritual of the Church, and a visiting priest who paid lip-service to feudalistic religion. Recreations included musical evenings, the reading aloud of classics, rather sedate walks and discussions – in fact all the elements of what Alexander Bakunin termed a 'European education'. But this education was abruptly terminated by the Decembrist Uprising; the second phase of influence in Michael's childhood had begun.

The uprising took place in Petersburg, three weeks after Alexander I died, and was swiftly and firmly crushed. The revolt was led by officers of the Guards – officers who belonged to the aristocracy – and aimed at establishing a constitutional monarchy or even a republic. Count Rostopchin, who had led the defence of Moscow against Napoleon, said that it was possible to 'understand the French citizen with his revolution for the acquisition of rights, but what idea can a Russian nobleman have in starting a revolution in order to lose his privileges?' Nevertheless the Decembrists typified the growing reaction of the intelligentsia against the old-style barbaric feudalism and, as Professor Lampert says in his *Studies in Rebellion*,[1]

This paradox became, in fact, a constant feature of the Russian revolutionary mind throughout the first half of the nineteenth century, when the squirearchical structure reached such a state of moral degeneracy that the mere fact of possessing a certain moral and social conscience dissociated them from their own class, which had become immune against moral problems and disquietude.

4

There were two Decembrist societies, one in northern and the other in southern Russia. The first, which encompassed both Moscow and Petersburg, mainly involved representatives of the army and of the civil service and was dominated, much to the embarrassment of Alexander Bakunin, by the Muravievs, his wife's family. Here the emphasis was on the involvement of the aristocracy and political discussion. The second group, centred at Kiev and containing officials from central Russia, was more revolutionary and certainly more democratic. For instance, Pestel, Colonel of the General Staff, did not think it was sufficient simply to liberate the serfs; they should also be regarded as owners of the land on which they had worked. Moreover he envisaged the demolition of Russian tsardom and its replacement by a federal republic on the lines of the United States of America. Also, unlike their northern 'colleagues', the southern Decembrists were not opposed to the much-discussed and highly controversial issue of Polish independence. In 1820 Pestel and two high-ranking fellow revolutionists were publicly hanged in Petersburg as a result of their radicalism.

The Decembrists were highly disciplined idealists and their courage was of an ennobled and select kind. They were not in fact true revolutionaries, as they had too much to lose and they considered their own actions too carefully and too politically. The prime importance of their movement lies in the social and political disillusion that was left amongst the intellectuals after their overthrow. It seemed that darkness had once more descended on Russia and the new Tsar, Nicholas I, did little to dispel this. He was obsessively bureaucratic, strengthened the position of the aristocracy and, despite his own doubts, fought vigorously against the growing need for emancipation. Alexander Herzen compared the new Tsar's attitude to 'the inflexible firmness that is to be found in cashiers, bailiffs, post-office clerks and sellers of theatre-tickets', whilst the despair of the intelligentsia is summarized in the diary of the liberal Nikitenko:

At first we craved frantically for light. But when we realized that it was no joking matter, that we were expected to hold our tongues and remain inert, that our talents and brains were condemned to petrify or putrefy at the bottom of the heart, which was to become their prison, that every fresh thought proved a crime against the social order; when, in short, we were told that educated men in our society were outlaws, that it can receive into its bosom only soulless compliance, and that military discipline is considered the sole principle on the basis of which action is permitted – then, suddenly, the whole young generation felt out of gear. All its lofty feelings, all the ideas which fired its imagination and inspired it to truth and goodness turned into dreams without practical significance: and for clever people to dream is ridiculous.[2]

But despite Nikitenko's views disillusion did not affect the intelligentsia so much as, say, the European despair following the failure of the French Revolution. Instead there was an atmosphere of questioning puzzlement which led to a vague interest in philosophy. The intelligentsia became highly academic in their social guilt, tsardom flourished and regimented convention advanced.

As a result of the Decembrist conspiracy Alexander Bakunin dropped the 'European' flavour of the household and much of its attendant liberalism. Instead he became determined to force his children into total submission to tsardom and for this reason he determined that Michael should go to the Artillery Cadet School.

When he left Premukhino Michael Bakunin was fourteen and a half, socially extremely naive, and with no experience of the outside world. He parted from Premukhino with bitter regret, for it was as if his entire spiritual life had been terminated. There was an extraordinarily intense relationship between Michael and his four sisters and a deep inner life burnt between the five of them. The girls, particularly Lyubov and Varvara, seemed to have inherited something of their aunts' passion, but this time the intensity was not turned towards religion but more towards the emotions. These were explored obsessively and as the five children were fairly isolated they were constantly absorbed in each other's feelings. Lyubov and Varvara in particular were vividly romantic and Michael followed suit. This romanticism extended into a passionate desire for adventure (which joining the Artillery School definitely was not) and he would listen for hours to his father recounting his European travels. In his early teens Michael was unaware that beloved Premukhino harboured the great social injustice of serfdom, but his later realization of this did not for one moment diminish his love for Premukhino and those memories of childhood years. These he was to cherish and often desperately recall: Premukhino was to become necessary therapy to Michael Bakunin.

II

Nineteenth-century Petersburg was the joint seat of culture and bureaucracy. The city was a conglomerate of many classes and varying degrees of wealth. Its atmosphere was tense and, compared to Moscow, cold-hearted and impersonal. Michael found it exceptionally unsympathetic. Desperately homesick for Premukhino, he lived unwillingly at the home of Aunt and Uncle Nilov (Alexander Bakunin's sister and her husband), a childless couple with an over-developed sense of discipline. In desperation Michael threw himself into hard work, passed the necessary exams and, in the autumn of 1829, entered the Artillery School.

This came as a rude shock to Michael and at first he experienced even more misery than in the months of loneliness in the dour Nilov household. Michael had never mixed with boys of his own age and was therefore bewildered to find that the position of authority that he had had over his four sisters was now totally annulled. He was a mere cipher, and was no longer able to have his every command satisfactorily obeyed. Physically Michael Bakunin was well-built, yet his strength was not outstanding and he found himself shy, isolated, and repelled by the male hurly-burly of the school. In fact so naive was Michael at this stage that he genuinely believed he had stepped into a truly demonic den of vice instead of a very average adolescent institution in which homosexuality, vulgarity, bullying and gambling all ran parallel to youthful high spirits and passive resentment towards military discipline. Money, always to be an alien system of barter to Michael and something of which he had had no experience at Premukhino, was inevitably a problem and he soon found that he was living well outside his income. So he borrowed and continued to borrow until he had run up some sizeable debts.

Alexander had sent Michael to the Artillery School to train for a life of service to the Tsar, but ironically many of the more radical students, far from idolizing the Tsar, worshipped the memory of the martyred Decembrists, many of whom had belonged to the Artillery School and the First Cadet Corps. This worship was highly clandestine and had many of the accoutrements of contemporary martyr-worship in any despotic state. Poems, reputedly written by the martyrs at their most traumatic hour, were handed round and cherished religiously, as were both anecdotes and artifacts. Those revolutionaries who had suffered death on the gallows were the most honoured, while those who had merely been exiled were much pitied for this unwanted evasion of the true martyr's death.

At first sight Michael considered the Decembrists to be enemies of Russia, plotters against the tsardom that he regarded as affectionately as Premukhino, as his family and as Russia itself. Sourly,

7

in his first year at Artillery School, Michael wrote home, pointing out how the school had shown him 'the black, foul, low side of life' and how because of this he had become used to lying 'because a clever lie is not counted among our cadets as a vice, but is unanimously approved'. He went on to add even more sourly that 'there reigns among the students a cold indifference to everything noble, great or holy'. This uncharacteristically priggish statement must have horrified Michael in later years, but in fact it was a genuine defence of the Tsar, whom at that time he undoubtedly saw as an avuncular and compassionate figure. Certainly, at this stage, there was nothing remotely radical about Michael's solidly conservative views.

For the next three years Michael Bakunin drifted in the mainstream of the Artillery School, distinguishing himself neither academically nor militarily. Gradually his naivety and unworldliness were painfully rubbed away, whilst his romantic and passionate nature longed for a quest that might fulfil a so far completely uncharted destiny. Yet the 'apartness' of his upbringing at Premukhino helped him considerably once he had got over the initial shock of the rough and tumble of Artillery School. He soon found himself able to stand somewhat aloof from the rigid aura of military discipline and find an essence of personal freedom within himself. At eighteen he passed his final examinations with some dexterity (considering that he rarely worked for an exam until the last moment) and in January 1833 he became an ensign.

This new rank gave him more freedom and more spare time than he had ever had before and he was also allowed to live outside the school, providing he regularly attended courses there. He at once moved back to the austere Nilovs (presumably because he could find nowhere cheaper to live), broke off relations with his fellow officers whom he found crude and banal, and immediately plunged into an idealistic and romantic love affair with a distant cousin – a girl named Marie Voyekov who was a year or so younger than himself. The affair was a direct result of the former privations of the Artillery School, his new-found comparative freedom and a desperate need for admiring company. He was even beginning to feel a creeping admiration for the Decembrists, largely based on his resentment of the autocratic discipline imposed by the school. Michael had no desire to indulge his physical passions with Marie, merely his spiritual passions. The friendship lasted a few heady months, during which Michael and Marie would discuss the meaning of love (carefully avoiding its physical overtones) and a number of other esoteric subjects. He would read aloud to her (while Marie, of course, sewed),

8

and they went to concerts and parties together. Marie later recorded that while attending a concert that included Beethoven's Ninth Symphony (Beethoven was Michael's favourite composer) she had been petrified by the expression on Michael's face. He looked, she said, as if he were 'ready to destroy the whole world'. Despite his rejection of the respectable religious values that were consistently drummed into his head by the Nilovs, Michael chose to attend Marie's First Communion, where he melodramatically went into a fervour of prayer on behalf of her and her family. All this was an excellent release for him after the discipline of the last three years, but it was a self-indulgence that was soon to be broken, for Marie Voyekov was swiftly taken away to the country by her aunt before her personality could be improperly inflamed by Michael's romanticism.

After Marie's departure Michael became inordinately restless and his need for rebellion increased. He soon found a ready target in the authoritarian figure of Aunt Nilov, who affronted his dignity by treating him in the same disciplined manner at eighteen as she had when he first entered her house at fifteen. She had already been nagging him about his intense relationship with Marie and had attempted to put an embargo on the affair by insisting that Michael did not leave the house without her permission. This he naturally refused point-blank to do. Notwithstanding this Aunt Nilov went on to criticize him for the vast array of debts he had run up in the last three years. As far as Michael was concerned this was the very last straw and he immediately withdrew from the Nilov household, stalking out in outraged dignity, at the same time uncomfortably aware that he had nowhere to go. Providence, however, came to his aid in the shape of the summer training camp, to which he went for the first time ever with some enthusiasm. He considered that honour was satisfied (Aunt Nilov had been a worthy opponent), swiftly forgot about Marie and settled down to commune with nature. At the camp, enjoying as he always had the countryside and open air, which so much reminded him of Premukhino, Michael had time to think, and the mood of sudden rebellion that had followed the misery of the years at Artillery School slipped away. Conservatism returned along with a need for reconciliation and a return to Premukhino, which he also saw as a means of repaying his now pressing creditors. His sentimental worship of Russia intensified and in one of his letters home, criticizing the French Revolution, he wrote, 'The Russians are not French. They love their country and adore their monarch. To them his will is law. One could not find a single Russian who could not sacrifice all his interests for the

9

welfare of the sovereign and the prosperity of the fatherhood.'[3]

III

Burning with patriotism, Michael returned to Premukhino on leave after an absence of almost five years. He received an ecstatic welcome from his father, sisters and brothers, and the usual pale dutiful affection from his mother. From Michael's point of view the sheer joy of returning to Premukhino and its all-embracing nostalgia was impossible to put into words. It was as enticing as he remembered it and so, in general, were his family. The reunion was perfection in every possible way, and just to make it even more perfect Alexander quickly paid off Michael's debts.

As Michael drank in the sweet freedom of Premukhino the grey conformity of Nicholas's reign was hardening. Bureaucracy was all, and through this the gentry gradually became more secure and more powerful. Admittedly some steps were taken in 'stabilizing the obligations of serf-owners towards their peasants',[4] but it gradually became clear that the aristocracy had total power over approximately twenty-three million human beings who were in the position of mere slaves. 'Orthodoxy, Autocracy, Nationality' became the official bywords, and disobedience of this dreary formula was looked on as something akin to heresy. The Church became the bulwark of conservatism and taught that man should stay in the situation in which birth and circumstance had placed him. Agitation was condemned and indeed the confessional was often used as a means of detecting this. However, this colourless and oppressive autocracy was not exceptional. After the French Revolution, much of Western Europe, with the exception of Great Britain, had come under despotic regimes – particularly those countries under the control of Austria. Liberalism was extinct and bureaucracy was gradually strangling the working classes.

Coincidentally, as the strands of bureaucracy tightened, Michael's libertarian instincts overrode his conservatism – at least on the home front. The disappearance of Marie had done nothing to quench the ardour of Michael's romanticism and at Premukhino he now extolled love as the ultimate perfection, the ultimate truth and the goal to which everyone should strive. Love was on a pedestal – it was unimpeachable and it was sacred. At the same time his recent victory over Aunt Nilov had greatly increased his self-confidence and his refusal to suffer personal oppression was considerably strengthened. Aunt Nilov had been a glorious conquest after the years of oppression at the Artillery School.

Almost immediately after Michael had arrived home at Premukhino he discovered an ideal opportunity to renew his campaign for the furtherance of spiritual love – and at the same time to rebel against the deadening orthodoxy of the older generation. The opportunity was Lyubov, his eldest sister, and her engagement to a wealthy cavalry officer named Baron Renne. Michael discovered that Lyubov had consented to the engagement because of pressure put upon her by Alexander, who considered the match to be eminently suitable, the only drawback being that Lyubov had not the slightest affection for her fiancé. But what particularly enraged the evangelizing Michael was that despite the fact that she did not love the Baron, Lyubov showed every sign of humbly obeying her father and going through with the marriage. Immediately Michael rushed into a determined campaign to force Lyubov to defy Alexander and to end her engagement to the Baron. The result was a major family rift in which the unfortunate Lyubov was torn both ways. Michael whipped up his sisters and younger brothers into a fever of rebellion against the stunned and enraged Alexander and Varvara. In fact he stage-managed the confrontation with tremendous panache, lobbying, negotiating and rampaging in great political style.

Alexander was considerably upset, both at the shattering of his carefully laid plans and at the mutiny of his children. He felt aggrieved too that Michael, having had his debts so discreetly paid, should bite so savagely the hand that fed him. After all he had reasoned that Lyubov would be making the most sensible, and surely the happiest, decision in marrying Baron Renne. Renne was a kind and honourable man, had no unpleasant vices and would give Lyubov the sort of background and security that she had become used to at Premukhino. Alexander loved his daughter dearly and was quite unable to accept or even to understand Michael's definition of romantic love. It reminded him too much of those cosmopolitan values that he had held in the pre-Decembrist days, and now within the current framework of conservatism and orthodoxy such feelings were quite unthinkable. However, one fact that Alexander Bakunin *had* overlooked was that his own marriage had been a love match, but now he was an old man and his memory was conveniently cloudy over such introspective issues.

The row continued, and rose to a level previously unknown in the normally placid Bakunin household. At the height of it Michael's leave ended and he was forced to return to Petersburg. However, the distance between Petersburg and Premukhino did not deter him in the least and he continued to bombard his father with letters, in repeated attempts to weaken his resolve, and also his sister, to strengthen her pallid and halting disobedience. Miraculously Michael even managed to enlist Aunt Nilov's support; under some extraordinary hypnotic spell she wrote to Alexander condemning him for trying to marry off Lyubov to a man she did not love. Winning over Aunt Nilov was an incredible feat indeed and was one of the first examples of the power of Michael's intense personal magnetism. Then suddenly it was all over; Alexander capitulated and Renne, no doubt sourly cursing Michael's sudden startling influence, left the district. Alexander, assailed on all sides and now aged sixty-five, had been defeated by his eldest son – a fact that bewildered and concerned him, for he loved all his children dearly. Michael was also surprised by his victory. First Aunt Nilov and then his father had capitulated, after being denounced for their reactionary emotional views. Michael had won, in the name of humanism, and above all freedom. Moreover, by this act of domestic rebellion he had given an early demonstration of the instinct for active revolution that was to dominate his future. Yet because of the rift life at Premukhino was never quite the same again. Authority had been challenged and vanquished and as a result an entirely different relationship had developed between Michael and his parents. They regarded him with bewilderment, as a dutiful fledgling who had somehow returned home an aggressive turkey-cock, whilst Michael regarded them, still with love, but also with the patronage of the conqueror. He had, rather to his own surprise, usurped parental authority, and having done this was now beginning to have the instinctive, if not the intellectual, confidence to question authority at other and higher levels.

IV

With the new and dangerous gift of inflated self-confidence Michael returned to the Artillery School, completely uninterested in his potential military career. He was out for romance and the pursuit of sacred, spiritual love and had no time for soldiery. Very soon he had further ingratiated himself with Aunt Nilov, who was by now unable to fight against her liking for her rebellious nephew, and shortly after that he scored a similar success with Nicholas Muraviev, one of his mother's relatives. In the autumn of 1833 he was a regular

caller at the Muraviev estate and became very friendly with three of Muraviev's daughters, all of whom were at a marriageable age.

The distinguished Muravievs, many of whom had played such a large part in the Decembrist Uprising, were an exciting and stimulating family. For some months Michael saw the Muraviev girls frequently and their intellectual and spiritual attainments soon overshadowed those of his first platonic girl-friend, Marie Voyekov. But, as was always to be the case, Michael's sexual interest was not aroused and his relationship with the Muraviev sisters was once again strictly spiritual.

Unfortunately Michael spent so much time with the Muraviev family that he was soon in trouble with the Artillery School, who found him considerably wanting in both progress and attention. This and his insubordination to a general resulted in his not only being dismissed from the school but, worse still, being sent to a brigade stationed on a remote part of the Polish frontier.

Unable to face his father's grief at his dismissal, Michael took a procrastinating course and repeatedly delayed writing home to Alexander about his disgrace. Because of this Alexander learnt of it through Nicholas Muraviev and from an item in the official gazette: far more galling sources of information than the pen of his own son.

Before going to Poland Michael paid a brief visit to Premukhino, a visit that considerably deflated his new-found arrogance. In the ensuing interview between father and son, Alexander, mindful no doubt of Michael's recent victory over him concerning Lyubov and her marital problems, was disinclined to show any mercy and it is certain that Michael was left in little doubt as to his fecklessness and general moral cowardice.

Morosely Michael departed for Poland, arriving in Molodechno in Minsk and eventually moving on to Vilna and then to Kartuz-Bereza in Grodno. Poland was at this time in a desperate state of misery. Three years before Michael's arrival the large-scale Polish insurrection had taken place and been ruthlessly crushed. But once again, despite his growing regard for the Decembrists, Michael was still conservative enough not to take the part of the rebels. He considered that the action taken against them was vitally necessary and not for one moment did any hint of his later sympathy for the persecution of Poland show through his current reactionary attitude.

As with the Artillery School students, Michael made no friends amongst his fellow officers, nor was he able to stand their company except when on duty. Off-duty life to these officers was a traditional recipe of cards, drink and women, congenial enough for the undemanding but regarded as a deadly bore by Michael. So he shut himself away, determined to evoke mental stimulation by a severe process of further education. Physics, Russian grammar, history and the Polish language dominated his self-imposed curriculum, to which was added the first threads of at least an awareness of German philosophy, given to him through a series of discussions with an army doctor acquaintance who was studying it. But unfortunately this ambitious programme was not enough and isolated study produced in Michael an unquenchable loneliness. He was desperate for company, but knew he was unable to find it within the intellectual limitations of the garrison. He needed soul-mates, debaters, fellow aspirants towards the self-improvement he was trying to attain. For Michael was not and never could be an academic – a scholar prepared to study alone. He wanted an exchange of ideas, the feeling of people around him; he wanted to argue, to laugh and to lovingly dominate some compatible fellow human beings. But he was not to find them in Poland and as his realization of this grew – and his academic world became more sterile and isolated – his loneliness increased until it became totally unbearable. His letters home to Premukhino reflected this, and in one he typically and rather melodramatically summed up his mental state.

> I am alone here, completely alone. Eternal silence, eternal sadness, eternal home-sickness are the companions of my solitude. ... Man is made for society. A circle of relatives and friends who understand him and share his joys and sorrows is indispensable to him. Voluntary solitude is almost identical with egoism, and can the egoist be happy?[5]

Meanwhile, at Premukhino, Varvara had married. Her husband was a dullish man named Nicholas Dyakov, a cavalry officer and landowner. It was not a love-match but a gentle and kindly acceptance of the inevitable. If Michael had not been isolated in Poland there is little doubt that he would have interfered and the marriage would not have had such a smooth beginning. As it was, Michael's jealous guardianship of his beloved sisters was temporarily checked and Nicholas Dyakov was able to become part of the Bakunin family.

Early in 1835 Michael returned to Premukhino – this time amidst a scandal that rendered Alexander almost numb with anger. He was ostensibly on military business in Tver but had travelled on to Premukhino. Whether or not his motive at this stage was desertion from the army it is difficult to say, but there is no doubt that Michael had instinctively returned home to find sanctuary. Once at

Premukhino he decided to feign illness, but was nearly arrested for desertion, and it was only Alexander's string-pulling that prevented a public disgrace. Eventually the military authorities allowed Michael Bakunin to leave the army on grounds of illness. It was a decision that pleased both parties.

V

For just under two months Michael thankfully relaxed at Premukhino, uncomfortably aware of the sardonic glances of his father. But the months of intellectual yearning in Poland were not an influence that was now dead. He was almost twenty-one and the even tenor of the pastoral life at Premukhino soon made him restless, despite its idyllic contrast to Poland. Varvara's marriage was a *fait accompli*, his parents thoroughly disapproved of him and the outside world was a tempting place, providing it had nothing to do with the army. So it was with both anticipation and excitement that Michael decided to go to Moscow, taking with him Lyubov and Tatyana.

Michael arrived in Moscow at a moment when Hegel, the German philosopher, had just died – an event which was to give added impetus to renewed study of his work amidst the philosophical circles in Moscow. The earliest circles, suppressed after the Decembrist Uprising, had been called the 'Wisdom Lovers', and had principally involved such distinguished personalities as Prince Vladimir Odoevsky, Dimitry Venevitinov (a cousin of Pushkin), and a large number of the older Slavophils and conservative publicists. These early circles tended to be highly emotional, metaphysically idealistic and nostalgic for a medieval past. Odoevsky, for instance, was one of the very first Russian writers to use such phrases as the 'decline of the West' and to write that Russia's mission was 'to save the soul of Europe'. This early thought was vague enough to adapt itself to the prevailing thought of the 1830s but the essence of its beliefs remained until Michael Bakunin's arrival in Moscow.

As much of Europe worked towards an age of science and materialism this Moscow school of Western European thought clung tenaciously to the romantic idea of attempting to reattain the medieval sense of corporate unity, 'an air of moral and artistic exultation and a taste for totality, for a universe of discourse, which is concerned with nothing less than the whole of knowledge, with the purpose and meaning of life, with God in the world and the world in God.'[6] Schiller, Goethe, Shakespeare and George Sand became the objects of the circles' infatuation, whilst German idealism and its philosophy as epitomized by Schelling, Fichte and later by Hegel were consistently enthused over by these desperately utopian Russians. But there was no other place in Russia where philosophical and intellectual liberalism could be practised and indeed Nicholas I was highly suspicious of the circles. He continuously harassed them and forced the universities to become seats of nationalistic, patriotic subservience. Original thought in Russia was almost completely stamped out, and it was only by the Moscow circles meeting secretly that utopian philosophical idealism, heavily influenced by German romanticism, continued. Moscow, it should be remembered, was the nucleus of surreptitious intellectual activity, whilst Petersburg represented the true Russia of Nicholas I – a city where bureaucracy was dominant and debauchery the only outlet from a grim morass of hypocritical conservatism.

The circles, which were always under surveillance by the Secret Police, recruited most of their more active members from the first- and second-year students of the University of Moscow, and they became dubbed 'the University of secret Hegelianism'. Alexander Herzen, on his return to Moscow from exile in 1840, five years after Michael's arrival, summed up the Hegelian influence on the circles as follows:

> They discussed these subjects incessantly; there was not a paragraph in the three parts of the *Logic*, in the two of the *Aesthetic*, the *Encyclopaedia*, and so on, which had not been the subject of desperate disputes for several nights together. People who loved each other avoided each other for weeks at a time because they disagreed about the definition of 'all-embracing spirit', or had taken as a personal insult an opinion on 'the absolute personality and its existence in itself'. Every insignificant pamphlet published in Berlin or other provincial or district towns of German philosophy was ordered and read to tatters and smudges, and the leaves fell out in a few days, if only there was a mention of Hegel in it. Just as Francœur in Paris wept with emotion when he heard that in Russia he was taken for a great mathematician and that all the younger generation made use of the same letters as he did when they solved equations of various powers, tears might have been shed by all those forgotten Werders, Marheinekes, Michelets, Ottos, Watkes, Schallers, Rosenkranzes, and even Arnold Ruge himself, whom Heine so wonderfully well dubbed 'the gate-keeper of Hegelian philosophy', if they had known what bloodshed, what declarations they were exciting in

16

Moscow between the Maroseyka and the Mokhovaya, how they were being read, and how they were being *bought* . . . Our young philosophers distorted not merely their phrases but their understanding; their attitude to life, to reality, became schoolboyish and literary; it was that learned conception of simple things at which Goethe mocks with such genius in the conversation of Mephistopheles with the student. Everything that in reality was direct, every simple feeling, was exalted into abstract categories and came back from them without a drop of living blood, a pale, algebraic shadow. In all this there was a *naïveté* of a sort, because it was all perfectly sincere. The man who went for a walk in Sokolniky went in order to give himself up to the pantheistic feeling of his unity with the cosmos; and if on the way he happened upon a drunken soldier, or a peasant woman who got into conversation with him, the philosopher did not simply talk to them, but defined the essential substance of the people in its immediate and fortuitous manifestation. The very tear that started to the eye was strictly referred to its proper classification, to *Gemüth* or 'the tragic in the heart'.[7]

There were two main circles: the circle of Herzen (founded before his exile) which was under a French political influence, and the circle of Nicholas Stankevich which was under a German philosophical influence. Stankevich was a year older than Michael and came from a similar aristocratic background. Although a weak personality, Stankevich was remarkable not just for being a leading member of the Moscow circles but for pioneering German metaphysics in Russia – and for being one of the first of the Russian romantics. Turgenev, the Russian novelist, later noted that Stankevich 'exerted such an influence over others because he was genuinely interested in every human being, and, without being conscious of it himself, carried him off into a sphere of the ideal'.[8]
Herzen added that,

Sickly in constitution and gentle in character, a poet and a dreamer, Stankevich was naturally bound to prefer contemplation and abstract thought to living and purely practical questions; his artistic idealism suited him; it was 'the crown of victory' on his pale, youthful brow that bore the imprint of death.[9]

Stankevich shared with Michael an ardour and craving for romantic, spiritual love but a fear of and a near-revulsion from its physical counterpart. For a time, Stankevich had found spiritual love and friendship in his relationship with Natalie Beyer, whose wealthy widowed mother owned an estate in Tver and was friendly with the Bakunins. But Natalie was unable to respond satisfactorily to the pressure of Stankevich's attempted spiritual communion; instead she became extremely sexually frustrated and relations, to say the least, became a little strained. But when Lyubov Bakunin had visited Moscow with her mother as Michael travelled lugubriously to Poland for the first time, Stankevich had immediately fallen in love with her. The mysterious and intense spirituality of the Bakunin sisters was particularly inherent in Lyubov, and Stankevich, detecting this, idolized her as a symbol of all he demanded in a woman. Unfortunately it was not in his nature to put thoughts of this kind into words. Lyubov and her mother returned home, and Stankevich continued his neurotic friendship with Natalie, who became more and more openly hysterical at Stankevich's lack of sensuality.

The emotional affairs of Stankevich, however, took a different turn on Michael's arrival in Moscow. Natalie Beyer, now obsessed by her failure to have a proper relationship with Stankevich, decided to become a martyr – which was obviously a considerably more interesting position than working to turn Stankevich's spirituality into sexuality and receiving only public sympathy for her efforts. On this basis Natalie Beyer decided against publicly abandoning her relationship with Stankevich, which would be extremely galling. Instead she resolved to re-match him with Lyubov Bakunin as soon as she arrived in Moscow with her brother. In accordance with her schemes Natalie told Stankevich how much Lyubov adored him and told Lyubov how much Stankevich adored her. Gradually she prepared for an ardent love affair, but Lyubov's return to Premukhino prevented it from coming to fruition. The seeds, however, had been sown and both Lyubov and Stankevich parted in a considerably unsettled state; the first merely uneasy, and the second wondering if at last his dreams might some day come true and the great spiritual romance, untarnished by physical crudity, be his.

Meanwhile Natalie had found that her manipulations had quite accidentally worked to her advantage, for during the sessions she spent with Lyubov assuring her of Stankevich's nobility and love she had met Lyubov Bakunin's fascinating brother Michael. Unfortunately Natalie was due for renewed and even more hopeless frustration, but at first she was hopeful, particularly when Michael's sisters returned to Premukhino and Michael stayed behind in Moscow for a week. During this week Natalie, her younger sister Alexandra and Michael formed an intense mutual admiration society. Michael needed admiring disciples and Natalie needed the hope of things to come. But almost immediately the dominating Natalie made a fatal mistake. Disloyally, but with an intention of gaining stronger sympathy, Michael had told Natalie that his sisters failed to understand him and treat him as a mature adult. Natalie somewhat foolishly took this typical ego-extension as reality and when Michael returned to Premukhino she sent a note with him that took issue with his sisters over their inability to see Michael as a man on the highest possible intellectual and spiritual plane. Their reaction was swift and positive. Tatyana, who was nearest Michael in age, looks and personality, and who was the closest of his family to him, sent a lashing letter to Natalie's sister Alexandra, succinctly encapsulating exactly what she thought of Natalie's condescending attitude to her and her sisters and of the false concepts she placed on Michael's personality.

It was at this point that Michael began to talk openly, if somewhat vaguely, of a sense of mission. He discussed it mainly with Natalie, who, unlike his sisters, had not formed a concrete impression of his personality. Because of this Michael felt able to aspire and to dream more unselfconsciously with her as a totally uncritical audience. But these plans, vague and only hinted at as they were, were in themselves a prevarication, for Michael used them as a barrier between himself and Natalie Beyer. Temporarily at least Natalie accepted these evasive tactics; Michael, she reasoned, would surely be unlikely to follow the romantic obsessions of Stankevich. He seemed more resolute, and certainly more virile. But Natalie was wrong.

Michael spent much of the summer of 1835 at Premukhino. During this period he indulged in deep introspection, and as a result his sense of mission began to grip him more strongly and he completely renounced any thought of sexual love. He wrote of this latter decision to both Natalie and Alexandra, but their reactions are not recorded. He offered them an egocentric and escapist explanation: 'I am a man of the times, and the hand of God has traced over my heart the holy words, which embrace my whole being: "He shall not live for himself." I intend to realize this fair future. I shall make myself worthy of it.'[10]

There is no doubt that Michael partly believed in these high-minded ideals, but there is equally no doubt that they were extremely convenient. They protected him from financial responsibility, from the horrors of getting a job and from the ever-pressing demands of women. In other words, Michael subconsciously forced himself on to an idealistic pedestal to avoid suffering from the conventional pressures of society, and in so doing launched himself into the far more intense suffering that was to be with him for the rest of his life. Dynamic personal energy formed an alternative outlet to sex, and the heady idealism of the Moscow circles, his first meetings with Stankevich and his friends and the intellectual excitement of German metaphysics gave him an increasing sense of ambivalent purpose – towards a misty futuristic goal that he assured himself was to be of international importance.

Musing at Premukhino, Michael extended the theme of his apologia to Natalie in the following letter to Efremov, a friend of Stankevich's, in whom he confided that 'our will is still undeveloped. It has not yet freed itself from the stifling swaddling clothes of our eighteenth century, the century of debauchery and charlatanism, of vulgarity and foolish pretensions to nobility, of scepticism in regard to everything lofty, and of petty fear of Hell . . .'[11] He went on to outline that man was at an unhappy transition stage between the eighteenth and nineteenth centuries where all was indecision and indifference to constructive thought. The solution was the development of the will: 'when we are able to say "ce que je veux, Dieu le veut", then we shall be happy, then our sufferings will cease. Until then we deserve them.'[12]

In October 1835 Michael was still at Premukhino. Alexander was playing a waiting game, confident that a few months of liberty would give Michael all the time he needed to work out his future. Tolerant, kindly Alexander had no intention of becoming a despotic disciplinarian in his handling of Michael, whom he obviously regarded as a healthy, if highly irritating, young reprobate. A reprobate who, however, would soon have to bow to respectability and conformity when confronted with the fact that if he was not going to serve the Tsar in the army then he must serve him in the civil service. But for the moment Alexander was prepared to stay his hand and, mindful of his own days spent in Europe, his former liberal outlook and his late marriage, was content to give his son one last summer's fling, watching with dry amusement Michael's absorption with ideology. The arrival of Stankevich and Efremov, however, in the same month, was considerably to dim Alexander's optimism over Michael's future.

Stankevich arrived amidst the pastoral bliss of Premukhino with high hopes of renewing his spiritual relationship with Lyubov. He would have to rely on fate to bring this about, for he was quite incapable of taking the initiative; but unfortunately fate was not to intervene and Lyubov and Stankevich merely longed for each other in their minds, going out of their way to prevent their feelings showing. But no such frustration existed over Stankevich's need to evangelize German philosophy to Michael, who was an extremely willing pupil. Stankevich, anxious to find a passion as strong as his hopeless yearning for Lyubov, decided to examine the philosophy of Kant, thus superseding his previous studies of the more simplistic Schelling. Both Michael and Stankevich spent much of the holiday trying to understand Kant while their romantic affairs faded into the background.

Stankevich soon had to return to Moscow but Michael remained at Premukhino, still immured in attempting to grasp the intricacies of Kant. But Alexander, once his son's friends had departed, viewed Michael's philosophical studies with increasing irritation. At first he contented himself with hints about entering the civil service, hints that Michael happily ignored. In fact the broader they became the harder he ignored them. Somehow the relationship between father and son survived the end of the year, but the tension grew until it came to a head at the annual family gathering at Tver to celebrate the New Year of 1836. There Michael apathetically met an old friend of the family, Count Tolstoy, who was Governor of Tver. But Michael's apathy turned to horror when Count Tolstoy, ignoring for Alexander's sake Michael's appalling military record, offered him a job in one of the Tver bureaucratic departments.

It was with feelings of great relief that Alexander received the offer. He was now seriously worried about Michael's future and felt the offer provided an excellent solution. Michael, however, viewed the position as something akin to a death sentence. Moscow, Natalie Beyer, Stankevich, Kant, discussion, good company, aspirations and dreams – none of this could possibly be forsaken for a respectable and totally boring job as a sinecured bureaucrat in Tver. But at this stage he did not have the courage openly to defy his father again. He loved him and he knew that he was growing feeble. On the other hand Michael was certainly not afraid of him. For some weeks he dithered, drank a good deal and toyed with the idea of staging a suicide attempt. But none of this was palatable and so he took what appeared to be the obvious, if the most cowardly, way out. Without even confiding in his beloved Tatyana, Michael packed his bags and ran away to Moscow.

Directly he arrived there he took up residence with Stankevich and wrote a carefully planned letter to Alexander saying that he would under no circumstances join the civil service. Instead he intended to study philosophy and scratch a living by teaching mathematics. Alexander, however, was unimpressed by Michael's continued idealism and decided that his liberal attitude to his son had had as little lasting value as his broader pre-Decembrist European liberalism. He wrote a furious letter to Michael, denouncing his philosophical views and reminding him of his responsibilities. The letter contained such phrases as 'True philosophy consists not in visionary theories and empty word-spinning, but in carrying out everyday obligations to family, society and country' and 'This dejection which weighs on you is the inevitable result of injured self-respect, of an idle life and of an uneasy conscience'. Alexander added that he had never been a despot, yet he had no intention of agreeing to Michael's current activities in Moscow. And he concluded emotionally with 'Reflect, come to your senses, and be, without reserve, a good and obedient son. Efface the past by your obedience, and rather believe your blind father than your blind – call it what you will. This is my last word.'[13]

But Michael had already determined to pay no heed to any pleadings from home and he made this clear in a letter to Varvara. Unwillingly, miserably, but with all the bravado he could muster, Michael turned his back on Premukhino and his parents. This dramatic gesture, however, was to be of short duration, for Michael's capacity to make his own living was, to say the least, extremely limited.

VI

Stankevich's philosophical progress was very much the reverse of the progress he made in his relations with Lyubov. By the time Michael arrived as a refugee from Premukhino he had already passed from Kant to Fichte. Michael, still prepared to play the role of keen disciple, followed suit and was soon eagerly translating a series of lectures by Fichte called 'On the Vocation of the Scholar' into Russian – a translation that eventually appeared in *The Telescope*, one of the leading intellectual journals of the day.

At this time Michael's only real soul-mates in Moscow were Stankevich and to a lesser extent Efremov. But he was soon to meet another important member of the Stankevich circle – Vissarion Belinsky. Some years later, Belinsky was described by Paul Annenkov in his *Reminiscences*:

I had been so impressed by the passionate tone of Belinsky's philosophical essays, and especially by his polemical ardour, that I naturally imagined him to be a person of extreme opinions, impatient of any views contrary to his own, always striving to lead and outshine others in conversation. I must confess, therefore, that I was rather surprised when at A. Komarov's party somebody pointed Belinsky out to me. I saw a short, stooping, flat-chested man, with large pensive eyes, who very unassumingly and simply, with a kind of spontaneous friendliness, returned the greetings of those who were introduced to him. There was certainly no sign of haughtiness or pose, no trace of the dictatorial manner I had feared; Belinsky betrayed, on the contrary, a certain shyness and timidity. . . . He was quiet and thoughtful, and, even more surprising to me, sad.[14]

Belinsky was indeed a sad figure, even at times a rather pathetic one, particularly in comparison with the blustering forcefulness which Michael had now developed as a shell around his all too vulnerable personality. Gone now was the timid boy of the Artillery School. A combination of freedom and homesickness had made him frantically self-confident in Moscow – a self-consciously pugnacious new boy in the intellectual rough-and-tumble of the new city school.

Belinsky, on the other hand, had not had the advantage of loving, if conventional, parents to rebel against. His parents were narrow, ignorant and, at times, violent. But somehow the years of brutal treatment at their hands brought about a dramatic intellectual emancipation in Belinsky although he was no conventional academic and quite unable to profit from the orthodox teaching at the University of Moscow. This factor, together with his writing a play that savagely attacked serfdom and the various rights of noble birth, earned him expulsion. Weeks later Belinsky was 'adopted' as something of a martyr by the Stankevich circle and through the circle's influence he joined the editorial staff of *The Telescope*. Belinsky was a charming, endearing personality who suffered from continuous ill-health and who had all the burning, frenetic energy of the consumptive. He was totally puritan in his anti-establishment views and Annenkov adds that he had an

inability to admit any bad faith, falsification, subterfuge in the world around him as in his own life, even when these things served to soothe wavering minds, and he felt an irresistible aversion from connivance with shallow and insincere judgments – even when they became apparent within his ranks.

Belinsky was attracted to Michael and indeed dominated by him, largely because of the latter's increasing personal magnetism. Indeed it was Michael's hectoring enthusiasm that first inspired Belinsky's feverish passion for Fichte. To Belinsky, who was intensely searching for the justification of man's presence on earth, the idealism of Fichte provided the necessary twin beliefs of moral progress and social freedom – a far more precise if less poetic philosophy than Schelling's, through which Belinsky, like most of the other members of Stankevich's circle, had progressed. Fichte for Belinsky, as for Michael, was an easy symbol of liberation, and provided a philosophical weapon for both men in their determination to establish control over their own fate and indeed to establish an independence of human destiny. 'Ideal life,' wrote Belinsky, 'is the only real, positive, concrete life, whereas so-called real life is negation, illusion, unmeaning and emptiness.' But unfortunately 'so-called real life' was soon to impinge heavily on Belinsky's 'ideal life'.

Michael, now enraptured by the free-thinking of his friends and the philosophy they all studied, had little interest in making a living – and little ability to do so anyway. He could of course borrow, which he was extremely good at doing, and for a while Stankevich and others were able to advance him a number of small loans on which he was able to exist for the first few months. He paid lip-service to financial independence by having a number of cards printed bearing the flamboyant inscription MONSIEUR DE BACOUNINE, MAÎTRE DE MATHÉMATIQUES, but for many months he was unable to obtain any pupils. Michael's attitude towards money was now beginning to set into an established pattern of borrowing, living and dining well – and borrowing again. He seemed to have no conception of the exact meaning of the word 'borrow'. Some basic confusion always existed, for by 'loan' Michael really meant 'gift' – a re-definition that his friends took some time in understanding. When they did finally realize that Michael never expected to pay a loan back, their reactions ranged from amused tolerance to cynicism and from cynicism to outrage.

One of the most attractive qualities in Michael's new-found self-confidence was enthusiasm, although his enthusiasm often bordered on propaganda. It had been immediately delightful to preach the gospel of Fichte to Belinsky and gain a convert, but it was even more delightful to preach the same gospel to a completely uncritical, unquestioning and always admiring audience in the shape of Natalie and Alexandra Beyer. Michael, who was now twenty-one, soon found the sisters a vital sounding-board to his own wrestling with Fichtean ideals and became even closer to the two girls, much to the frustration of Natalie. So close did he become, in fact, that he was able to use the same rebellious influence on the Beyers as he had on his own family when Alexandra was hotly pursued by a family-approved but unloved suitor. Alexandra, horrified by the yawning chasm in front of her, immediately took steps to enter a convent – a situation that was saved by Michael persuading his long-suffering but still devoted sister Varvara (who in fact had little sympathy for the Beyer girls after Natalie's ill-timed letter) to provide a temporary refuge for Alexandra in Tver.

The ruse was successful and much to her mother's fury Alexandra sought temporary sanctuary with the Bakunin girls, who were soon irritated and made jealous by her constant paeans of praise of Michael.

Meanwhile Natalie, in Moscow, received the full onslaught of Michael's Fichtean ideology. Staggering under the sterile weight of this lecturing, Natalie threw both strategy and subtlety to the winds and voiced her physical frustration. Uneasily Michael countered with some appropriately high-minded comments about the 'inner life' conquering physical passion. Natalie, however, had no intention of being crushed by these intellectual excuses and broke off all friendship with him, having finally realized that Michael's outwardly robust personality concealed the same shrinking from sensuality as Stankevich's had. Undeterred, Michael continued to see Natalie Beyer, until her mother, all too well aware of his destructive influence upon her daughter, bore Natalie off to the country – and, hopefully, more promising masculine horizons.

It is difficult to decide whether Michael's naive disappointment at the split should be taken at face value, or whether it was merely a cover for the hardening of such evasive tactics. It is true to say that he was subconsciously unable to face up to the fact that so far all the women in his life – Marie Voyekov, the Muraviev sisters, and now Natalie Beyer – had been impressionable in terms of intellect but were instinctive in terms of sex. Michael was attractive and virile to look at and there was every reason to suppose that he would give a good performance in bed, but he intellectually scorned and physically drew away from the entire process of sexual passion, telling even himself that the mind was higher than the body. Yet if Michael had had his own frustrations eased by sexual intercourse it is possible that he would not have had such an incredible amount of energy. He was always to be astonishingly mentally virile and energetic and there is little doubt that his sexual sterility was a contributory factor. He plunged himself into ideals, within his romantic boundaries of 1836, as many young men would have plunged themselves into sex.

With Natalie away, Stankevich inconveniently on holiday, and many of his other friends unavailable, Moscow suddenly became an area of disenchantment. Fichte was certainly stimulating in company because company meant explosive debate, but without it life was very grey. It was also May, the beginning of summer, and inevitably Michael's thoughts turned to Premukhino and the rural joys from which he had isolated himself. It suddenly occurred to him that it was at least four months since he had left home, and to Michael at this time four months were an eternity. Without giving it any further thought he packed his bags, borrowed the fare home and arrived at Premukhino as a familiar but hopeful prodigal son.

Alexander Bakunin's immediate reaction is not recorded but it is possible that a grim amusement may have overcome his disapproval of Michael's unpatriotic and, to his mind, highly unconstructive actions. All that can be said is that Michael spent the summer at Premukhino, recharging himself for the coming philosophical ardours of Moscow. The Bakunin sisters were delighted to see him and had fortunately forgotten the disruption caused by Natalie and Alexandra Beyer. Alexander, old and blinder than ever, did not have the energy to battle against his unsatisfactory son. He regarded Michael's present life-style with extreme disapproval and his future with the utmost horror, but he was surprisingly content to receive Michael at Premukhino once more, and even to welcome any of Michael's friends who decided to join him. In fact Michael had invited Belinsky to join the family party and it was his visit that was to heighten the emotional temperature once more. However, before Belinsky's arrival Michael spent many weeks preaching Fichtean idealism to his most receptive sisters. Certainly the role of brother was the one in which Michael felt most at home and with Tatyana in particular he had an incredibly intense rapport. In Tatyana Michael invested all his frustrated love and in Michael Tatyana invested all hers. They adored and worshipped each other, working themselves into a near-hysterical frenzy. Michael, aware of his negative physical feelings towards women, found in his love for Tatyana a built-in safety device. She was his sister – and because of this there could never be any hint of a sexual relationship between them. Secured by this protection, Michael felt himself able genuinely and romantically to love and enjoy perfect, if at times somewhat feverish, spiritual union between himself and a woman who could never make unwelcome demands on him. Tatyana, however, although similar to Michael in temperament, had two drawbacks that were to drain much of the colour from her life. She was completely unemancipated and lacked her brother's drive and initiative. In addition to this her chances of marriage, never very strong as she was not at all beautiful, were consistently ruined by Michael, who became intensely and selfishly jealous each time a man came near her. But although there is no doubt that Michael's relationship with Tatyana was far too close for Tatyana's future happiness, the intensity of love between brother and sister was an attitude typical of the romantic movement and therefore was not regarded as either extraordinary or eccentric.

The idyllic summer wore on, and the uneasy truce between father and son, the delights of Tatyana and the mental euphoria of Fichte calmed, refreshed and stimulated Michael. He was king-pin in his own family unit. There was no one to compete with him; there were no embarrassing money problems; and he was stimulated by the increasing sense of freedom and exploration that his reading was giving him. The 'inner' life became his most evangelized theme whilst the 'outer' life was dismissed as being convention-ridden, hypocritical and utterly superficial. The soul became all-important and Michael spent fervent hours in contemplation of his own. This, together with a broad diet of romantic reading, including Schiller and Goethe, made him both fantasize more, and at the same time live an enthusiastic but not particularly profound interior life.

Belinsky's arrival at Premukhino, however, effectively shattered Michael's sun-lit days of self-indulgence. Belinsky came nervously, all too well aware of his poor background, trembling at the thought of breathing the refined air that the aristocratic Bakunins breathed in Premukhino. Conscious of the social horrors of coming from the looked-down-upon professional classes and wondering how he would cope with the mysteries of Michael's much fabled esoteric sisters, Belinsky wallowed in his own inadequacy. He wanted to be liked but feared that he would be despised. Perhaps it was partly due to this desperate need to conform that Belinsky soon joined in the Fichtean euphoria that Michael was spreading about Premukhino like an anxious but dominating mother hen. There was, in fact, a stronger reason for Belinsky's immediate attraction to Fichte. It soon became firmly lodged in his mind that Fichte provided a substantial basis and rationale for both the freedom and the moral ambition of mankind. He was also considerably more logical and down-to-earth than Schelling. Even more important, Fichte seemed a necessary catalyst to Belinsky's ever-pressing search for the 'justification of man'. He felt liberated and took hold of Fichte almost as if it were a weapon – a weapon that man could use to control his own fate. This mind-over-mystery Fichtean approach was only to last the year, but nevertheless the studies that Michael and Belinsky made that summer of 1836 at Premukhino were to bring the two young men very close together.

Fichtean theory was based upon the premise that man creates the world from the depths of his mind. As Lampert puts it,

> Life becomes a dream in which man creates the objects that come before him, and when he ceases to dream the world ceases to be . . . The mind retraces its steps over the road it had travelled towards abstraction until it regains the world of phenomena, and subsequently declares the phenomenal world to be a necessary condition for its activity.[15]

But, Lampert goes on,

> That idealism, pursued to its ultimate consequence, should end by denying the world seemed to philosophers and laymen alike to be carrying the joke too far. People grew rather merry over the Fichtean Ego which produced by its mere thinking the whole external world. It is not surprising, therefore, that his philosophy has always had to endure much from satire. Some asked with understandable annoyance if the Ego of Johann Gottlieb Fichte implied a negation of all other existences? Fichte's lady friends are said to have enquired anxiously whether he does not at least believe in the existence of his wife: and if not, whether Frau Fichte puts up with this?[16]

But Belinsky, like Michael, was not in the least abrasive over Fichte. And indeed he wrote, from Premukhino, a eulogistic analysis of the Fichtean doctrine for *The Telescope*. He went into some detail on the ideology of self-development and ended the article on a futuristic note.

> In the distance, beyond the hills, appears the horizon of the evening sky, radiant and aglow with the beams of the setting sun, and the soul dreams that in the solemn stillness it is now contemplating the mystery of eternity, that it sees a new earth and a new heaven.

The shy, gauche and subservient Belinsky by degrees became extremely happy during the high summer at Premukhino. He was enthralled and committed to Fichte, he was grateful to Michael for introducing the philosophy to him, and he loved the pastoral beauty of the Bakunin estates. The fact that the estates were entirely worked by serfs he found hard to ignore, but as he was considerably in awe of the Bakunins he made no comment. Michael, for his part, still easily ignoring the plight of the serfs, further indulged himself by patronizing his intelligent and stimulating pupil, playing the part of mentor with relish.

But then in September 1836 things began to go badly wrong and the idyll was shattered. Naively, and with a complete absence of tact, Belinsky hotly defended the French Revolution (the event that gave rise to Alexander Bakunin's former liberalism), implied that many other celebrated heads had yet to roll and was later seen by Alexander to be reading his *Telescope* article on Fichte to Lyubov and Tatyana. Alexander was furious at this all-encompassing display of radicalism and, instead of aiming his fury at Belinsky, angrily harangued a highly indignant Michael. Belinsky was not to stop at political and philosophical disruption; he also made the mistake of falling in un-reciprocated love with Alexandra, at the same time guilelessly succeeding in capturing the attention of Tatyana. Quite by accident the sincere, humble and naive Belinsky had not only excited the fury of Alexander Bakunin but had also considerably enraged Michael. For Belinsky had done the unforgiveable: he had poached on Michael's own very special territory. He had unconsciously dared to arouse Tatyana's intellectual interest and as a result Michael was bitterly jealous. The image of the friendly patron, the self-indulgent mentor, was gone, for Michael had replaced his affection for Belinsky with intense hatred. Immediately, and with considerable panache, Michael went out of his way to make the sensitive Belinsky's life at Premukhino a living hell. He teased him, snubbed him and embarrassed him at every opportunity in front of his entire family, and particularly in front of Tatyana.

The golden spell of sun and study and joyful philosophical debate was over and in its place was bitterness, unrest and misery. Yet Michael's sadism seemed equally matched by Belinsky's masochism: neither would give ground. Belinsky remained, albeit miserably, at Premukhino, while Michael made no really decisive move to evict him from the house, away from his purely intellectual relationship with Tatyana and back to Moscow. Belinsky's relationship with Alexandra also had unfortunate echoes of Stankevich's pallid relationship with Lyubov – and indeed Michael's relationships with all women – but Belinsky's attitude was infinitely purer and far more unconscious than Stankevich's evasive tactics or Michael's manipulative defence-mechanism. In the belief of the romantic movement of the times to which Belinsky subscribed, a woman was on a pedestal – and womanhood itself was a bastion of the ethereal and of the sublime. Women were creatures of mystery with whom near-sacred friendships were struck.

With open warfare against Belinsky still being maintained, but now in a state of deadlock, Michael restlessly turned his attention to the affairs of the other members of his family. Now that the idyll had collapsed he was anxious for a rebellious cause to stimulate his mind. At the moment Michael confined his attentions to the family and his immediate friends, so he was pleased to find that several opportunities presented themselves. The first was the large-scale spreading of revolution amongst his younger brothers; the second was the more small-scale disruption of Varvara's now failing marriage. In the first insurrection Michael played a revolutionary followed by a surprisingly censorious role. In the second he was to be a permanent influence. All in all Michael thoroughly enjoyed every moment of plotting, planning and dramatic denouement.

As I have already made clear, Michael, born the only boy in a group of four sisters and before his five brothers, was in an extremely influential position. He had already succeeded in dominating the lives of his sisters, and now, as the elder brother, he was about to seize the opportunity of dominating his brothers. Nicholas, the eldest, was at the Artillery Cadet School in Petersburg, Ilya was attached to a cavalry regiment as a cadet and Paul, Alexander and Alexis were at school in Tver, living in a flat supervised by Grandmother Poltoratsky – an old lady who was as dominating as her eldest grandson. In August, just before Belinsky's arrival at Premukhino, Michael had returned to Tver with his three youngest brothers at the end of their school holidays. Naturally he converted them to the 'inner' meditation of Fichte, taking a fortnight or so in Tver to do so. Later, Alexander, at fifteen, was to write home to his sisters, talking of their indoctrination by their hitherto only vaguely-known elder brother. 'The more we get to know Michael, the more we feel how indispensable he is to us. He has raised us high above our former state, and we have for the first time enjoyed a happiness unknown to us before . . . Now we truly understand the great vocation of man . . .'17

The great vocation of man, however, had no place in the uniformity of school life in Tver and with Michael's return to Premukhino all three boys felt an appalling sense of loss and an unbearable restlessness, so powerful was their brother's personality. Michael had sown the seeds of unrest particularly successfully. But he had not finished with them yet. At half-term in October, Paul, Alexander and Alexis returned to Premukhino, looking forward to a renewed course of Michael's Fichtean evangelism. But Michael, to their great joy, went even further by asking Alexander if the boys could leave school and accompany him back to Moscow in the autumn where he would become their self-styled philosophical tutor. Alexander's reaction was predictable. The very thought of his three so far untainted (or so he believed) younger sons going to live in Moscow with their reprobate elder brother was an impossible proposition. Already Michael's friend Belinsky had been openly preaching revolution within the hallowed portals of Premukhino, and now Michael was suggesting that his three babes were to be contaminated by philosophy and radicalism. The thought was unbearable. On the contrary, Alexander stated firmly that Paul, Alexander and Alexis must grow up as loyal servants of the Tsar, and that meant them pursuing their present line of study.

The boys returned to school before Alexander's decision was known to them but, unable to bear the tension any longer, they hired a coach and told the driver to head swiftly for Premukhino. This act of rebellion was forestalled by a combination of a suspicious coachman, a dominating grandmother and general inefficiency of planning. But the attempt itself caused a vehement family upheaval. The blame of course was considered by all adult members of the family to lie squarely on Michael. Alexander told Varvara's husband Dyakov to go immediately to Tver and lecture his sons, giving them all a thrashing if needs be, the elder Bakunin children remonstrated with their father at his fascist means of putting down the mutiny (especially by introducing an outsider like Dyakov) and Michael wrote his three youngest brothers a stern letter. This accused them of general lack of discipline and of taking action that their years did not qualify them for. Tatyana also took the three strongly to task, pointing out brusquely that they had caused serious trouble for their elder brother. No doubt the tone of Michael's letter was mainly caused by this, for he was beginning to realize that if he ever wanted to persuade his father to give him an allowance when he returned to Moscow, he was certainly not going the right way about it. The Tver revolt was finally crushed by the intelligent intervention of Dyakov, who invited the boys back to his own estates for a short holiday rather than attempting to punish them.

But it was not just Michael's incitement of the younger Bakunins – or his introduction of the outspoken Belinsky to the family circle – that rendered his father so desperately angry. There was a third and final piece of revolutionary encouragement that Michael gave in the already incident-packed summer of 1836, and this was once more contained within the family circle. This time it concerned Varvara and her relationship with the colourless Dyakov. When Michael first arrived at Premukhino at the beginning of the summer he found Varvara already firmly in residence. Her marriage to Dyakov, who was considerably older than her, had always been somewhat inexplicable. Perhaps it had been her strong sense of religious discipline or religious sacrifice that had forced her to maintain the unfortunate match. Whatever the reason, she was most unhappy; in fact she was so miserable that after the birth of her first baby in November 1835 she made the excuse to the humble and undemanding Dyakov that she needed her mother at this time of domestic crisis and set off for the protective confines of Premukhino. She was still there the following summer and once he had discovered how deeply miserable Varvara was as a married woman, Michael immediately set out to persuade her to remain at Premukhino and never to return to Dyakov. A combination of her own misery and her admiration for Michael resolved her to accept the advice, whilst Michael saw the entire Varvara situation as unemancipated – typical factors of a society that had not as yet universally accepted Fichtean philosophy. Michael's influence over Varvara, however, was only to last as long as he was at Premukhino; some months after his return to Moscow she wrote to Dyakov begging his forgiveness and inviting him to Premukhino.

And so the tumultuous summer at Premukhino passed – a summer that had begun swamped in high-mindedness and Fichtean ideology and had ended in small-mindedness and jealousy. Michael's continuous interference in his family's motivation and his bullying domination of their minds were symptomatic of the state of insecurity and flux in his own. He had incurred Belinsky's fear and his father's wrath, and there was only one relationship that he could look at with love and with approval and that was the passionate love of Lyubov for Stankevich – and the evasive love of Stankevich for Lyubov. As yet the relationship was undeveloped, but to Michael its possibilities were not only a warm spot in a cold world but a relationship fully worthy of the approval of Johann Gottlieb Fichte.

At the beginning of November, however, Belinsky, who had already suffered much at the hands of Michael that summer, was now to have his suffering – and indeed his means of livelihood – further impinged upon by the State. Publication of *The Telescope* was suddenly and forcibly terminated. The journal had become too liberal and too outspoken for the censor and its life was at an end. Belinsky immediately returned to Moscow to view the disaster at closer hand. A few days later Michael, smarting under the verbal chastisement of his father and with his Fichtean ideology battered and bruised by the family traumas, followed him.

VII

The last few weeks of 1836 and the first few months of 1837 in Moscow were very much the reverse of the previous winter's idyll. Michael, Stankevich and Belinsky were all in moods of considerable dejection. Michael was suddenly aware of a gradual and then quickening loss of faith in Fichtean ideology. It was not working for him and his former enthusiasm turned to irritable disillusion. Both his interior and his exterior life seemed empty and were still somehow utterly superficial. At the same time the cold wind of conscience struck him, mixing uneasily with his new philosophical scepticism. He saw himself as vain, arrogant and pretentious. He looked back on the domination of his family with disgust and his jealous bullying of the defenceless Belinsky with self-loathing. In retrospect the whole of last summer seemed an unintellectual and immoral sham and Michael sank into an abyss of dejection. His friends felt little better. Stankevich was trying unsuccessfully to quell an uneasy conscience over his evasive affair with Lyubov, whilst Belinsky's sense of inferiority and inadequacy – redoubled as a result of his Premukhino experiences – were not improved by the fact that a major source of revenue had disappeared with the closure of *The Telescope*, for he did not find living off the charity of friends as easy as Michael did.

But Michael was too active and too hopeful a person to sink into a slough of despond for long, although it was Stankevich, always the intellectual catalyst to the group, who provided Michael's next springboard in the shape of the German philosopher Hegel. Berdyaev considered that Hegel had the same importance for Russian thought as Plato had for the patristics and Aristotle had for scholasticism. Stankevich, on making the transfer from Fichte to Hegel, made the remark that he had 'no desire to live in the world until [he] found happiness in Hegel', and, strange as it may now seem, Hegel caused more debate and comment than any philosopher since the Middle Ages. Despite the many attacks that both Schelling and Fichte made on Hegel there are some similarities between all three philosophers. All, for instance, believed in a metaphysical teaching which stated that the universe was a unity in which was contained all historical and naturalistic occurrences. They also believed that this unity produced the Absolute, or ultimate reality, and that this Absolute appears in the shape of experience in the human mind. Hegel, however, differed from Schelling and Fichte in adopting a dialectical method. He claimed that his theory of method was not only a theory of logic but also one of reality. This was based upon the premise that the difference between knowledge and its object and, as a result, between logic and metaphysics is unreal. Hegel went on to state that this method, as well as implying a description of reality, also 'helped to constitute that which it described, so that reality itself was seen by him as behaving according to this method'.[18]

In Hegel's view man continually forges his way through the creation, and the overcoming, of opposition – so that inevitably the mind is always driven forward by conflict towards a horizon of greater truth and experience. Every historical process is a dialectical process demanding both realization and movement. Life is no longer static and, Lampert states, 'Without Hegel there would have been no Darwin, for it is Hegel who stopped at no logical usage or fastidiousness, who ventured to teach that the conceptions of kinds develop out of one another'.[19] But Hegel differed from Darwin's evolutionary theory in that he did not believe that change was merely a development due to environmental changes but rather that it was a dialectical movement of the spirit that resulted from inner conflict. In this way Hegel could be interpreted in a revolutionary sense, with the state of 'becoming', or destructive creation, taking precedence over the state of 'being', or stability and permanence.

Michael was instantly and obsessively converted from Fichte to Hegel and immediately wrote to his sisters, briefing them as to his change in direction. He also exactly defined where he had gone wrong in his philosophical past and once this definition had been somewhat conveniently made there was every excuse for his old mood of elation, intolerance and optimism to return. Michael discovered that, according to Hegelian philosophy, man developed in three specific phases or periods: the instinct period, the feeling period and the thought period. He decided that his recent Fichtean period was the Hegelian 'feeling' period and although his inner soul was now at rest the greatest danger that faced him was a form of simplistic complacency. It was therefore necessary to have his inner self assaulted by outside controversy, by outside influence and by continuous and progressive thought. Above all it was German Hegelian thought that was essential.

In the late autumn of 1836, as Michael was on the threshold of Stankevich's revelation of Hegel, Lyubov appeared in Moscow and Stankevich took the unprecedented step of arranging to correspond with her secretly. He also agreed to see his own father in the new year and afterwards make a formal declaration about his feelings towards Lyubov. Michael, of course, saw fit to organize the sending of the correspondence between Lyubov and Stankevich and read, and even warmly commented on, the letters before passing them on. Michael approved of the sentiments which Stankevich expressed and, despite the suspicion of his other sisters concerning the validity of Stankevich's intentions, hotly defended the friend whom he so much admired.

In April 1837, as Michael grew more and more committed to Hegel, Stankevich, much to everyone's relief, officially, if rather abstractedly, proposed marriage to Lyubov. But this happy news came as an ironic parallel to further misery for Varvara. Having had Dyakov to stay with her at Premukhino, all her resolutions to be a perfect wife vanished once again. She found that even a few hours in his company was intolerable; the very thought of being with him for the rest of her life was too appalling to countenance. Despite model if colourless behaviour on Dyakov's part, Varvara wrote to Michael in Moscow saying that although she was obsessed with guilt about the way she was treating her husband, she could not bear to be in his company. Her only hope lay in immediate flight. Michael, now a professional family conspirator, wrote back saying that he would help her plot on his return to Premukhino in the early summer.

Almost as soon as Stankevich had proposed marriage to Lyubov events began to take a sinister turn. The unwilling fiancé left Moscow for his father's estate, preparatory to taking a journey to Karlsbad. Coincidentally he had announced this intention in March 1837, a fortnight before he proposed marriage to Lyubov. But the reason for the trip to Karlsbad was real enough. The spa was a popular retreat for those suffering, like Stankevich, from the early symptoms of T.B. Despite this, Stankevich was still being evasive, for the very thought of the moral obligations and responsibilities that would be imposed upon him by linking closely with another human being were as intolerable to him as the person of Dyakov was to Varvara or Michael's revolutionary behaviour was to Alexander. The facts were becoming all too clear to Lyubov; nevertheless, being an exceptionally understanding and compassionate person, she decided not to admit them even to herself. Alexander, however, was neither understanding nor compassionate. His only concern was that one of his daughters had been proposed to and his prospective son-in-law seemed to be taking an inordinately long time in conducting her to the altar.

In the early summer of 1837, while Lyubov yearned for Stankevich, while Stankevich guiltily evaded his commitments, while Alexander Bakunin fumed at his elder son's waywardness and while Varvara wrestled with her conscience and the distaste that the presence of her husband brought her, Michael continued to immerse himself in Hegelian ideology at Premukhino. Belinsky, meanwhile, licking his wounds in the Caucasus, had yet to explore Hegel. His meeting in Moscow with Michael, following the disastrous Premukhino episode, had been moderately successful. They had both been miserable and they sought solace in their shared depression. It was this unification that tempted Belinsky to write a letter to Michael from his Caucasian retreat rationalizing the lack of rapport between them at Premukhino, and describing their loss of faith in Fichte as their personal gain. Michael, however, was prepared for no such confidences and Belinsky's tentative attempts at renewed intimacy were rudely brushed aside. In fact Michael found Belinsky's missive claustrophobic in the extreme. This resuscitation of the past – this gentle inquest on shattered ideology and battered friendship – was not to Michael's taste, immersed as he was in a powerful and all-embracing new ideology. He wrote a stiff note back to Belinsky, pointing out that the events and aspirations of the previous year were very much a thing of the past and that Hegel had shown him a final, positive philosophical solution to his life. He was extremely patronizing, despite the fact that he was desperately anxious not to allow any chink in his own Hegelian armour.

But Michael's attempted patronizing temporarily liberated Belinsky from trying to please him and from being so much under his influence. He was furious at the letter and wrote a particularly strong reply, pointing out the obvious facts concerning Michael's lack of affection for him. Belinsky's letter is important, for it drew an accurate, surprisingly objective and really rather unpleasant picture of Michael's current values and personality. Belinsky dispassionately pointed out that Michael was arrogant, selfish, unfeeling, unscrupulous and feckless, for ever living off other people and their money. This then was Michael's Fichtean 'outer life' in all its squalidity. As for his Fichtean 'inner life' – well, he spent too much time inside it, hence the reason for his neglect of the outer surfaces.

Michael's reaction to Belinsky's letter proved, however, that despite his selfishness, his domination and his procrastination he was basically sensitive and suffered from a conscience that was easily touched. At the same time he justified Belinsky's telling criticisms by the comforting thought that this onslaught had been directed at a Fichtean-orientated Michael rather than a Hegelian-orientated one. With great panache he sat down to compose a confessional letter to

Belinsky that ranged from total self-abasement and huge modesty to the surprisingly honest statement that his shabby treatment of Belinsky at Premukhino was entirely due to his own personal jealousy over Tatyana's affection for him.

Michael wrote the letter in November 1837 from Premukhino. Next month he returned to Moscow, his head spinning with Hegelian doctrine. There he met Belinsky; they embraced each other warmly and were reconciled. At once Michael's domination was reaffirmed, for Belinsky had been immensely flattered by Michael's letter and his well-established feelings of inferiority had received a pleasant, if temporary, salve.

Meanwhile the affair between Lyubov and Stankevich was now no more than a tragic farce, and the weakening physical health of both protagonists was a further stultifying factor. In August 1837 Stankevich departed as promised to Karlsbad without visiting Lyubov, while Michael, immersed as he was in Hegel, showed more of the tender side of his personality by showing a considerable amount of devoted attention to the one sister for whom he had rarely had much time. However, the change in Michael's personality was not so deep that he could resist the temptation of encouraging a now distracted Varvara to leave Premukhino and her unbearable allegiance to the unloved Dyakov. She had decided that she must escape somewhere abroad, possibly to Berlin, and Michael was not only prepared to arrange the escape but also to accompany her, for he was now enthusiastically planning to leave Russia for Germany – and in particular for Berlin – to pursue his Hegelian studies in an atmosphere saturated by the master himself. How he and Varvara would exist in Berlin was quite another matter. Little trivialities like this would normally not have troubled Michael, but Varvara was more practical. She could sell her jewellery, of course, and maybe she could even extract money from Dyakov, but the main stumbling-block was Alexander.

This proved to be very much the case, but not as far as Varvara herself was concerned. In this matter Alexander was still liberal enough to understand, and, up to a point, to sympathize with his daughter's sufferings. But when he discovered that Varvara was to be accompanied to Berlin by Michael he flew into a rage of such intensity that his other bouts of fury were made to look like mere irritation. Accordingly, in December 1837 Michael's reconciliation with Belinsky and his Hegelian euphoria were rudely interrupted by the arrival of a letter from Alexander denouncing him for his subversive influence over the entire Bakunin family. In the letter he listed the domestic revolutionary activities that Michael had been

37

responsible for at Premukhino, and indeed the charges, had they been of national or international significance and read out in a High Court, would have hung Michael many times over. There was the desertion from the army, the refusal to join the civil service, the breaking up of the Lyubov–Renne affair, the subversion of his younger brothers and the encouragement of their short-lived rebellion, the interference between husband and wife in the Varvara–Dyakov affair, Belinsky, and so on. The list seemed endless. Alexander then pronounced sentence by telling Michael that either he must mend his ways or he must not return to Premukhino. Michael retaliated at the end of December 1837 by writing Alexander a letter, amounting to a short autobiography, which examined every part of their relationship since childhood. It was, however, merely an ingenious justification for all he had done and all he intended to do. It was also a precedent for other documents – documents which would be on a far broader, more international scale. Michael had begun his career as a revolutionary at home. Now he was ready to step outside and to use the tactics of subversion he had learnt at home to less parochial effect.

VIII

Michael spent the spring of 1838 continuing to study Hegel, and continuing to interfere with the affairs of both his family and his friends. A job, he considered, would not further any of these activities; in fact it would be a definite drawback. In January he relinquished the post of tutor to the son of the extremely rich Levashovs after a short period of a week. He then moved rapidly from the Levashov mansion into the lodgings of Belinsky, who was only too happy to give a home and no doubt money to his old friend. At once Michael settled down to tutor Belinsky in Hegelianism – a tutorship that lasted euphorically until March 1838. During this period Michael turned again to his old sounding-boards, Natalie and Alexandra Beyer. But this time it was Alexandra who did the wooing while Natalie provided a cynical background to her sister's open adoration for Michael. Taking the bull by the horns, Alexandra openly told Michael how much she loved him. He, now professionally adept at dealing with high emotion, took her avowal lightly and continued to write her passionately spiritual letters. His ego boosted as usual by adoration, Michael almost made the fatal mistake of genuinely falling in love – this time with another member of the Muraviev clan, a distant cousin named Sophie. But as always he was able to switch his thoughts to matters of greater interest, such as Hegel.

Meanwhile the effect of Hegel on Belinsky was completely shattering. The fogs of the more intransigent Fichtean ideology cleared, Belinsky found himself entering into a new reconciliation with reality. 'I look at reality,' he wrote to Michael during this reversal of thought, 'which I used to despise so much, and feel strangely stirred by a sense of its rightness; I realize that nothing can be banished from it, that nothing can be imprecated and rejected.' But Belinsky's use of the word 'reality' was limited to the Hegelian vein – and, as Lampert points out,

> He intended it to have a Hegelian connotation. But in his hands it acquired a somewhat different meaning. Hegel's idea of reality is part of his monistic conception of the relation between the whole and its parts. The whole, according to Hegel is, as it were, there from the beginning, and being there, it expresses itself in parts whose nature it pervades and determines. The whole, therefore, is more real than its parts: reality is proportional to the mass and richness of the elements which go to make it. The model for Hegel's conception of reality is the all-inclusive whole which contains and gathers up into itself the abstract universal of Platonic philosophy and the raw matter of sense experience. And it is in this sense that Hegel asserted in the Introduction to his *Philosophy of Right* 'the rationality of the real' or the 'reality of the rational'. To regard something as real, and therefore as rational, was for him to regard it as an aspect of the whole.[20]

Thus Belinsky, under Michael's dominating tutorage, was initiated into Hegelian philosophy.

Three traumatic events occurred in the spring of 1838. The first was the beginning of a second and final quarrel between Michael and Belinsky. The second was the worsening physical condition of Lyubov. The third was the departure of Varvara for Karlsbad. The quarrel began when a new and exciting opportunity presented itself to Belinsky. In March 1838 he was offered the editorship of a moribund newspaper called the *Moscow Observer*. Now owned by a liberal publisher, the idea was to restyle the paper and remove its highly reactionary editorial tone. Belinsky, jobless since the closure of *The Telescope*, and, unlike Michael, uneasy at borrowing and living off his friends, was only too pleased to take advantage of the opportunity. For his part Michael viewed the new development with very mixed feelings. On one level he saw the new *Moscow Observer* as a source of employment and on the other he viewed Belinsky's job as editor with increasing jealousy. However, the first issue carried Michael's first-ever printed contribution – a translation into Russian of three lectures by Hegel together with his own introduction. Its publication gave him a great deal of satisfaction but unfortunately it did nothing to improve the growing feelings of jealousy.

In many ways these were understandable enough. Michael loved to dominate and it was not in his nature to play a secondary role in his conversations, his relationships or indeed in his ambitions. He was too forceful and at the same time too insecure to allow or indeed to trust others to dominate him. As a result he was becoming more and more overbearing, but despite this he was never a bore. For those who based their judgements on first impressions Michael's immediate confidence and enthusiasm compelled his listeners to admire and to follow him. It was only after they had grown to know him better that sudden feelings of cynicism and disillusionment gripped them.

Meanwhile Michael's philosophical beliefs had taken a slightly different slant. For instance, in his introductory article to the Hegelian essays in the *Moscow Observer*, he talked in great detail of the importance of the Hegelian 'rational reality'. Gone were the idealistic connotations and in their place was reality, or at least Hegelian reality. Here Belinsky's influence shows and it must have been strong, for Michael had now adopted some uncharacteristic philosophical attitudes and, like Belinsky, he turned on Kant and his former beloved Fichte and accused them of wallowing in 'self-loving, egotistical self-contemplation'. As a contrast to what he considered was the spiritual perversion and squalor of the French Revolution he wrote that

> happiness lies not in fancy, not in abstract dreaming, but in living reality. To revolt against reality means to kill in oneself the living source of life . . . Let us hope that the new generation will reconcile itself with our beautiful Russian reality, and that, abandoning all empty pretensions to genius, they will feel at last the legitimate need to become real Russians.

A far cry indeed from the 'inner' and 'outer' life of Fichte. Total orthodoxy and total conservatism became the order of the day and as a result the entire structure of the archetypal conservatism of the Russian State was fully accepted, as was the Church. An extraordinary volte-face for Michael, but a comparatively short-lived one.

For Belinsky, however, this orthodoxy was a pattern for the future and his Hegelian 'reality' was already set on a highly conservative course which included the acceptance of the grey and bureaucratic reality that stretched around him in the shape of the Russian State.

As spring merged into summer Michael grew more and more jealous of Belinksy in his position of editor of the restyled *Moscow Observer*. In fact the jealousy grew to such a pitch that it totally outweighed his need for prestige or money. As a result, confident that he still had Belinsky under his control, Michael decided to kill the whole concept of the journal and in a grandiose way calmly told Belinsky that after due consideration he considered that they were both too intellectually and philosophically immature to control the journal in this way. Unfortunately Michael's over-confidence was about to receive a severe set-back, for Belinsky firmly stated that he had no intention of accepting this, going on to make it very clear that their master–pupil relationship was at an end. Michael was furious. His pride was thoroughly offended, and, bewildered by Belinsky's sudden independence, he at once gave up writing for the *Observer* and immediately began to plot solidly against Belinsky. It was not difficult to find support, for already Belinsky was committed to the change from an ultra-revolutionary to an ultra-conservative. Alexander Herzen was later to say to him scornfully, 'Do you know that from your point of view you can prove that the monstrous tyranny under which we live is rational and ought to exist?' whilst Annenkov said of him that after a few months of editing the magazine he had reached

a gloomy stage, where one could see a remarkable and original thinker in the humiliating position of a martyr pining under the impact of a cruel intellectual discipline which he obstinately persisted in imposing on himself, although it deprived him of his power, refusing to admit that it was a punishment.[21]

Meanwhile poor Belinsky firmly stated that

The word 'reality' has for me the same significance as the word 'God'. Now that I am in the position of contemplating the infinite, I begin to understand that everyone is right and no one is guilty, that there are no false, erroneous opinions, and that all things are different facets of the Spirit.[22]

It was absolutely essential to Michael's self-esteem to replace

Belinsky as quickly as possible – and luckily for him he did not have to look very far. Vasili Botkin, the son of a merchant and therefore socially inferior to Michael, Stankevich and Belinsky, had been introduced into the Stankevich circle some two years before. With no university education and all too aware of his social inferiority, Botkin was highly intelligent, humble and apologetic – an ideal disciple for Michael. Their relationship was not destined to last long, for Botkin was not a doer, being something of a dilettante, but he was useful at that time, especially as a base, for Michael, now openly quarrelling with Belinsky, could hardly remain as his guest. For the rest of the spring, therefore, Michael resided at Botkin's lodgings, only leaving them in May to return to Premukhino.

At Premukhino Michael found that Lyubov was dying. Still the arid, hopeless correspondence with Stankevich continued. Two sick, anaemic lovers – the one at Premukhino, the other at Karlsbad – both ill, both drifting, both in love with the idea of being in love. Meanwhile Varvara's position, as an ironic contrast, had improved. Alexander, softened no doubt by a combination of age and the absence of Michael, had agreed to Varvara and her son's journey to Germany and the requisite amount of money was gallantly provided by the brother of the unfortunate and unwanted Dyakov. They departed in June, leaving Michael even more frustrated, for despite his genuine horror and concern over Lyubov's condition he was becoming more and more desperate each day over the organization of his own trip to Germany. It was all a question of raising the money and Michael had already worked through most of his patrons. His own family, he knew, would definitely not finance him, nor would the Muravievs, and Michael's friends saw no reason to increase his state of indebtedness to them. All, that is, except Stankevich, who before going to Bohemia the year before had rashly promised Michael that he would pay his debts and give him an allowance in Germany of 1500 roubles a year. However, Stankevich first had to obtain this money from his father, who was an extremely generous and open-handed man. So open-handed was he, in fact, that Stankevich was wary of asking him for so much, particularly for such a spendthrift as Michael. Earlier that year Stankevich had whittled down the expected amount to a round sum of 2000 roubles, which was certainly not enough for Michael to make the journey and live in Germany. Gloomily Michael decided to play a waiting game and to pray for a suitable benefactor.

One afternoon, soon after Varvara's departure, Michael and his brothers and sisters lit a bonfire in the garden and Lyubov was brought out to watch it. She came in a carriage, pale, listless, her dead-white face lit by the scorching, flickering red darts of the bonfire. It was an afternoon of rapture, of time suspended and of time retrieved. Two months later, in August 1838, Lyubov was dead.

Over the period of Lyubov's impending death both Belinsky and Botkin drifted like grey ghosts through the grief-stricken atmosphere of Premukhino. They had been invited down somewhat tactlessly by Michael's mother and his younger sisters, who had been visiting Moscow while Michael was down at Premukhino. Still entranced by Alexandra, Belinsky had come, though much against his better judgement. Fortunately there was too much on Michael's mind for a renewal of hostilities and the period passed off peacefully, if apathetically. But once Belinsky was back in Moscow, he sent a number of letters to Michael at Premukhino, all written with the intention of forcing Michael to recognize him as a person. In these letters Belinsky hotly defended his theories and acceptance of reality in Hegelian terms, contrasted these with the vagaries of Michael's motives and personality, and then proceeded to launch into a surprisingly accurate and extremely bold personal attack. He ranged from references to Michael's lack of sexual experience to his domination over his sisters, and from Michael's rather academic idealism to the way he had calmly projected a series of theoretical and philosophical values upon his sisters rather than encouraging them to face the 'realities' of life. Michael reacted to the Belinsky letters with fury, with venom and with fear, for he was dimly aware that Belinsky had come all too near the truth. No longer was he a disciple, instead he had become a probing and exceptionally accurate realist.

This final quarrel led Michael to reject Belinsky's interpretation of Hegel with its merciless discipline. The friendship having split, so did their mutual line of philosophy. Belinsky rushed, impelled by his own honesty, into a dark corridor of unmitigated orthodoxy. Michael, on the other hand, rescued himself from this by his own cowardice. Belinsky had threatened him by arriving too near the truth, by stripping Michael of all his vanities and worse still by breaking down the wall he had carefully built up around his inadequacies. Now Michael was well and truly on the run – from Hegelian 'reality', from Belinsky and even more strongly now from Moscow.

But escape was not so easy, and return to a relatively friendless Moscow, with the Stankevich circle broken up and a hostile Belinsky, was an unpalatable proposition. Instead Michael moped around Premukhino, which in itself was suffering the gloom of the aftermath of Lyubov's death and Varvara's departure. Even the closeness of Tatyana could not shift the grey depression that had taken possession of Michael's mind. Cut off from intellectual stimulation by his quarrel with Belinsky and from romantic stimulation by having squeezed out the last drops of the Beyer sisters' hysteria, Michael turned to books and to academia as both a means of escape and of occupation. But a great deal of his time was spent in plotting how he could raise enough money to go to Germany. Stankevich, whose health was deteriorating in Karlsbad, was obviously not going to be able to finance Michael's trip and so there was only one other person to whom he could possibly turn in his desperation – his father. Alexander, very old now and nearly blind, was still far from senile, particularly in his attitude to Michael's philanderings, and Michael, for his part, was aware of his father's cynicism. Somehow, though, he would have to convince Alexander that funding a trip to the seat of Hegelianism was a viable project, and that would need the manipulation of a genius. But Michael's outward self-confidence was rarely lacking; it was only in his inner core that there lay curled a sensitive and lonely spirit. The opening of a paper factory on the estate and the extra income it brought into Premukhino eventually provided the opportunity – an opportunity that Michael was to grasp with both hands – but for the moment his tactics were to give a surprising outer show of being a loving and dutiful son to his father. This new role must have considerably surprised Alexander, but it is not on record whether or not he was able to see through the ruse.

Meanwhile Michael sporadically read more Hegel, a number of books on religion, various grammars, the Koran and a diverse selection of contemporary and ancient historians. His concentration, although often forced, showed remarkable consistency, and it is here, studying alone, that Michael's outstanding will-power begins to reveal itself. He had set himself to read, to understand and to annotate – and this he did by the hour. Still fearful of Belinsky's grim Hegelian reality, Michael returned briefly to the abstract idealism of Schelling and Fichte, and then went on to read Strauss's *Life of Jesus*, which represented Christ as an important historical figure rather than a spiritual leader. Guy Aldred, in his pamphlet on Bakunin, wrote that 'Strauss viewed Jesus as a Socrates misconceived by Christian tradition as a magician.' As a result Strauss had had his theological chair taken away from him in Germany and the German Hegelians had split into two very specific wings: the Left supporting Strauss and the Right refuting his theories.

At this point Michael made another extremely important discovery: Ludwig Feuerbach. He first heard of him through Botkin, who sent a magazine to Michael which laid out Feuerbach's ideas.

Feuerbach had been born in the same year as Kant's death and it was George Eliot (who also translated Strauss) who first translated Feuerbach into English. He taught that belief in God and the after-life was merely the dreams and desires of a terrified race living on a tiny and insignificant planet. Feuerbach, however, also claimed to be a Hegelian, which seemed to Michael totally alien and completely paradoxical. He admired Strauss but, unlike the more superficial Botkin, took up a conservative position on the right wing of Hegelian thought. Despite this, Strauss's rebellious theories, within the Hegelian framework, became increasingly attractive, but it was not the theories that interested him so much as the mere factor of their rebellion.

IX

With the exception of two brief visits to Moscow in the company of Tatyana, Michael stayed at Premukhino studying and waiting for the right opportunity to ask his father for the necessary money for his visit to Germany. In July 1839 Michael made a serious, if refreshingly uncalculating, tactical mistake. He went to Petersburg in an attempt to begin the impossible task under Russian law of securing Varvara's divorce. In fact it was an excuse for an adventure but once again it caused the fury of Alexander to come down venomously on his son's head over his further interference in the Varvara–Dyakov tragedy. Michael failed to secure the divorce, spent four months in Petersburg, visited the Muravievs but left because the girls were away, met and impressed Kraevsky, the editor of the popular journal *Notes of the Fatherland*, agreed to produce two articles for him, continued to argue by post with Alexander – and, in October 1839, suddenly ran into Belinsky.

At first the meeting was awkward and then suddenly, with a mixture of horror and delight, Belinsky found himself slipping into his old subservient position. Michael's feelings about this reconcilia-tion were far more superficial than Belinsky's and their new-found friendship had a shallower quality to it, almost as if it were a scratched recording of times remembered.

While Michael drifted aimlessly around Petersburg Alexandra Bakunin and her parents paid a visit to Moscow. Naturally Alexandra sought out Michael's only remaining friend, Botkin, who, following in the true tradition of Michael's other friends, fell in love with her. Unfortunately Botkin's passion was of an inferior nature to the spiritual passions of Stankevich and Belinsky. Botkin was not only of a more superficial intellect, but he was also socially taboo. Alexandra, however, feeling it was time that she was paid some attention, agreed to correspond secretly with Botkin with Michael's connivance. Surprisingly Michael did not object to Botkin as a suitor and told Alexandra, no doubt bearing in mind his hopeless mission to Petersburg and the past miseries of Varvara, that she should marry Botkin if she loved him. Soon the Alexandra–Botkin affair became the subject of gossip that eventually reached the ears of Alexander, who predictably refused to agree to the marriage. Michael, his old fire returning as he slipped back into his identity of family trouble-shooter, hurried back to Premukhino in November 1839. There he had a final, furious confrontation with his father. There is no doubt that this marked the last battle between Alexander and Michael. Michael spent only a few days at Premukhino and then left for Moscow in high dudgeon, having failed to wheedle or bully the old man into an acceptance of the woeful Botkin as a prospective son-in-law. Denouncing his father roundly, Michael determined more strongly than ever to leave Russia. But the question was, now that he had quarrelled with Alexander, how was he going to do it?

In Moscow Michael desperately sought new friends. Botkin was inadequate to his needs and he could not bear the time-slip relationship with Belinsky, or indeed his reactionary Hegelian views. Providentially two particularly important figures from the political Moscow circles now began to play a substantial role in Michael's life. They were Alexander Herzen and Nicholas Ogarev.

The political activities of Herzen and Ogarev had already brought both men to the attention of the authorities. As a result Herzen had been banished to Perm in the Urals, and Ogarev, who was considered to be less of a public danger, spent his banishment in his own native area of Penza. Herzen was two years older than Michael and had been born the illegitimate son of a nobleman named Ivan Yakovlev. Tutored by a revolutionary exiled Frenchman, Herzen learnt his radical beliefs young and the Decembrist Uprising left a vivid impression on his childhood memories. One of his most vivid memories was of the *Te Deum* sung in praise and honour of the victory of Tsar Nicholas over the five leading Decembrists who had been executed. Herzen was only a boy of fourteen at the time. Twenty-nine years later[23] he recalled that

In the midst of the Kremlin the Metropolitan Philaret thanked God for the murders. The entire Royal Family took part in the service, near them the Senate and the Ministers, and in the immense space around packed masses of the Guards knelt bare-headed; they also joined in the prayers. Cannon thundered from the heights of the Kremlin. . . . On this spot and before the altar defiled by bloody rites, I swore to avenge the murdered, and dedicated myself to the struggle with that throne, with that altar, with those cannons.

Herzen met Ogarev when both were young men and together they battled for liberalism. After leaving Moscow University, Herzen and Ogarev dominated their political circle until they were arrested when Herzen was twenty-two. Penalized by the State as a 'daring free-thinker, extremely dangerous to society' and sentenced to 'civilian duty for an indefinite period to remote provinces', Herzen emerged from exile in Perm in 1840 and became a leading intellectual in Moscow. At the same time he began a highly academic and highly concentrated study of Hegelian philosophy. His mind was far better trained than Michael's, or indeed that of any of his contemporaries, but although he was to be very much a theoretician in later life, Herzen now longed for Hegelian philosophy to become activated.

Nicholas Platonovich Ogarev was the son of a rich landowner who was in the Penza administration. Highly romantic, he fell in and out of love during his enforced sojourn away from Moscow, and a year later was married. He inherited his father's estates and liberated the serfs on one of them, selling it to them on a hire-purchase basis. In the autumn of 1839 Ogarev and his clever but socially aspiring wife Maria were permitted to return to Moscow. At once their marriage began to founder as Maria took on the role of socialite while Ogarev returned to his friends and their philo-sophical and political circles. Maria soon quarrelled with Herzen and, bored with her husband, started a flirtation with a mutual friend of Ogarev and Herzen, Ivan Galakhov.

Michael found Herzen to be an extremely pleasant companion, yet at no time was he excited by his personality or his political views. His article for Kraevsky (his second published work) was due to appear in the spring, yet nowhere in the article had Michael indicated that his Hegelian philosophy was adaptable to politics, and indeed to revolution. In fact during this winter Michael became something of a socialite himself, taking advantage of the frequent receptions given by the Ogarevs and the musical soirées given by Botkin. It was during this period that he witnessed Ogarev's wife Maria in a compromising situation with Katkov, another member of Herzen's circle, and lost no time in informing everyone of this incident. Both Ogarev and Katkov were furious and Moscow hummed with discreditable stories about Michael: about his debts, the way he lived at the expense of others, and the way he had interfered to a large extent in many people's lives. Michael quickly realized, to his own intense discomfort, that his reputation in Moscow was rapidly veering towards that of a philanderer, and a dilettante. As a result he grew even lonelier and in February 1840 he wrote a sad and objective appraisal of his state at the time in a letter to the now severely ailing Stankevich.

> My whole life, my whole virtue have consisted in a sort of abstract spiritual force, and that force has been shipwrecked on the sordid trivialities of everyday family life, of empty family quarrels, and of quarrels between friends, and perhaps also on my own incapacity. There still survives within me the old strong need, predominating over everything else, for living knowledge – a thirst which is still unsatisfied despite all my poor, laborious efforts. All my knowledge is limited to the fact that I know nothing – a necessary transitional state as a prelude to true knowledge, but a very poor and unrewarding one for anyone who is condemned to remain in it.[24]

Now more than at any other time he must at all costs escape to Germany, and he would have to humble himself before Alexander to do it. Alexander was now his only hope, for with Michael's personal reputation at its current level there was obviously no hope of borrowing from anyone else in Moscow. In desperation, therefore, Michael sat down and wrote a long and very emotively phrased appeal to his parents. In it he acknowledged his father's cherished but pessimistic hopes of his either going into the civil service or alternatively, as the eldest son, returning to manage the family estates. He felt that if he could obtain a degree and acquire a professor's chair he could serve the Tsar in this capacity, but first, before any of this happened, he must go to Germany for three years. Within this three-year period he would gain his doctorate at the university and would return to Moscow as a professor. All this could be achieved for as little as 1500–2000 roubles a year. Having wrapped up this bargain offer in a welter of pleas and apologies for the past, Michael waited tensely for his father's reaction. Eventually it came, and the answer, with many provisos and complaints, was yes, on the basis of the lowest allowance of 1500 roubles. But Michael, with the gossip increasing around him, was only too glad to accept anything. The amount, however, was slightly increased when Michael, playing safe, borrowed a thousand roubles from Herzen, who, not knowing him as well as he should and choosing to ignore the gossip, paid up fairly willingly.

In May 1840 Michael returned to Premukhino, to take leave of his family. Out of Moscow, away from the gossip, and assured of a new and intriguing future, Michael was on top of the world. He was charming to his family, to his parents and to the recently rather neglected Beyer girls. He wished to depart without recrimination and without unpleasantness. Genuinely he wished everyone well and he went about setting up a number of cherished memories to look back upon. In his own mind Premukhino became a happier place and his father a gentler and less aggressive patriarch. The only dramatic incident that occurred was the news that Varvara had joined the now seriously ill Stankevich in Rome. She had increasingly admired Stankevich and it was strangely logical that she should be with him now. No one, not even Alexander, registered surprise or disapproval.

Michael's farewell to Premukhino was heavily emotional, particularly in his parting from Tatyana. Paul and Alexis accompanied him for a small part of the journey towards Petersburg from where Michael's ship would sail to Germany. They all wept most of the way.

On 26 June 1840 Michael eventually reached Petersburg. However, during the three days he spent there before his ship sailed Michael had one final humiliation, and worst of all a humiliation that was aided by Belinsky, who was still residing in Petersburg. Katkov, who had been largely responsible for spreading rumours about Michael in Moscow, discovered that Michael was paying a visit to Belinsky in Petersburg and decided to lie in wait for him there. Belinsky, on welcoming Michael to his house, was distinctly cool. He felt that Michael had been manipulative once again over the short-lived Botkin romance, and was therefore not averse to witnessing an unpleasant scene between Katkov and Michael. He had decided that Michael thoroughly deserved retribution and was unhappy to see him escape scot-free from Russia. An unpleasant scene there certainly was. The confrontation began with Katkov accusing Michael of having interfered in his affairs and ended with him calling Michael a eunuch. It was this insult, touching on Michael's greatest vulnerability, that roused Michael to real fury and the conversation gave way to blows. The outcome of the struggle was a tactical victory for Katkov and talk of a duel between them. Michael was totally humiliated, but Belinsky looked on dispassionately. He had been savaged too mercilessly by Michael in the past to feel really sorry for him and now was only conscious of revulsion at Michael's beaten expression. Later that day Michael extricated himself from the duel by passing a note to Katkov, via Belinsky, which pointed out that as duelling was forbidden on Russian soil it would be better to transfer the encounter to Germany. Katkov's reply is not on record but one can assume that Michael was not going to run the risk of a duel cutting short his cherished plans. In fact Michael's natural optimism easily dismissed the antagonism and humiliation that he was leaving behind him in Russia and he looked forward instead to a nobler, more stimulating and more harmonious life in Berlin. While he made final arrangements for the trip, Michael insulated this optimism by spending his time with the Herzens, who he considered were infinitely better friends to him in Petersburg than the new, independent and now hostile Belinsky and the thoroughly offensive Katkov.

With the relish of the true romantic Michael then sat down to write farewell letters to his brothers and sisters and Natalie and Alexandra Beyer. Then in the early morning of 29 June 1840 Alexander Herzen walked down with Michael to the rowing boat that was to take him down the River Neva to Kronstadt where he was to catch a steamer that would take him across the Baltic. After a false start during which the boat quickly had to return upstream in the face of a storm, Herzen at last said goodbye to Michael, leaving him alone, setting out again once the wind had dropped, into a blinding rainstorm.

As the boat edged its way down river Michael did not indulge in any traditional retrospection. He was twenty-six, and he was leaving failure behind him. Much of his plotting and manipulation had ended in hate or apathy. His 'career' had disintegrated long ago. He had recently been abused by a bully and one of his original victims had looked on uncaringly. Lyubov was dead and Stankevich was dying. Philosophically Michael had only dabbled, if concentratedly and obsessively, in Fichte and in Hegel. Indeed he had done worse than dabbling. He had approached philosophy subjectively and had turned it to his own needs and requirements. 'Eunuch', Katkov had flung at him, but Michael did not brood on that, for he had the ability to forget the deeply unpleasant, or rather to secrete it in some dark hollow of his mind that was reserved for the truth. But it was a very dark hollow and long ago it had been plugged with delusion, in the shape of Marie Voyekov – and the Muraviev sisters – and Natalie and Alexandra Beyer. They hovered in his mind, phantom-like, passionately clinging to a hope about him that could never be fulfilled. Eunuch: the echo was muffled and was losing impact as the boat furrowed on through the dark water.

50

Michael was looking forward – not back. Forward to a rosy, fantastical future. Belinsky, plodding further and further into the grey corridors of Hegelian reality, was a far more unfortunate man than Michael, who, self-delusionist or not, was looking forward to seizing the opportunity of a new and exciting rebirth.

PART TWO

Academy of Unrest: 1840–8

I

Michael Bakunin may have had more than his fair share of human frailty, but he also had far more than his fair share of intellectual and physical energy. At twenty-six he was an unharnessed dynamo – a massive engine that yearned for something to drive. It was this energy that continued to generate his enormous optimism, optimism that grew greater as the slow, arduous voyage to Hamburg slowly unwound and he left behind him the humiliations and despairs of Russia. Berlin – the fount of Hegelian wisdom – seemed a new and mythical place. It was a fresh start, a new adventure and perhaps there, somewhat mystically, Michael would find something to which he could harness his energy.

Five days later the steamer reached Lübeck and Michael, after spending some days surveying Hamburg, went on to Berlin, arriving there on 25 July 1840. He discovered that Varvara was still in Italy. The reason for her non-appearance was an immediate shock: Stankevich was dead. He had died towards the end of June and Varvara had been with him. Michael's reaction was muted by the incredibility of it all and by the fact that the non-existence of Stankevich seemed too absurd to believe in. Stankevich had been a brilliant and essentially good man – a fact that Michael had not failed to realize – but to Michael, Stankevich had been something more. He had represented complete security despite his wraith-like personality and indecisiveness. He was the only one of Michael's friends who had not criticized him, he had been a willing if not always effective provider of funds – and he would have made an ideal brother-in-law if only he had been able to marry poor Lyubov. Later, Michael was to sum him up effectively as follows:

> It was impossible to be near him without becoming uplifted and ennobled. In his presence no one could have a cowardly or trivial thought; no unpleasant instinct was possible. The most ordinary man ceased to be ordinary under his influence. He belonged by nature to that category of men who are at once rich and refined . . . who are endowed with a great genius, but do not manifest it by any singular great historic act, nor by any creation, be it scientific, artistic, or industrial; who attempt nothing, do nothing, write nothing, and whose total activity is concentrated and embodied in their personal lives, but who nevertheless leave after them in history, by exclusively personal but at the same time very powerful activity, in fact, a profound mark on those who are close to them.[1]

Michael had described a man who was without avarice, and without jealousy – a near-saint in his dealings with his fellow human beings – and perhaps that is why he did not grieve for Stankevich for long, for in his opinion Stankevich was almost too good to live.

A few weeks later Varvara returned from the small Italian village where Stankevich had died and joined Michael in lodgings. He was pleased to see her and delighted to find that she would see to his needs, for he had little time for housekeeping as he began to feel his feet in Berlin. Professor Franco Venturi sums up Michael's personality at this time as follows:

> When he finally went abroad in 1840, Bakunin had broken with everyone. He felt isolated. His political conceptions remained those of a conservative by philosophical choice; his ideas were those of a convinced Hegelian. Yet he felt profoundly dissatisfied. He was now in agreement with no one. His anxiety was expressed in personal quarrels, which grew increasingly complicated, and in polemics, which now lost all theoretical meaning, and degenerated into conflicts of temperament. . . .
>
> Strange as it may seem, Hegelian orthodoxy helped him – once in Germany – to abandon all philosophy. In the meantime, it brought him into direct contact with the discussions of the Hegelian Left, which he had scarcely been aware of in Russia. His very desire for the Absolute prevented him searching for a philosophical ladder to help him from speculation to action, an abstract justification for practical activity. His philosophy collapsed once it had fulfilled its purpose . . . There remained his

detachment from the surrounding world, and above all the wish to give an absolute value to the new direction of his life. He disdained as worthless anything not directed to this end.[2]

At this time Berlin was, from a Russian émigré's point of view, delightfully liberated and excitingly Bohemian. Despite the fact that Hegel had been dead for some years now, his philosophy was the only philosophy practised in the city. Beethoven, the musical interpreter of Hegelian ideology, was extremely popular and much performed, and salon-like evenings, devoted to literary readings and philosophical discussion, completed the esoteric form of life lived by the intelligentsia.

Michael soon found that Varvara and her small son were neither particularly stimulating company nor able to contribute any major source of income, but fortunately he met Ivan Turgenev, who admirably fulfilled both his needs.

Turgenev was then twenty-two, and had been living in Berlin for two years. He was all too happy to draw Michael into Berlin society and was prepared, like Belinsky and Botkin before him, to adopt the role of disciple. Michael was delighted. He had Varvara to housekeep for him, he had Turgenev as guide and disciple – and he had Berlin with its wondrous Hegelian treasures ready to be explored. As expected, the next two years, from 1840 to 1842, were both stimulating and exciting for Michael and saw a change in the whole concept of his philosophical attitude. However, the image of Premukhino was never far from his mind and as usual he found it easy to forget the rows and strife he had had with Alexander. Instead he remembered only the good times. The long summer days . . . the dreamy, dusty foliage . . . the silver thrust of the river . . . Tatyana . . . Lyubov . . . Stankevich . . . even Belinsky. Living with Varvara, however, was a comparatively short-term project, for Michael soon found that Turgenev's company and lodgings were preferable. Moreover, Turgenev was able to borrow convenient sums of money from his widowed mother, who was still living in Russia.

Michael often wrote home, giving detailed accounts of his life in Berlin, his Hegelian studies and particularly his friendship with Turgenev. He even went so far as to tell his sisters that Turgenev held fourth place in his most intimate affections (the first being taken by his sisters, the second by the Beyers and the third by Stankevich). Varvara acted as hostess for the friends of Michael and Turgenev. She enjoyed entertaining them but was more interested in meeting Werder, Michael's Hegelian professor, than many of the pedantic and rather sombre German students. Michael, however, was anxious to import more of his family into Berlin (on Turgenev's money) and elected Paul, his favourite brother and already a confirmed Hegelian, to be the lucky protégé. When Paul had arrived, Michael was anxious, once again presuming on Turgenev's money, to import Tatyana. But she was not to come, for she was not anxious, however much she wanted to see Michael, to cause a major family row. Paul, however, was a different case. He had become over-friendly with the ever-eager Alexandra Beyer and, as a result, Alexander was only too happy to let him leave the country for a period, particularly if Turgenev was paying. Taking the choice between having the boy entangled with the infamous Alexandra and having his mind totally polluted by Michael's teachings and life-style, Alexander chose the latter, which indicated just how much he must have feared the Beyer sisters.

Paul, just twenty-one, arrived in Berlin during August 1841, joined Michael and Varvara on holiday near Frankfurt and then took lodgings with Varvara at Dresden for the winter while Michael returned to Berlin. Meanwhile Turgenev, on holiday in Russia, paid a short visit to Premukhino. He instantly became popular with the family and especially with Tatyana, who after her disastrous intellectual rapport with Belinsky had loved nobody except Michael and her immediate family. Turgenev's effect on her was instantaneous. With all the ardour of her passionate nature she fell in love with him, but Turgenev never responded to her love, although tragically it affected the whole of her life. She continued to worship him until he married. By then she had become a determined spinster.

In June 1842 Varvara returned to Russia. She went because she was still feeling guilty over depriving Dyakov of his child when he was so humble and acquiescent to her and also because Alexander had written to her pleading for a reconciliation with Dyakov. Michael, of course, did not let her go easily and for a brief period he returned to his role of family liberator. He attempted to dissuade Varvara but eventually failed, although he tried everything – even down to rewriting Varvara's letters to her husband. Varvara, almost always dominated by Michael and fully aware of it, was this time determined to lead her own life and take her own decisions. Using evasive tactics she quietly slipped out of Germany for Russia in June 1842 without telling her domineering brother that she was going, and in the autumn of 1842 Paul followed her, his love for Alexandra Beyer now a thing of the past and his philosophical studies hardly started.

Michael was not as sorry to see him go as might have been expected. He was gradually undergoing a major change and his preoccupation with philosophy was being replaced by politics. Because of this he had no intention of returning to Russia himself. He hinted in letters to Alexandra Beyer and to his sisters at Premukhino that it was unlikely that he would ever return and in November 1842 after he had said goodbye to Paul Michael wrote a long letter to Premukhino. It was very much a letter of farewell.

> Do you remember how once, late on an autumn evening, we imagined pictures in the hedgerow between Lopatino and Mytnits wood? Do you remember how a flock of cranes flew over? Now I am in the country to which the cranes fly from you. Do you remember our walks in Mytnits wood? Have you been along my favourite path this summer? What has happened to my trees in the little wood? We lighted a fire there one spring, in Holy Week. Lyubov was ill then and near to death, and she came in a carriage to join us . . . Then I went away. God! How my heart was breaking when I said good-bye to Papa . . . now he has completely shut me out from his heart. If only he knew how I love him! . . . Did you feel then that we should never see one another again? Then do you remember, Alexis, how the three of us drove and cried as we went, and the thrush was singing in the bushes.[3]

With this poignant farewell Michael proceeded to dismiss Premukhino from his mind and concentrated on his new interest in the Hegelian Left.

November 1842 also saw the departure of Turgenev for Russia; in fact he and Paul travelled home together. Michael and Turgenev had been very close friends indeed, one of the great links between them being Stankevich, whom Turgenev had worshipped ever since he had first met him in Berlin. For Turgenev Michael took over from Stankevich as an object of worship, despite the fact that although he too was a Hegelian he was a rather more ebullient mentor than Stankevich. Michael found Turgenev infinitely more stimulating than his last disciple Botkin and together they formed an intense friendship, despite the fact that Turgenev was not particularly interested in philosophy except for its modishness. Turgenev was probably one of the best friends that Michael ever had and the fact that he had money and good connections were minor, if useful, points in his favour. They genuinely liked each other and Turgenev accepted the fact that Michael's ideal of friendship had to involve the master–pupil relationship. Through Turgenev Michael met various other friends of Stankevich, Russian émigrés who happened to be in Berlin at the time. Even Katkov blusteringly arrived for a period and was amazed to find that Michael appeared to have little or no memory of their last violent encounter in Petersburg. In fact so urbane was Michael that the usually confident Katkov retreated in some confusion. Michael also met a number of important Germans, such as the critic and journalist Müller-Strübing, and Varnhagen von Ense, who took enormous interest in Russian literature and its *personae*.

Together Michael and Turgenev had a vivid social life throughout the first eighteen months of Michael's period in Berlin, and much time was spent elegantly visiting the salons of various cosmopolitan Berlin ladies whose *raison d'être* was either the theatre, music or literature. Politics was rarely discussed. When alone, Michael and Turgenev spent hours discussing their future, their philosophy or their dreams. It was a very good friendship, warm, sincere and mutually stimulating.

Michael's philosophical studies, however, were far more disciplined. At Berlin University Professor Werder faithfully translated and taught the thinking of the Master. Michael totally committed himself to study although his ambition to learn often outstripped his powers of concentration. Eventually, however, he obtained a diploma and also gained Werder's friendship, for his classes on Hegelian philosophy were, to say the least, underpopulated. The unambitious Werder admired the passionate zeal of the two young Russians and found that their enthusiasm rekindled much of the Master's fire.

Michael also met Schelling and although he was unimpressed by Schelling's lectures at this stage Schelling was, in fact, already promoting the attack that was more and more forcibly to be made on the major concepts of Hegelian philosophy by the Hegelian Left or, as they were later to be known, the Young Hegelians. Broadly, Schelling attacked Hegel's philosophy as being negative, 'comprehending merely potential being but not real being as it comes to the attention of thought'.[4]

Schelling made the further point that his new advocation of a 'positive' rather than a 'negative' philosophy was an attempt to go beyond Hegel's teachings rather than return to Kant's.

Michael himself was not greatly influenced by Schelling's teaching and it was not until the winter of 1841, when Turgenev was visiting Russia and Paul and Varvara were in Dresden, that Michael seriously started studying the views of the Young Hegelians. However, Schelling's attack on Hegelian philosophy was of importance, for

Schelling was not alone in his opinion that Hegel's ontology lacked

57

immediate reference to real existence and observation; the Young Hegelians agreed with him. His statement that Hegel only 'affects' the real and transforms it into a 'wasteland of being' agrees with the criticisms of Feuerbach, Marx and Kierkegaard; the latter defends Schelling against Hegel because he, at least, made an attempt at putting a halt to the reflection of thought upon itself. Therefore Schelling was justified in stating that it was superfluous to come to the defence of the Hegelian philosophy against him. Even those who took Hegel's part and opposed him 'did so partially at least not in order to oppose positive philosophy; on the contrary, they themselves also wanted something of the sort. Only they were of the opinion that this positive philosophy would have to be erected on the basis of the Hegelian system and could not be erected upon any other; further, the Hegelian system lacked nothing more than their effort to continue it in a positive direction. This, they thought, could come about in a continuous progress, without interruption and without any turning back'.[5]

When lecturing in Berlin, and knowing full well that he had many, if not all, of the Hegelians in his audience, Schelling could congratulate himself that 'The tension is unbelievable, and already . . . all precautions have been taken to see that the enormous pressure to get into the largest lecture room, itself relatively small, does not cause any difficulties'. But Schelling was not to emerge victorious and indeed the Young Hegelians soon rejected his diatribe as Schelling's 'latest attempt at reaction'.

In the winter of 1841–2, without any of his faithful disciples, Michael was left alone to study and to think. It was during this period that he was faced by a distinct challenge, and in fact the year 1842 was, without doubt, the threshold of Michael's transition from abstract philosopher to abstract revolutionary. Before this period it could still be said that Michael was basically a conservative. He treasured what was unchanging – Premukhino, the Russian countryside, Tatyana – yet his instinct was for change, and often for destruction. It was as if the beloved realities of his life were the wings and stage of a theatre, and within the confines of this immovable structure Michael would create a world of his own that was either a better way of presenting the old world or an optimistic assessment of a possible future. In this void between basic conservatism and instinctive rebellion Michael invariably found himself alone and painfully isolated from those around him. Never a man to face unpleasant realities if he could help it, Michael was curiously objective about his lack of fulfilment. In 1840 he had written to

Stankevich saying, 'My whole life, my whole virtue has consisted in a kind of abstract spiritual force, and that force has been shipwrecked on the sordid trivialities of life, on empty family quarrels and quarrels between friends, and on my own . . . disablement.'[6] Without Paul, without Varvara and without Turgenev, Michael became an island of solitude, of frustrated aspiration and of halting self-knowledge. Beyond this loneliness was the inevitable sexual aridity of which he knew himself to be a victim and to which Katkov had so brutishly drawn public attention. Yet, unbeknown to Michael, the sexual drive that eluded him and caused much of his inner loneliness had drained into the enormous drive of energy that seemed so spectacular to outsiders. For despite Michael's continued inner feelings of inadequacy and failure his outer personality remained both dynamic and magnetic. Turgenev, for instance, had written to Michael in 1840, saying, 'I arrived in Berlin. I devoted myself to science – the first stars were kindled on my sky, and at last I knew you, Bakunin. Stankevich brought us together – and death will not part us. I can scarcely put into words what I owe to you.'[7] Turgenev was not always to have such a high opinion of Michael and indeed few were who had known him over a long period. In the words of some anonymous contemporary, Michael could be compared to 'a great ship, without rudder, drifting before the wind and not knowing why or whither'. The ship was fully rigged and very spectacular to look at but nevertheless Michael himself was afraid of the unknown spectral figure at the wheel. Who was this inner being? Was he a charlatan? A fool? A hypocrite? Or, worst of all, was there nobody there at all? Professor Lampert says of Michael,

His ideas were neither philosophical concepts, nor intellectual propositions, nor intuitions: they were neither guides nor – at any rate, until he embarked upon his revolutionary career – materials for action, but mental states. He seemed to acquire them, not by thought or insight, but by breathing the haunted air. They thronged his mind with all the vividness of sensation. For ordinary men an idea, an image is less alive than sensation. Day-dreams satisfy emotional needs and fulfil frustrated desires; but they are pale shadows of real life, and at the back of man's mind is the awareness that the demands of the world of sense have another validity. With Bakunin it was not so. His ideas and day-dreams were so significant to him that it is the world of sense that was shadowy and he had to reach out to it by an effort of the will.[8]

Despite Michael's vision of it as a vital environment for the liberated mind, Berlin was, like Russia, also subjected to the persecution of intellectual thought. In 1840 Wilhelm IV became King of Prussia and by 1841 this highly reactionary monarch had launched into a series of attacks on radical philosophical thought. It was largely because of these attacks that books such as Feuerbach's *The Essence of Christianity* were received with so much interest, and it was this book that was to make the most significant contribution towards the cause of the Young Hegelians. Broadly speaking, Feuerbach brought Hegel's philosophy more into keeping with the changing times, whilst Bauer and Stirner, representing a second attack, 'brought all the philosophy to an end in radical criticism and nihilism'. Later Marx and Kierkegaard each produced his own radical conclusions from this drastically altered situation, Kierkegaard philosophically destroying the bourgeois-Christian world and Marx the bourgeois-capitalist world.

Feuerbach, like Michael, was lured to Berlin by its promise of liberated intellectual stimulation, studied for two years with Hegel, and immediately took steps to make radical changes in the basic concepts of Hegelian philosophy. But the Young Hegelians, in their interpretations of Feuerbach's *The Essence of Christianity*, managed to find powerful reasons for turning politically dormant Hegelianism into revolution. It was worked out as follows: if everything real is in itself rational, nevertheless the method of dialectics proves that everything real is subject to change. Hegel had viewed history as a reflection of a dialectical process in the development of various ideas. Feuerbach and later Marx simply reversed this dialectical principle

denying the dominant role of ideas in history claimed by Hegel, and declaring that material things, while actually developing as dialectical processes, do so in their own right, as it were, and not as reflections of the development of independently existing ideas. On the contrary, it was the ideas which were the reflections of material reality.[9]

Thus was born the Young Hegelians' conversion of Hegelianism from acceptance to rebellion on the basis that a rigid acceptance of the status quo could hardly be rational.

In the sphere of influence upon Michael during this period the name of Feuerbach is inseparably linked with that of Arnold Ruge. It was Ruge who first introduced Michael to the new interpretation of Hegelianism and it was Ruge who was initially responsible for Michael's break from conservative thought. Ruge based his philosophy upon the statement that 'everything depends on history', which was a more complete view than Feuerbach's despite the fact that Ruge had qualified his remark in Hegelian tradition as 'philosophical history'. Ever since 1838 Ruge had issued a review of politics and philosophy which had gradually become the more or less official journal of the Young Hegelians. It was produced in Halle and called the *Hallische Jahrbücher* and Michael had already been familiar with it before he had left Russia. But by 1840 Wilhelm IV, already incensed by the Strauss scandal, attempted to suppress the diminutive group of the Hegelian Left by ordering the journal to cease publication. Ruge, however, merely moved from Prussia to the more liberal Saxony, and from Dresden republished the review under the title of *Deutsche Jahrbücher*. Amongst the journal's distinguished contributors were Feuerbach, Strauss and Bauer, and Karl Löwith states that Ruge was justified in being proud of it as

> no other German scholarly periodical ever experienced such satisfaction, seeing its discussions became events which went far beyond the circle of theoreticians, becoming involved in all of life. To the present day, German philosophy has nothing comparable to this journal which could equal it in critical forcefulness, effectiveness, and influence upon political theory.[10]

The critical content of the *Jahrbücher* was mainly concerned with politics and religion and Ruge's own writings had a brisk 'atheistic-republican' tone to them. But in fact, compared with Bauer's later outstripping of the criticism of religion made by Strauss and Feuerbach, Ruge was a moderate. Ruge's own explanation of the differences between Young and Old Hegelians was also published in the *Jahrbücher*. He said that the Old Hegelians adapted Hegel's philosophy to what actually existed whilst the Young Hegelians turned the philosophy of right and the philosophy of religion into a 'negating and postulating activism'. The Young Hegelians then made two major protestations. The first was the revolt against the limitation of Hegelian thought in transferring actual political reality from its contemporary course back to a situation that was now totally out of date. The second protestation was made against the blatant arrogance of total philosophy which

> seeks to be a 'present-day apocalypse' through recollection of what has been, whereas philosophy actually merely begins the future through its criticism in the present. Instead of constructing an absolute State by means of the categories of logic, the present existence of the State must be criticized historically with reference

to the immediate future. For only the spirit of the age, as it realizes itself, is truly comprehended reality, as Hegel himself teaches 'in a hundred passages', although he avoided everything that might give offence to the Church and the State.[11]

Michael had met Ruge briefly before being converted to the Hegelian Left. He found him interesting if highly materialistic and also saw him as a strong challenge to the complacent German temperament of the times that Michael was learning to dislike intensely. It took Michael the winter of 1841–2 to become a convert to the Hegelian Left. During this period the Young Hegelians had, to the infuriation of Wilhelm, distributed a vast amount of propaganda concerning their cause in the form of leaflets and pamphlets. Michael read every one of these and gradually his instinct overrode his conservatism and he began to interpret Hegel in a revolutionary sense. In the spring of 1842 Michael moved to Dresden to be nearer Ruge and the passionate focus of the Hegelian Left.

II

Michael had now completely lost sight of preparing for a professorship at Moscow University. He had done three terms at Berlin University and even this sustained effort had seemed an eternity. Ruge, Dresden and the revolutionary concepts of the Young Hegelians were eminently more attractive. Ruge and his journal, the *Deutsche Jahrbücher*, very much appealed to Michael and he felt sure that he would soon be able to penetrate its columns. In October 1842 Michael did succeed in publishing an article in the *Deutsche Jahrbücher*; it was a vital milestone in his awakening revolutionary consciousness as well as being one of the best-composed essays of his career. It was also one of the best articles that the *Jahrbücher* itself had published. Written under the French pseudonym of 'Jules Elysard', the essay was entitled 'Reaction in Germany: From the Note-books of a Frenchman'. Basically the essay was couched in Hegelian philosophic language and its aim was to argue the theme of permanent social and political revolution. However, its flavour was very much in accord with Michael's own personality and its target was the liberals or, as Michael preferred to call them, 'the compromisers' who sat on the fence without being committed to the Left or to the Right. It criticized the Jews, for whom Michael often barely concealed his dislike, and much of the content had religious overtones. These were to appear continuously in his writings until 1860, when his later studies of socialist ideas had determined his public acceptance of atheism.

To the compromisers we can only apply what was said in a French journal: 'The Left says, two times two are four; the Right, two times two are six; and the middle-of-the-road compromisers say two times two are five.' They never answer yes or no; they say: 'To a certain extent you are right, but on the other hand . . .' And if they have nothing left to say, they say: 'Yes, it is a curious thing.' . . . And as it is said of the Polish Jews that in the last Polish war they wanted to serve both warring parties simultaneously, the Poles as well as the Russians, and consequently were hanged by both sides impartially, so these poor souls vex themselves with the impossible business of the outward reconciliation of opposites, and are despised by both parties for their pains. No, the spirit of revolution is not subdued, it has only sunk into itself in order soon to reveal itself again as an affirmative, creative principle, and right now it is burrowing – if I may avail myself of this expression of Hegel's – like a mole under the earth.[12]

The impact of social revolution was clear. The essay also included a clarion call which was to become a continuous crusade – that the lowest classes of the poor held the greatest revolutionary potential. The essay ended on an impassioned exhortation:

To the Positivists we say: 'Open the eyes of your mind; let the dead bury the dead, and convince yourselves at last that the Spirit, ever young, ever newborn, is not to be sought in fallen ruins!' And we exhort the compromisers to open their hearts to truth, to free themselves of their wretched and blind circumspection, of their intellectual arrogance, and of the servile fear which dries up their souls and paralyses their movements.
Let us therefore trust the eternal spirit which destroys and annihilates only because it is the unfathomable and eternal source of all life. The passion for destruction is a creative passion, too.[13]

Michael also pointed out that true democracy was as yet a pure ideal which could only come to fruition when it had overthrown reaction and achieved its own totally independent existence. There could be no compromise between democracy and reaction, and when the last famous phrase of the essay, 'The passion for destruction is a creative passion, too!', is applied both politically and socially it must become clear that Michael, all too often vague and woolly in his future writings, had written a fresh, vivid and well-reasoned essay.

Not only did the piece mark the end of his philosophical era and the beginning of his revolutionary one but, as implied by the French pseudonym, Michael was becoming more and more enamoured with the practicalities of French theory, which left the idealism of German metaphysics in a void of its own – an unreal, impractical world in which revolution could not flourish. Already Michael had been enormously impressed with *Politique du Peuple* by Lemennais and had become acquainted with the political philosophy of Proudhon, Fourier and Stein. *Politique du Peuple* appeared about the time of the publication of Michael's essay in the *Jahrbücher* and suddenly a new and positive world was opened up to him on which to focus his new revolutionary concepts. Russia, apart from its desperately-clung-to family memories, was now an impossible base for his activities and the much-longed-for Germany was now also an ideal of the past. Now Michael was looking towards France and the theories of men like Proudhon as a pointer to that previously ill-defined sense of mission that now seemed to him to be gathering more substance.

Meanwhile, reactions to the essay came in a series of glowing tributes to Michael from many of his older Russian friends. The pseudonym was never given much credence and once it had leaked out that Michael had written the piece Herzen confided in his diary that 'the article is wonderful from beginning to end'. Expressing his full agreement with Michael's sentiments, Herzen also added that 'He [Michael] is wiping out his former sins – I am completely reconciled to him.' Botkin wrote Michael an enthusiastic and friendly letter whilst even Belinsky was moved to say that 'Michael and [he] had sought God by different paths, but met at last in the same temple'.

But there was another reason – a very powerful reason – for the use of a pseudonym. Even if the Saxon Government was fractionally more liberal than the Prussian Government, it certainly regarded the article as extremely inflammatory and although no immediate action was taken it was clear that the *Deutsche Jahrbücher* and its contributors were in some jeopardy.

That October a young German political poet named Georg Herwegh arrived in Dresden on a short visit. Herwegh, the only son of a famous Stuttgart restaurateur, had given up a theological career for the law and had then given up the law for literature; he also had considerable medical knowledge. In 1841 he had published in Zurich a collection of political poems called 'Poems of One Who is Alive'. Herwegh's poems were echoes of the new young and democratic German movement. They were revolutionary in content and extremely stimulating. At the time, Herwegh's poems were a best-seller and he was precipitated into instant and dangerous fame – fame that severely sabotaged an already self-indulgent personality. Herwegh became the darling of German democracy and even the reactionary Wilhelm IV of Prussia received him, muttering something about respecting honourable opponents.

The good-looking young poet, who was later to cause such tragic emotional strife in the Herzen family, made a favourable impression on Michael. 'Young Germany', the movement that looked towards the progressive political-philosophical views in France and of which Herwegh was a representative, to a large extent expressed Michael's new conceptions. Not only was all this in Herwegh's favour but as Turgenev and Paul would soon be returning to Russia there would be a vacancy for a disciple. Michael was immediately attracted to Herwegh and wished to protect his new-found friend from the realities and responsibilities of life that Herwegh was so keen to avoid. For his part, Herwegh was content to allow Michael to indulge himself by dominating him. Despite his physical delicacy Herwegh professed to be a man of action and Michael, full of his new revolutionary zeal, welcomed this, for he too was a man of action now that he had realized the ethereal dangers of German metaphysics. In addition, Herwegh not only had plenty of money but he also edited the *Deutsche Bote*. This radical journal, published in Switzerland, might well become an outlet for Michael's articles. Michael was now back on top of the world. The days of grey indecision were over and although the 'interior' loneliness persisted, life was infinitely more exciting. The future was full of unexplored possibilities and, as ever, Michael managed once more to create a generous supply of his own adrenalin.

On leaving Dresden for Berlin Herwegh met Emma Siegmund, the daughter of a rich Berlin Jewish silk merchant, whom he later married. At the same time the reactionary Wilhelm IV, who had recently been remarkably courteous to Herwegh, suddenly banned the circulation of *Deutsche Bote* in Prussia, which was a serious blow. Herwegh, arrogant and furious, wrote an outspoken letter to Wilhelm which coincidentally or otherwise was published in the press. Wilhelm's reaction was to give the illustrious Herwegh twenty-four hours to leave the country. Michael decided to join him in his speedy return to Switzerland.

Although Michael was eager to leave Germany he was not solely motivated by his desire to substitute revolution for metaphysics. Owing to his controversial article, and his association with Ruge and Herwegh, the Prussian and Saxon authorities both regarded him with suspicion, and he suddenly had the unpleasant thought that if the authorities *did* decide to expel him in the same manner as Herwegh then it was possible that they might hand him back to Russia. Moreover, he was loath to lose the companionship of Herwegh of whom he had become extremely fond, so in early January 1843 he joined him in Karlsruhe en route for Switzerland, leaving behind him a mass of debts.

III

The transition from Berlin to the heavy conservatism of Zurich unsettled Michael and made him lethargic. Suddenly his self-confidence failed him and the 'inner' isolation became more apparent. This may in part be due to the fact that just before he left Dresden he had made a very genuine friendship – perhaps the most genuine he ever had – with an apolitical musician named Adolf Reichel. Reichel, at that time a music teacher at the Conservatorium, was a gentle and 'whole' person. He admired and liked Michael but was not dominated by him, and neither did Michael, for once, feel the need to dominate or to protect Reichel. Reichel's sister Matilda, however, developed what was now the routine ardour women seemed to have for Michael, and he took the usual avoiding action. Despite this, Matilda, like her brother, always retained a very warm place in her heart for him and perhaps it was the fact of leaving such steadfast friendship behind that increased Michael's sense of isolation in Zurich. It was Adolf Reichel who was later to summarize Michael's character by remarking that he would 'grow in a hurricane and ripen better in stormy weather than in sunshine'.

Nevertheless Michael remained depressed. Herwegh was his only friend in Zurich and he was now completely wrapped up in preparations for his marriage. Dreamily Michael lived alone, absorbing the brilliance of the landscape with its mountains and lakes, yet finding all this pastoral beauty very unconducive to work or to future planning. A kind of sad nostalgia filled him, in the foreground of which was Herwegh, on whom Michael now doted as if he were one of his own sisters. Herwegh's forthcoming marriage held a gentle delight for Michael, as if he were personally about to arrange the marriage of two children. Steeped in sentimental delight Michael wrote to Paul Bakunin in February 1843:

> Sometimes I lie here for hours together on the divan, gazing on the lake and the mountains, which are specially beautiful in the setting sun, watching the tiniest changes in the picture, changes that follow one another without ceasing; and I think, think of everything, and feel sad and cheerful and merry; and everything in front of me is hidden in a mist.[14]

Michael was in dreamland; it was as if he were enchanted and able to move lightly through an insubstantial world.

In March 1843 Michael was best man at Herwegh's wedding to Emma, which took place in the canton of Bâle where Herwegh was now sheltering. The authorities in the canton of Zurich had asked Herwegh to leave because of the revolutionary nature of his work and his expulsion from Prussia. Herwegh and Emma then left for Italy and publication of the *Deutsche Bote* fell into abeyance. A book appeared containing material originally intended for the Journal but Michael had done no work to include in it.

In April Michael visited some Italian friends from Dresden, a singer named Pescantini and his wife, on the shores of the Lake of Geneva for a few days. There Michael idolized Pescantini's wife Johanna, considered she was too 'perfect' for her husband and started vaguely to think in terms of 'liberating' her from her unworthy husband as he had tried to liberate Varvara. Michael began to emerge from the temporary shadows he had dreamily slipped into as once again he began to play his favourite role. At the same time, the question of money, particularly since the departure of Herwegh, was becoming a major problem. Somewhat ungallantly, particularly bearing in mind his intentions towards his wife, Michael had borrowed money from Pescantini. However, this was not a ready means of supply and with Belinsky, Botkin, Herzen and Turgenev still in Russia, Ruge in Dresden and Herwegh in Italy, Michael's previous sources of ready money had now dried up. Ruge now began to press for repayment (being owed over 2000 thalers) and Michael, who was meeting no response to his desperate appeals for money to Premukhino, finally drew a cheque on Turgenev's bank to pay off the by now highly indignant Ruge. Unfortunately the cheque bounced and Ruge, now near apoplexy, could no longer be silenced. Suddenly life was no longer nostalgic or pastoral; it had become a nightmare of manipulative thinking and in the end he wrote another desperate letter to Premukhino (addressed to his more sympathetic brothers) pleading for cash to prevent him going into prison (which he feared) or facing dishonour (which did not worry him quite so much). Both Paul and Nicholas were most concerned. Encouraged by the ever-faithful Natalie Beyer they made plans which resulted in Tatyana ironically writing to her adored Turgenev and squeezing money out of him for Michael, while Alexander made up the rest. As usual with this kind of situation trouble quickly developed. Turgenev wrote Tatyana a brusque letter which considerably upset her and made her frustrated love for him all the worse, and Alexander Bakunin, old and feeble as he was, grew more cynical than ever about his eldest son. But at least Michael was in funds again.

The final catalyst to the renaissance of Michael's activity was Wilhelm Weitling. Michael had already made the acquaintance of a number of radical Swiss thinkers. He had met the liberal Professor of Natural Sciences, Vogt, and his wife Luisa (who were to become as firm friends as Reichel and his sister), Follen, the leader of the Zurich radical party, Julius Fröbel, August Becker and many others. Inevitably Becker told Michael of the ideas of Georg Büchner, of whom he was a friend and associate, whilst Vogt contributed towards Michael's gradual loss of the sense of a spiritual world. But it was Weitling who was the most important corner-stone, not just in Michael's progress towards becoming a revolutionary but in his first conceptions of anarchy.

Weitling was an extraordinary man. Highly articulate and often fanatical, he was more than a match for even Michael's ebullient personality. His book, *Guarantees of Harmony and Freedom*, contained a sentence which made an immediate impact on Michael. The sentence read, 'The perfect society has no government, but only an administration, no laws, but only obligations, no punishments, but means of correction.' Michael did not question whether or not human frailty was up to this kind of test. Instead he suddenly seized the sentence as an instinctive goal – something that he must fight towards. It was also a logical extension to the concluding paragraph of Michael's essay, 'Reaction in Germany', when he stated that 'The passion for destruction is a creative passion too!'

In May 1843 Weitling visited Michael in Zurich with an introductory letter from Herwegh. The illegitimate son of a German girl and a French officer, Weitling, a tailor by trade, escaped military service and wandered from country to country. In Paris, where he arrived in 1835, Weitling studied the principles of both communistic and revolutionary practice. In 1839, however, he was asked to leave the country and spent the remainder of his years before meeting

Michael wandering in Switzerland, working towards the practical implementation of the vital paragraph in *Guarantees of Harmony and Freedom*. Michael, who had already read and admired the book some weeks before Weitling appeared, was delighted to meet him.

Basically Weitling's influence on Michael's fluid revolutionary zeal can be divided into three main areas. Firstly, he directed Michael's attention towards the labour movement and the proletariat. Secondly, by his utopian conceptions Weitling pushed Michael a long way towards his eventual anarchism. Thirdly, he made Michael realize how important in terms of revolutionary conspiracy were the *déclassé* groups in society. But despite the major role these influences played in Michael's life, Weitling was totally unable to convert him to true communism. In fact, in an article in *Der Schweizerische Republikaner* (which was edited by Fröbel) in June 1843 Michael roundly condemned communism. He said,

> once and for all we announce that we are not communists. We have as little desire as the gentlemen from the *Observer* to live in a state built according to Weitling's plan, one which is not the expression of a free society, but rather a herd of animals organized by compulsion and force and concerned solely with material interests, ignoring the spiritual side of life.[15]

But Weitling's basic attraction for Michael was that unlike Ruge or Herwegh, who would only preach revolution in theoretical or poetic terms, Weitling was an activist. His fanaticism demanded action, violence and the overthrow of those who opposed communism. It was this very fanaticism which Michael instinctively sympathized with so much and made him shrug off his temporary vagueness. Now Michael was beginning to subjugate himself, in theory at least, to the industrial proletariat – the poorest of the poor whom he now firmly assumed were to be the very nub of the impending revolution.

Weitling, however, had attracted the attention of the Zurich authorities. Owing to the impending publication of his new book, *The Gospel of a Poor Sinner* (which depicted Christ as rebel, communist and illegitimate son of Mary), he was arrested, sentenced to six months imprisonment and then expelled.

It was Weitling's arrest that set in motion the active persecution of Michael's own political freedom. Observing how closely associated Michael had become with the politically dangerous Weitling and having already noted the content of 'Reaction in Germany' and Michael's relationship with Ruge and Herwegh, the Russian Legation at Berne showed paternalistic displeasure in their erring

Russian son of noble birth. While Michael spent the summer with the Pescantinis and the autumn and winter in Berne, where Reichel came to join him, Alexander Bakunin was instructed by the Russian Government to order his son home, and not to send any more money abroad to him. Alexander obeyed the second command but was unable to comply with the first. For after all, no matter how he worried over Michael's future, Alexander knew that he had no control over it, for he obviously had no influence over his eldest son.

On 6 February 1844 Michael was told by the Russian Legation in Berne that he was to return home to Russia immediately. Despite a self-acknowledged fear of the retribution that would face him if he did not comply with the order, Michael steeled himself to disobey. Instead of returning dutifully to Russia, in company with Reichel Michael compromised by leaving for Brussels.

IV

Two further vital influences on Michael's life presented themselves during the next three months in Brussels. The first was the result of a visit to Paris and the second was the cause of the Polish émigrés. At this time Paris was the focal point of those requiring political asylum. Ruge had moved there, the Herweghs were living there in some style and Michael immediately found the atmosphere to be one of satisfactory revolutionary fervour. The city thronged with émigrés, largely from Germany, who continuously advocated the overthrow of the bourgeois State.

Arriving in Paris in March, Michael discovered that a short-lived successor to the *Deutsche Jahrbücher* was being published by Ruge under the name of the *Deutsch-Französische Jahrbücher*. The first – and in fact the last – number carried a great scoop: an article by Karl Marx on Hegel's *Philosophy of Law*. The journal also contained a letter, written to Ruge by Michael the previous May, which urged Ruge not to despair (if indeed he did) of revolutionary ideals and prospects. Michael went on to add that it was France which would be the hatching-place of future revolutionary plans. Ruge, however, needed no such personal bolstering for he saw himself, somewhat egocentrically, as the catalyst if not the principal figure in a new revolutionary movement set in Paris and spiralling all over Europe. To marshal his would-be lieutenants, Ruge convened a meeting during Michael's stay of those with revolutionary commitment and it was at this conference that Michael was to meet Karl Marx.

The electric environment of revolutionary Paris did not impress Marx. He had an unemotional personality and distrusted enthusiasm and melodrama. He had simply chosen Paris because it was convenient to utilize the potential of the *Deutsch-Französische Jahrbücher*, which was meant to attract both a German- and a non-German-speaking public. He was also trying to define the factor responsible for the failure of the French Revolution. Originally a Hegelian convert, Marx was rapidly making himself familiar with the economic and political teachings of both French and English thinkers, looking at them carefully in contrast to his Young Hegelian thought and slowly working towards the establishing of his own attitude. In 1843, for instance, Marx had written of France,

> In France every class is tinged with political idealism, and feels itself a representative of general social needs . . . whereas in Germany, where practical life is unintelligent, and intelligence unpractical, men are driven to protest only by the material necessity, the actual chains themselves . . . but revolutionary energy and self-confidence are not sufficient by themselves to enable a class to be the liberator of society – it must identify another class with the principle of oppression . . . as in France the nobility and priesthood were identified. This dramatic tension is absent in German society . . . there is only one class whose wrongs are not specific but those of the whole society – the proletariat.[16]

At the first meeting between Michael and Marx neither particularly registered their common dislike of German society or the totally opposite nature of their personalities. At Ruge's meeting, which was held on 23 March 1844, the German contingent was represented by Ruge, Marx and Bernays (a journalist); the French by Blanc, Pyat and Leroux; and the Russian by Botkin, Tolstoy and Michael.

Some days later Michael returned to Brussels and to the dull job as a Conservatorium teacher that the forward-looking Reichel had obtained for him to prevent him running into debt again. But Reichel's hopes of Michael settling down in a steady job with a steady income were soon to be dashed as Michael's boredom with Brussels and enchantment with Paris increased. There was only one diversion: the Polish cause.

Directly Michael had arrived in Brussels he had seen the first of the Polish émigrés and become friendly with Joachim Lelewel, one of their more powerful representatives. Gradually Michael had become familiar with one of the chief Polish goals – the demand for the reclamation of the 'historic Poland' of 1772 which included in its territory White Russia, Little Russia and Lithuania. In fact Michael disagreed with this imperialistic desire, considering that these areas had every right to maintain their independence. But despite his lack of sympathy for these territorial requirements, Michael had every sympathy for the Poles themselves as refugees and victims of Russian and Prussian overlordship. They, however, largely regarded Michael as more of a nuisance than anything else in terms of their future plans. Nettlau points out in an essay that has been used as a Preface to Maximoff's selection of Michael's political philosophy that

> since the Poles as well as Bakunin saw in each other a revolutionary factor of some real value, the subject was rarely discussed frankly, and all attempts at mutual action were destined to failure. To this was added the fact that the question of liberation of the peasants and the distribution of land naturally separated Bakunin from the powerful aristocratic Polish party, as did also their extreme clericalism.

In July 1844 Michael persuaded Reichel to leave Brussels and to come and live with him in Paris. Unwillingly Reichel agreed, probably realizing what a costly sojourn it would prove to be for any friend of Michael's. Yet Reichel was too fond of Michael to try to dissuade him and indulgently he accompanied his ebullient friend to Paris.

V

Michael lived in Paris for the next three and a half years and there he first encountered Proudhon. Pierre-Joseph Proudhon came from genuine peasant stock. He was born in 1809 in Besançon, son of a poverty-stricken free-lance brewer and a servant. At eight the boy became a cowherd, but by twelve he was already reading intensively. As a result his mother managed to get him into college as a day boy and he finally attained the top class before his father insisted that he earn his living. He entered the printing trade and used his position as apprentice, printer's reader and compositor to further his education. After a short period in Paris, Proudhon toured France, completing his course as a compositor, and then returned to Besançon where he started a printing shop. Later he gained the Suard scholarship at Besançon Academy and in 1840 he published the pamphlet entitled *What Is Property?*, the text of which began:

If I were asked to answer the following question: *What is slavery?* and I should answer in one word, *It is murder*, my meaning would be understood at once. No extended argument would be required to show that the power to take from a man his thought, his will, his personality, is a power of life and death; and that to enslave a man is to kill him. Why, then, to this other question: *What is property?* may I not likewise answer, *It is robbery*, without the certainty of being misunderstood; the second proposition being no other than a transformation of the first?

This pamphlet was the first step in Proudhon's philosophical career and when Marx and later Michael arrived in Paris he was at the height of his success. Isaiah Berlin sees him as

a man of narrow, obstinate, fearless, puritanical character, a typical representative of the French lower middle class which, after playing an active part in the final overthrow of the Bourbons, found it had merely succeeded in changing masters, and that the new government of bankers and large industrialists, from whom Saint-Simon had taught them to expect so much, had merely increased the tempo of their destruction.[17]

Proudhon had two main targets: the accumulation of wealth and the way this accumulation was used to dominate the poor and associate political authority with economic control. In other words he considered that the State practised a legal form of theft. He later modified this extremely radical statement on the basis that a minimum of property was required by each man in order to retain independence and dignity, but throughout his life Proudhon considered that monopoly was one of the greatest destroyers of mankind's potential for a fair and equal society.

Proudhon rejected God in the same way as he rejected the political institution and establishment. Indeed he regarded God as personified by the institutionalized Christ as totally evil, and believed that Christianity would break down once a true age of scientific knowledge and reason had been achieved.

Michael introduced Proudhon to Hegel, and Proudhon, who knew no German, was extremely grateful to the blustering young Russian.

73

Michael found Proudhon better company than the obsessive and highly aggressive Weitling, and it was Proudhon, with his attack on the State, on God and on private property, no matter how fluid or subject to change his ideas were, who became the major catalyst to Michael's anarchism. They spent days and nights together with Proudhon talking of his own form of liberation and Michael of Hegel, and as a result there was considerable cross-fertilization. This was evident for instance in Proudhon's *Economic Contradictions*, published in 1846, with its slogan '*Destruam et Aedificabo*'. The whole work was not only distortedly Hegelian in style but also had echoes of Michael's now famous phrase 'The passion for destruction is a creative passion'. Michael was always to acknowledge his debt to Proudhon and never to accept that he himself had been a considerable influence over Proudhon. At the same time he realized that Proudhon was too much of an individualist to weld others together in any organized political movement. In 1870, for instance, Michael was to write,

> As I told him a few months before his death, Proudhon, in spite of all his efforts to shake off the tradition of classical idealism, remained all his life an incorrigible idealist, immersed in the Bible, in Roman Law and metaphysics. His great misfortune was that he had never studied the natural sciences or appropriated their method.[18]

Of course these rather patronizing comments themselves fail to indicate just how important Proudhon had been to Michael's development towards anarchism. Something of the man's personal force, however, comes across as Michael continues by pointing out that

> He had the instincts of a genius and he glimpsed the right road, but, hindered by his idealistic thinking patterns, he fell always into the old errors . . . Marx as a thinker is on the right path. He has established the principle that juridicial evolution in history is not the cause but the effect of economic development, and this is a great and fruitful concept . . . On the other hand, Proudhon understood and felt liberty much better than he. Proudhon, when not obsessed with metaphysical doctrine, was a revolutionary by instinct; he adored Satan and proclaimed Anarchy. Quite possibly Marx could construct a still more rational system of liberty, but he lacks the instinct of liberty – he remains from head to foot an authoritarian.[19]

The strange point about this piece of writing is that Michael, in describing Proudhon's idealism, could well be describing himself. Equally strangely, in the light of the events to come, Michael could, even in 1870, apparently fully appreciate Marx's qualities. But at this particular stage, in 1844, Michael saw Proudhon as a major social revolutionist whilst Marx saw him only as a utopian and a reformist.

Michael's relationship with Marx was very different from his relationship with Proudhon. For two people who were poles apart in temperament, it was ironic to see how much Michael and Karl Marx had in common. They both disliked the coldly impersonal and power-hungry Ruge. They both admired the work of Herwegh. Both disliked the backwardness of German thought and both hoped that French thought would inspire European if not international revolution. Michael later (in 1871) wrote about his early encounters with Marx in Paris.

As far as learning was concerned, Marx was, and still is, incomparably more advanced than I. I knew nothing at that time of political economy, I had not yet rid myself of my metaphysical aberrations, and my socialism was only instinctive. Although younger than I, he was already an atheist, a conscious materialist and an informed socialist. It was precisely at this time that he was elaborating the foundations of his system as it stands today. We saw each other often, I greatly respected him for his learning and for his passionate devotion – though it was always mingled with vanity – to the cause of the proletariat. I eagerly sought his conversation, which was always instructive and witty when it was not inspired by petty hate, which alas! was only too often the case. There was never any frank intimacy between us – our temperaments did not permit it. He called me a sentimental idealist, and he was right; I called him vain, perfidious and cunning, and I also was right.[20]

This was another objective piece of hindsight by Michael.

In 1844, however, Michael was mixing with a wide circle of German exiles, many of whom had been associated with the now defunct *Deutsch-Französische Jahrbücher*. In its place was a less costly news-sheet called *Vorwärts*, which was edited by Bernays and a fellow Jew, Bernstein. Michael wrote a number of essays for *Vorwärts* in 1844. His views here, as in his letter to the pompous Ruge in 1843, indicate a kind of sympathetic hopefulness concerning the socialist ideas of the day. He approved of them and indeed applauded them, but privately Michael felt frustrated over what he considered to be their limited aims. The socialists did not contemplate doing away with the old order and Michael was becoming more and more convinced that this would be more effective than attempting to 'improve' it. They would not liberate, they would only alleviate – and that, as far as Michael was concerned, was not aiming high enough. Nevertheless in 1876 Michael was to tell a French socialist that, during those early Paris days, 'we arrived at the firm belief that we were witnessing the last days of the old civilization, and that the age of equality would soon begin. Very few could resist this highly charged emotional atmosphere in Paris; two months on the boulevards was usually long enough to change a liberal into a Socialist.' However, despite the fact that many advanced ideas were put forward, no one idea was more forceful than the other. Meanwhile the bourgeois system continued to blossom.

During the summer and autumn of 1844 Michael, as usual, undertook no financially rewarding tasks. He lodged with one of Bernstein's brothers for a while and then returned to Reichel, presumably for reasons of greater financial security, remaining there for some time. He met George Sand, Lemennais, Cabet (who wrote *Voyage en Icarie*), Considérand, the leader of the Fourierists, and the Decembrist Russian Nikolai Turgenev, but without doubt Michael was mainly attracted to the radical journalists of the time. Unfortunately they were theorists – there was no action, only words – and it was the torrent of revolutionary, idealistic words that Michael was beginning to abhor. Certainly he still preferred the Paris socialism to the now despised German world of metaphysics, but the inaction of it all was beginning to gnaw at him. It is certainly significant that Michael spent very little of his time writing articles.

In December 1844 the Tsar issued a decree which condemned Michael to the loss of his noble rank and, in his absence, banished him to a period of hard labour in Siberia. He also confiscated all Michael's property in Russia and consigned it to the care of the State. Now Michael was completely exiled from the country and the home he had loved so dearly.

VI

In January 1845 *Vorwärts* published two anti-Prussian articles by Karl Marx. Immediately the incensed Prussian Government asked for Marx's expulsion from France. The French authorities complied with this request, at the same time suppressing the two articles. As a result the Marx family moved to Brussels. Now without Marx and having quarrelled with Ruge, Michael depended for company on the rich, socially conscious Herwegh, who took little interest in Michael's political ideology. The Herweghs led a superficial, highly fashionable life, and when Herwegh took a mistress the censorious Ruge was heavy in his condemnation. But, as usual, to Michael Herwegh could do no wrong. Indeed his fashionable life-style attracted Michael, who, with Reichel, spent a lot of his time at the Herweghs' house. There is little doubt that Michael thoroughly enjoyed the glossy intellectualism of Herweghian life, but this socializing and its attendant pleasures were to come to an abrupt end in January 1845 when Michael read in the *Gazette des Tribunaux* the Tsar's sentence upon him. This sentence also applied to another Russian whom Michael intensely disliked, a man named Ivan Golovin who at that time was also living in Paris. Annoyed, perhaps, that another shared his martyrdom, Michael wrote furiously to the radical French newspaper *La Réforme*, mainly in answer to a letter that Golovin had written in the *Gazette des Tribunaux* complaining that the Tsar's decree was a violation of the 'charter granted by the Romanovs to the Russian nobility'. Michael disagreed with this and wrote pointing out that the laws of Russia were basically the will of the Tsar. He then went into an impassioned defence of democracy, particularly as applied to oppressed peoples such as, in Michael's experience, the Russians and the Poles. Driven on by anger rather than logic, Michael penned his first positive revolutionary article against Russia, thereby cementing his position as traitor to his native land in the eyes of its authorities. Apart from criticizing Russian society and predicting a revolution, Michael also talked of his interest in the liberation of the Poles (as a prelude to revolution in Russia) and also the persecution of the Slavs by the Austrian empire – a subject that was to come to the fore in Michael's proclamations late in 1845.

Now, realizing more than ever his permanent isolation from Russia, the waves of Michael's homesickness rapidly began to intensify. It had been impossible to correspond with home since 1843, when Michael had become first politically undesirable and then an enemy of the Tsar, for the censor would have opened any attempts at communication. To have absolutely no news from home was becoming too much to bear and Michael would even have welcomed an angry letter from Alexander. But there was nothing, until, with his usual initiative, Michael found a way of sending letters from Paris to Premukhino via a returning Russian friend. He wrote to Paul and Tatyana both individually and jointly, for it was only those two whom he now really cared about. To his soul-mate Tatyana he sent a copy of his revolutionary letter to *La Réforme*, but she continued her two-year silence, despite his entreaties.

Michael managed to send these letters in the spring of 1845 and until the end of 1846 an irresolute mood settled on him, similar to the mood that had descended upon him in Switzerland a few years before. Having made his initial outburst in *La Réforme*, Michael did little to follow it up, and for a year life for him was trifling, lazy and dreamy. Various Russian visitors arrived in Paris and Michael seized on them eagerly, questioning them again and again on the news of the country from which he had exiled himself. He spent a considerable amount of time with Grigori Tolstoy, Reichel and Johanna Pescantini, with whose emotions and possible liberation from her undeserving husband Michael still toyed. He was genuinely fond of her but little came of it. Ogarev arrived in a desperate state of mind, his wife having left him, and so did Nicholas Sazonov, a former associate of the Herzen-Ogarev circle. Sasonov lived over-indulgently and was imprisoned for debt, causing the arrival from Russia of his horrified and hopefully counselling sisters. Ironically Maria, the elder, in trying to enlist Michael's support and advice, fell blindingly in love with him and the affair followed the usual course. Michael did not feel a great deal for Maria, or at least not as much as he felt for the cause of Johanna's liberation, yet this sort of affair was becoming a recurrent episode in Michael's life. Apart from these events and the publication of a long letter on the persecution of the Catholics in Lithuania and in White Russia in *Le Constitutionnel* on 10 March 1846, life was relatively without incident.

1847 was a far more positive and significant year in Michael's life. A number of his old friends arrived in Paris and life became more stimulating. First to arrive was Alexander Herzen, with his wife and entourage. Herzen found Michael superficially unchanged. As ebullient as ever, he retained the same eccentric mannerisms of enthusiasm and indeed his outward personality seemed exactly the same as it had been in Moscow a decade ago. However, Herzen soon discovered that even if Michael was unchanged superficially, his spiritual and political experience had broadened considerably. His years of liberation in Europe, the way he had turned Hegelian philosophy into a revolutionary code, his meetings with Proudhon and Marx – all this was almost overawing to Herzen, who, freshly arrived in Western Europe, felt himself to have stagnated in Russia for years. But his admiration was not to be of any long duration, and in his memoirs Herzen recalled that

In 1847 I still found the old Paris – a Paris, moreover, with a quickened pulse, that had been singing Béranger's songs, with the chorus 'Vive la réforme!' unexpectedly changed into 'Vive la Republique!'. Russians in those days continued to live in Paris with an ever-present, conscious sense of thankfulness to Providence (and to the regular despatch of remittances) that they were living in it, that they were strolling in the Palais Royal and going aux Français. They frankly worshipped lions and lionesses of every kind – celebrated doctors and dancing-girls, the dentist Désirabode and the mad Ma-Pa, and all the literary charlatans and political jugglers of the day.

I hate the systematic, prémédité insolence which is the fashion among us. I recognize in it the family traits of the old dashing arrogance of our officers and landowners, like that of Danthès, adapted to the manners of Vasilevsky Island and its streets. But it must not be forgotten that our servility to West European authorities also has come out of the same barracks, the same government offices, the same antechambers, though it has come out of the other door and is addressed to the grand gentleman, the officer chief or the commanding officer. In our lack of anything whatever to which to do homage, except brute force and its symbols, stars and ranks in the service, the demand to have a moral Table of Ranks is easy to understand; but, to make up for that, to what men have not the best of our contemporaries bowed down with tender devotion? Even before Werder and Ruge, those mighty dullards of Hegelianism. From this reverence for Germans it may easily be gathered how far they went in their attitude to Frenchmen, to men who are really remarkable – to Pierre Leroux, for instance, or George Sand herself . . .[21]

But as fast as Herzen acclimatized himself to the tatty, often superficial and debt-ridden society that existed behind the more grandiose revolutionary plotting, the more sceptical he became as to its real, intrinsic value. In their turn Michael and his friends were disappointed that Herzen did not bring better news from Russia. Even when writing 'Reaction in Germany' Michael had optimistically expressed the opinion that surely revolution, or at least the shadow of it, must be growing in his native land, but Herzen brought no such tidings. Herzen recalls that

After the first, noisy days in Paris more serious conversation began, and at once it became evident that we were tuned to very different keys. Sazonov and Bakunin ... were displeased that the news I brought referred more to the literary and university world than to political spheres. They expected to be told about parties, secret societies, ministerial crises (under Nicholas!) and the opposition (in 1847!), but I told them about professorships, Granovsky's public lectures, Belinsky's articles, and the mood of the students, and even of the seminarists. They had been too much separated from Russian life, and had entered too thoroughly into the interests of the 'all world' revolution and French problems, to remember that among us the appearance of *Dead Souls* was more important than the appointment of a couple of Paskeviches as field-marshals and a couple of Filarets as metropolitans. Without regular means of communication and with no Russian books and periodicals, they were related to Russia theoretically and from memory, which throws an artificial light on everything far away.[22]

As a result there was a slight flaw in the mutual pleasure of Herzen's reunion with Michael. Herzen, once he had returned to his normally analytical state of mind, saw the ineffectiveness of these 'world revolutionary' plotters and through the torrent of words only perceived that 'five men listened and did not understand, and five others did not understand and talked'. On the other hand, Michael, although disappointed that no revolutionary storm-clouds were immediately apparent on the Russian horizon and saddened to find matters so passive, was for the moment filled with a heady optimism. The new arrivals, the talk and the aspirations were as satisfying to Michael's nature as they were frustrating to Herzen's.

A few weeks after Herzen's arrival Belinsky also appeared in Paris. He was only to stay for a few months and returned to Russia in September 1847. To Michael, Belinsky was changed in both mind and body. He had finally renounced Hegel and the ardours of Hegelian reality and like Michael he was now looking towards France and its political philosophies as the great liberating and activist fount of wisdom. But he was also in an advanced stage of consumption and, like Stankevich before him, was slowly burning away. A shell of his former emphatic self, Belinsky was a pallid listener to the euphoric discussions and the liberated thought about him. 'It is strange', wrote Annenkov, 'that this admirer of the West and the western culture, on his way through the West, stood mute and listless before the monuments of that culture, as if absorbed in a wholly other, alien thought.'[23] Turgenev, however, who also briefly visited Paris that summer, put the situation rather more matter-of-factly by saying that Belinsky was 'too much of a Russian, feeling like a fish out of water outside Russia'.[24] He did, however, write a letter from Paris to Gogol, who that year had published in Russia a book called *Selected Passages from a Correspondence With Friends* in which he rejected his own art as a novelist and attributed a form of divine right to the established order of life. Professor Lampert interpreted his theory as follows: 'It is not "in vain" that God has decreed some women to be beautiful and others ugly; that some men are Governors General and others their clerks, some slaves and others slave owners; that some are oppressed and others their oppressors.'[25]

Belinsky's letter, bitterly attacking Gogol, began,

Russia needs no sermons (she has had enough of them!), but an awakening among the people of the sense of human dignity lost in dirt and dust during so many centuries . . . She presents the ghastly spectacle of a country where human beings are sold without even that justification of which American plantation lords cunningly avail themselves, by maintaining that a negro is not a man . . . The most vital national questions in Russia now are the abolition of serfdom, the abolition of corporal punishment, the implementation of at least those laws which already exist.[26]

But apart from this outburst Belinsky was finished – as was his former involvement, be it disciple-like or vengeful, with Michael. In June 1848 he died in Petersburg.

VII

At this time a revolutionary cause presented itself to Michael and ironically it was one that he had rejected several times during his years in Paris. Originally, in his Tsar-loving days, Michael had been totally uninterested in the fate of Poland. As far as he was concerned it was simply a boring country in which he had unwillingly been stationed, whose subjects were often disloyal to the Tsar. But gradually he became aware, via the French socialists, that the Polish cause was the darling of all enlightened liberal political thought, and Poland's oppressors – Austria, Russia and Prussia – were the archetypal triumvirate of bullies who gave the thought indisputable credence. The idea then occurred to Michael that by supporting

Polish nationalism as a revolutionary cause he could provide a stepping-stone to revolution in Russia itself. He had already come across Polish refugees in Germany and Prussia, had met more in Brussels, had underlined the oppression in both Poland and Russia in his article in *La Réforme*, and as a result had been approached several times by a number of exiled Polish representatives to whom he had responded somewhat unenthusiastically. Then, in 1846, the Polish insurrection ended with Cracow, the remaining free republic of Poland, being annexed by Austria with the approval of Russia, and at last Michael realized that the Polish problem was a fully-fledged revolutionary cause.

In Paris, more than anywhere else, the crushing of the Polish revolt caused immense reverberations. The exiled Poles were particularly powerful there and exerted considerable influence over both exiled and native intellectuals. Michael followed the short-lived rebellion throughout its course and at its collapse wrote a furious article in *Le Constitutionnel* supporting the liberation of Poland from the oppression of the Tsar.

The article, however, was not enough, for Michael was determined to show some practical involvement with the Polish cause. On this basis he immediately offered himself as an anti-Tsarist agitator either in Poland or elsewhere. The Poles were frankly suspicious of this young Russian who was offering his services in this magnanimous way, and anyway it was not altogether clear what he could actually do. Michael, however, was not in the least dismayed by the apathy of the exiled Poles to his grandiose offer of assistance, and although they did not call upon his services for some time, in November 1847 he agreed to speak at a banquet organized to celebrate the anniversary of the 1831 Polish insurrection.

The speech Michael gave, apart from proving him a remarkable orator, is clearly a landmark in his public career as a revolutionary in search of revolution, and the furore that followed it and culminated in his expulsion from France only served to enhance that reputation further. Pan-Slavism became Michael's specific revolutionary cause – a cause that he optimistically hoped would set off a great European revolution which in turn would lay the foundations for revolution in Russia. Realizing this potential, Michael spent a considerable time preparing his speech. It began,

Gentlemen: this is indeed a solemn moment for me. I am a Russian, and I come to this great assembly, gathered here to celebrate the anniversary of the Polish revolution. Your very presence here is a sort of defiance, a threat and a curse thrown into the face of all the oppressors of Poland. I have come here, gentlemen, inspired by a profound love and unshakable respect for my country.

I am not unaware of how unpopular Russia is in Europe. The Poles consider her, not without reason, as perhaps one of the principal causes of all their misfortunes. Men of independent opinion from other countries view the very rapid development of her power as an ever-growing danger to the liberty of peoples.[27]

He went on,

Almost a year ago – I believe it was after the massacre of Galicia, a Polish nobleman made you an extraordinary proposition, in a highly eloquent letter addressed to Prince Metternich, which has since become famous. No doubt carried away by his hatred for the Austrians which, by the way, was quite justified, he suggested nothing less than that you should submit to the Tsar, surrender yourselves, body and soul, to him, without drawback and without reservation. He advised you to do voluntarily what you had so far done under duress, and he promised you, in compensation, that as soon as you ceased to pose as slaves, your master would, in spite of himself, become your brother. Your brother, gentlemen, do you hear this? Emperor Nicholas your brother!

The oppressor, your bitterest enemy, the personal enemy of Poland, the executioner of so many victims, the man who ravished your liberty, the man who is pursuing you with relentless perseverance, as much through hate and by instinct as through political strategy – would you accept him as your brother? Each one of you would rather see Poland perish than consent to such a monstrous alliance.[28]

Michael proposed a form of revolutionary alliance between the Russian and Polish oppressed. He emphasized how miserable the Russian people were under the regime of Nicholas I, 'for if happiness were possible for the Russians in their present abject state, ours would be the basest, vilest people in the world'. Finally he summed up the idea of a revolutionary alliance by pointing out that,

To the extent that we have remained disunited, we have mutually paralysed ourselves. Together we shall be all-powerful for the good. Nothing could resist our common and united action. The reconciliation of Russia and Poland is a tremendous task, well worth our total devotion. This will be the emancipation of sixty million men, the deliverance of all the Slav peoples who are groaning under a foreign yoke. It will be, in the end, the fall, the definitive collapse of despotism in Russia.[29]

Michael's powerful oration and his grandiose urging of revolutionary conciliation between the Poles and the Russians made a tremendous impact on his audience, and sustained, wildly enthusiastic applause followed his speech. It is obvious that Michael's personal magnetism and his super-charged energy were as vital as ever, despite the fact that he had little or no idea how his ideas could be put into operation. For the moment it was enough that he had found the Polish cause and into this he was able to channel both his immense energy and the ebullient enthusiasm that was so contagious.

However, the Russian Ambassador, Count Kiselev, was far from enthusiastic over Michael's latest exploit and was furious when he heard the full content of his anti-Tsarist speech. He immediately took two lines of action. Firstly, he asked the French Government to expel Michael from France on the grounds that he had roundly attacked and preached revolutionary propaganda against a Government friendly to France on French soil. Secondly and far more subtly, in order to undermine Michael's good reputation with the Poles, Kiselev spread the rumour in Polish circles that Michael was a Russian agent planted amongst the émigrés and refugees in order to betray them.

More ambitiously, Kiselev also demanded the disbandment of all Polish organizations and committees in France, together with the expulsion of all Polish radicals or revolutionaries from the country. The French authorities, however, though they needed to pay lip-service to the Russian Government, were sympathetic to the exiles. They therefore refused to disband the Polish societies or to expel any Poles, and instead, on 14 December 1847, sent an expulsion order to Michael. He queried it but received no reply. As a result Michael unwillingly left for Brussels, leaving behind the shadow of suspicion that he was a Russian agent – a shadow that was to grow rather than lessen as the years passed.

Some doubt that Kiselev started the rumour and put the blame instead on groups of Polish exiles who still distrusted this extraordinary Russian noble who seemed to subsist without occupation or any obvious means of financial support. Certainly the suspicion of Michael being a Russian agent is mentioned in a police report of February 1847, months before Kiselev reportedly began it. Either way, whether Kiselev simply capitalized on an earlier rumour or not, it was a slur that Michael found very hard to remove. Moreover, it was a slur that, in the future, his enemies were to use much to their advantage.

VIII

Michael unwillingly remained in Brussels for two and a half months, from mid-December 1847 until February 1848. He found the revolutionary atmosphere much less vibrant than in France. The Polish refugees, for instance, were much more insular and ineffective than their more radical brethren in Paris. Lelewel was there but Michael considered that he had become decrepit and ineffective. He also disapproved of his new colleague, Lubliner, a Polish Jew. Considering Michael's affection for minority groups and his championship of the oppressed, it does seem extremely out of character for him to be anti-Semitic. But the reason really lies in his enmity with Marx and other Jews. (His anti-Semitism predictably grew worse during his confrontations with Marx.)

The Poles themselves were now suspicious of Michael's motives and on 10 February 1848 he published in *La Réforme* an open letter to Count Duchâtel, French Minister of the Interior, trying to scotch the increasing and by now very damaging rumours about his being a Russian agent. He was still unable to regain his former status, however, and the only public appearance he made in Brussels on behalf of the Poles took place on 14 February, when he gave a speech at a Polish banquet which was basically an extension of his first famous speech to the Poles in Paris.

Inevitably he and Marx met once again. Marx and his family had been living in Brussels since his own expulsion from Paris in 1845 and was only able to remain there on condition that he would publish nothing political. He renounced Prussian citizenship, ran into extreme financial difficulties, and was given allowances by such people as Jung and Engels. Annenkov, who visited Marx in Brussels, left this particularly evocative portrait of him at this time:

He was typical of the kind of man who is made up of energy, will-power and unshakable conviction, a type that is highly remarkable even at first glance. With a thick black mane of hair on his head, his hands covered with hairs, his coat buttoned up awry, he nevertheless gave the appearance of a man who has the right and the power to command attention, however odd his appearance and his actions might seem. His movements were awkward, but bold and self-confident; his manners ran positively counter to all the usual social conventions. But they were proud, with a trace of contempt, and his harsh voice which rang like metal was curiously in keeping with the radical judgments on men and things that he let fall. He always spoke in imperative phrases that would brook no resistance; moreover his words were sharpened by what seemed to me an almost painful tone which rang through everything that he said. This tone expressed a firm conviction that it was his mission to dominate other minds and prescribe laws for them. I was faced with the incarnation of a democratic dictator, such as one's imagination might have created.[30]

Marx's main energies in Brussels were channelled into trying to create an international socialist organization, and as a step towards this he founded a seventeen-member group which he called the Communist Party. The group was linked to a number of correspondence committees in London, Paris and Germany. There were no proletarians on these committees, as they were already organized into other groups. It was Marx's intention to co-ordinate all these committees into one Communist League and with this idea in mind he and Engels went to London towards the end of November 1847 to attend a congress of the League. As a result they were asked to write a public manifesto. Michael, however, showed little interest in Marx's activities, although he did join Marx's Democratic Federation. Gradually his views of Marxism began to indicate a sharp division between the thinking of the two men. He instinctively disliked the Germans and he wrote to Herwegh saying that Marx's group

poison the atmosphere. Vanity, malevolence, gossip, pretentiousness and boasting in theory and cowardice in practice. Dissertations about life, action and feeling – complete absence of life, action and feeling . . . The epithet BOURGEOIS! is shouted *ad nauseam*, by people who are from head to foot more *bourgeois* than in a provincial city – in short, foolishness and lies, lies and foolishness. In such an atmosphere no one can breathe freely.[31]

But basically this was subjective intolerance on Michael's part, for he was becoming as intolerant of Marx's theorizing as he was anxious to return to action in Paris. In Brussels there was only the Polish cause to interest him – a cause that had become necessary therapy for a man frustrated in his search for positive radical change. A fortnight after the publication of Michael's letter in *La Réforme* revolution broke out in France. Proudhon, writing a year later, described his own impressions of its beginnings.

> Placed at the very bottom of the social edifice, in the midst of the working masses, and being myself one of the sappers who had undermined the foundations, I could see, better than the statesmen who were arguing on the house-tops, the approach of danger and all the consequences of collapse. A few more days and, at the first parliamentary breeze, the Monarchy would crumble and with it the old structure of society ... The Houses of Parliament had not yet met for the 1847–8 session when I came to the conclusion that all was lost. I went straight to Paris. The two months that passed before the explosion – between the opening of the session and the fall of the throne – was the saddest, most wretched time I have ever been through in all my life.[32]

The actual events that occurred were swift and unpredictable. On 22 February both the French Government and its Republican Opposition were entirely convinced that nothing was going to happen and in fact demonstrations, organized by the Republicans, and security precautions, organized by the Government, were cancelled. What neither side had counted on, however, was the people of Paris. Sensing drama and overtly curious, they thronged the streets and came to the collective decision that Louis-Philippe and his Government would have to go. Louis-Philippe countered by dismissing his Prime Minister, Guizot, and appointing Louis Thiers, who was less right-wing. It was too late; there were clashes between the army and the crowd, shots were fired, shops looted and barricades erected. By the morning of 24 February 1848 revolutionaries controlled the centre of Paris and at 1 p.m. Louis-Philippe abdicated. In the afternoon the Opposition had set up one government while revolutionaries at the Hôtel de Ville had set up another, and in the evening the two governments merged and the Second French Republic was proclaimed.

Alexander Herzen, who was in Paris at the beginning of the Second Republic, described the atmosphere in the streets as follows:

> At last columns were formed; we foreigners made up an honorary phalanx immediately behind the leaders, among whom were E. Arago in the uniform of a colonel, Bastide, a former minister, and other celebrities of 1848. We moved down the boulevard, voicing various cries and singing the 'Marseillaise'. One who has not heard the 'Marseillaise', sung by thousands of

voices in that state of nervous excitement and irresolution which is inevitable before certain conflict, can hardly realize the overwhelming effect of the revolutionary hymn.

At that minute there was really something grand about the demonstration. As we slowly moved down the boulevards all the windows were thrown open; ladies and children crowded at them and came out on to the balconies; the gloomy, alarmed faces of their husbands, the fathers and proprietors, looked out from behind them, not observing that in the fourth storeys and attics other heads, those of poor seamstresses and working girls, were thrust out – they waved handkerchiefs, nodded and greeted us. From time to time, as we passed by the houses of well-known people, various shouts were uttered.

In this way we reached the point where the Rue de la Paix joins the boulevards; it was closed by a squad of the Vincennes Chasseurs, and when our column came up to it the chasseurs suddenly moved apart like the scenery in a theatre, and Changarnier, mounted upon a small horse, galloped up at the head of a squadron of dragoons. With no summons to the crowd to disperse, with no beat of drum or other formalities prescribed by law, he threw the foremost ranks into confusion, cut them off from the others and, deploying the dragoons in two directions, ordered them to clear the street in quick time. The dragoons in a frenzy fell to riding down people, striking them with the flat of their swords and using the edge at the slightest resistance. I hardly had time to take in what was happening when I found myself nose to nose with a horse which was almost snorting in my face, and a dragoon swearing likewise in my face and threatening to give me one with the flat if I did not move aside. I retreated to the right, and in an instant was carried away by the crowd and squeezed against the railings of the Rue Basse des Remparts. Of our rank the only one left beside me was Müller-Strübing. Meanwhile the dragoons were pressing back the foremost ranks with their horses, and people who had no room to get away were thrust back upon us. Arago leaped down into the Rue Basse des Remparts, slipped and dislocated his leg; Strübing and I jumped down after him. We looked at each other in a frenzy of indignation; Strübing turned round and shouted loudly: '*Aux armes! Aux armes!*' A man in a workman's blouse caught him by the collar, shoved him out of the way and said:

'Have you gone mad? Look there!'

Thickly bristling bayonets were moving down the street – the Chaussée d'Antin it must have been.

'Get away before they hear you and cut off all escape. All is lost, all!' he added, clenching his fist; he hummed a tune as though there was nothing the matter, and walked rapidly away.[33]

Michael's reaction to the revolution was predictable. He could hardly believe that the opportunity he had been awaiting for so long had come at last. He immediately flew into a wild frenzy, was quite unable to contain his excitement and set off immediately for France. He arrived at Valenciennes, a town near the frontier, just as the Republic was proclaimed.

IX

Michael arrived in Paris on 26 February 1848. At once the atmosphere of dew-fresh, as yet untarnished revolution fascinated him and for the brief period of a month he found the infancy of the Second Republic wholly delightful, completely engrossing and, most important of all, a fulfilment of his sense of mission. His restless neurosis faded away, his nagging home-sickness temporarily disappeared and his habitual feeling of isolation from his fellows was replaced by a sense of total involvement. The barricades, the red flags and the notable absence of the moneyed from the streets suited Michael's romantic nature, and the average working man, with whom he had had no practical dealings in the past, became both hero and martyr. For a while Michael stayed with the new National Guard under the equally new Police Chief Caussidière, whose caustic comment on Michael's involvement was 'What a man! On the first day of a revolution, he is a perfect treasure; on the second, he ought to be shot.'

Michael, however, impervious to the jaundiced view that his associates soon took of him, remained euphoric. As he later wrote, in the forced tranquillity of a prison cell,

I breathed through all my senses and through all my pores the intoxication of the revolutionary atmosphere. It was a holiday without beginning and without end. I saw everyone and I saw no one, for each individual was lost in the same innumerable and wandering crowd. I spoke to all I met without remembering either my own words or those of others, for my attention was absorbed at every step by new events and objects and by unexpected news.[34]

Michael was not interested in creating order out of the chaos of the first few weeks of the Second Republic, and while others struggled around him to create some form of social and logical pattern, Michael merely talked of further destruction and disorder. Meanwhile, the *Communist Manifesto* had just been published in Germany – a fact that moved the Belgian authorities to arrest Marx and his family and subsequently expel them from Brussels. Fortunately at that very moment Flocon invited Marx to come to Paris. He immediately established a new base for the Communist League and began to take a critical interest in the activities of his former associates. He started by opposing Herwegh (who was being pushed by his wife into living up to his literary reputation and becoming a more practical revolutionary) and his plan to found a German legion in order to overthrow the German leadership. He also, via his new Central Committee of the Communist League, drew up a seventeen-part programme for the pre-revolutionary Germans entitled 'Demands of the Communist Party'.

With revolution having broken out in France and hopefully about to break out in Germany, Michael's sense of euphoria continued unabated for about a month. However, he gradually realized, with sudden desolation and despite the heady atmosphere, that this was not his cause. It was a cause he had been happy to join, but now that he had joyfully witnessed his first revolution at first hand, he returned to the Polish cause which was closer to his heart. With this, he reasoned, he would be able to initiate and be responsible for his own personal revolution.

On 13 March Michael wrote a letter to *La Réforme*, which included the following words:

> Soon, perhaps in less than a year, the monstrous Austrian Empire will be destroyed. The liberated Italians will proclaim an Italian republic. The Germans, united into a single great nation, will proclaim a German republic. The Polish democrats after seventeen years in exile will return to their homes. The revolutionary movement will stop only when Europe, the whole of Europe, *not excluding Russia*, is turned into a federal democratic republic.[35]

Already, however, some of Michael's old friends were learning that it was better to avoid him. Turgenev, for instance, took great care not to be seen with Michael, and so did Annenkov. Both were fully aware that if Michael continued to act in the same manner as he was doing now, his friends would eventually have to answer to the Russian authorities for their association with him. Michael was now a marked man. If he ever fell into the hands of the authorities he would either be executed or at best be sentenced to life imprisonment.

PART THREE

Seeds of Revolution: 1848–51

I

In comparison with the rational Marx and the intellectual propagandist Herzen, Michael, if judged superficially, is in danger of emerging as a somewhat comic figure. Yet despite his self-admitted non-intellectualism and his extreme illogicality, he had by this time become an instinctive activist, and because of this refreshingly practical quality he had also become a natural and self-confident leader. Eugene Pyziur says of him,

> In the revolutionary firmament of the nineteenth century, his star was one of the brightest. His revolutionary performance was unprecedented, for he was not only a leading actor but also his own stage manager and scenario writer. In his performances, he usually, though not always, had a small supporting cast, but he reduced its members to supernumeraries.[1]

So far, the entire motivation for Michael's revolutionary activities had been an instinctive passion for the liberation of, first, the members of his own family who had drifted into the misery of compulsory conformity and then later, on a broader scale, the beleagured Poles. His energy, undiminished by domestic or sexual responsibility, was enormous and his inner loneliness acted as a continuous spur to bring about the freedom of the oppressed.

Michael was now thirty-four, penniless, and still able to blinker himself effectively against the realities of life that either did not interest him, made him feel guilty or inconveniently wormed at his always empty pocket. The sense of mission he had recognized so long ago still burned, and he felt all the time that he was heading, rudderless, towards a notable and idealistic future. The lines he had written to his family from Berlin in 1842 still held true.

> A great future still awaits me. My presentiments cannot deceive me. Oh, if I can only achieve a tiny part of all that is in my heart, I ask nothing more. I do not seek happiness. I do not think of happiness. Deeds, holy arduous deeds, are what I ask. Before me lies a broad field, and my part will be no mean one.[2]

Michael's avowed selflessness seems out of character with his protected egocentricity, but in fact many of his associates were at pains to point out that despite a large number of glaring personal faults he was generous and unselfish. It is to his credit that although he had every wish to bring about a widespread revolution, he had no desire to hold high office in the post-revolutionary administration.

1848 was a vital turning-point in the history of European Socialism, for it was in this year that radicalism really became socialism. Michael himself was now gradually becoming more and more loyal to the working class, but in fact the 1848 revolution was the very last time the French workers allowed their interests to be looked after entirely by middle-class politicians.

In the same year Herzen left Paris for Geneva and also exiled himself from Russia. He denounced the despotism of the Tsar, and proclaimed his 'gospel of universal negation'.[3] Herzen wanted a social republic and his goal was the destruction of existing political structures. His theories went far beyond Proudhon's and in this extract from his memoirs he explains why:

> A thinking Russian is the most independent being in the world. What, indeed, could stop him? Consideration for the past? But what is the starting point of modern Russian history other than the entire negation of nationalism and tradition? . . . On the other hand the past of the western nations may well serve us as a lesson – but that is all; we do not think ourselves to be the executives of their historic will. We share in your hatred, but we do not understand your attachments to the legacies of your ancestors. You are constrained by scruples, held back by fraternal considerations. We have none . . . we are independent, because we start a new life . . . because we do not possess anything – nothing to be loved. All our recollections are full of rancour and bitterness . . . We wear too many fetters already to be willing to put on new chains . . .

What matter for us, disinherited juniors that we are, your inherited duties? Can we, in conscience, be satisfied with your worn-out morality, which is non-Christian and non-human, and is evoked only in rhetorical exercises and judicial sentences? What respect can we cherish for your Roman-Gothic law: that huge building, lacking light and fresh air, a building repaired in the Middle Ages and painted over by a manumitted bourgeoisie? . . . Do not accuse us of immorality on the ground that we do not respect what is respected by you. Maybe we ask too much – and we shall not get anything . . . Maybe so, but still we do not despair of attaining what we are striving for.[4]

Ironically, on the day that Michael published his article in *La Réforme*, the Viennese rebelled against Metternich's Government. On 17 March a constitutional ministry was established in Hungary, and the people of Italy rebelled against their foreign leadership while Venice declared itself a republic; on 18 March, amidst all this European revolutionary fervour, the people of Berlin demanded from Wilhelm IV the guarantee of a constitution. France had set in motion a wave of revolutionary activity.

But to Michael these European revolutions were a mere beginning. It was Russia where revolution was needed and Poland was the only place from which it could begin. The Prussians had allowed the Poles to form a Polish National Committee in Posen and it was in Posen that Michael knew he had to be. Already the Polish leaders were on their way there and Michael was determined that he should follow. However, lack of money, he realized, was going to be a major deterrent and there was nobody he could possibly think of borrowing from. Turgenev and Annenkov were still determinedly avoiding him for their own safety, Herzen had left Paris, and his Polish associates, like him, had no money. Then Michael had a brainwave. With European revolution in full swing, surely the French Provisional Government would lend him money? He approached them immediately and Flocon was delighted to pay off Michael, who was now a very doubtful asset to the shaky foundations of the Second Republic. As a result of their discussions Michael received the sum of 2000 francs as a grant towards his revolutionary work in Posen. In addition, Caussidière, the new police chief, gave him one passport in his own name and another as a Polish subject named Léonard Neglinski. Armed with this booty, Michael left Paris on 30 March 1848 for Posen, elated that after a revolutionary practice-run in Paris he was now setting out to bring relief and freedom to his own country. He was once again boundlessly and naively optimistic, and it is possible that at this moment his thoughts were with Premukhino and Paul and Tatyana, for in his mind Michael had already effected the liberation of the Poles and was now jumping dozens of stages, looking forward to the liberation of his own people. He could see himself returning triumphant to Premukhino, to confront the amazed Alexander, with Moscow in flames behind him, the Tsar deposed and the serfs running free. (Now that he had accepted the validity of the working man's cause Michael's conscience was troubled about the serfs – a factor that he had hardly considered before.) But this dream was not to be, and Michael was eventually to arrive home at Premukhino in a very different manner. Disaster was ahead and he was moving steadily towards it.

II

Michael started out for Posen, fully aware that he hardly knew anyone there and that he would have to operate alone. He also heavily resented the current condemnation of Russia and looked at the increasing union between the Poles and the Germans with horror. Another factor of this journey to Posen, he determined, would be to do everything he could to end the Polish–German union. To effect this he would appeal to all other Slavs and the Polish Russians (those Russians who lived in Poland) to unite, for without help the Poles obviously had no hope of achieving anything. The plan was specific. 'To unite all Slavs, Poles and Russians . . . under the battle cry of liberating the Slavs living under the rule of Prussia, Austro-Hungary and Turkey.'[5]

But Michael's journey to Posen was packed with melodramatic incident. After a brief stay in Frankfurt, when he gloomily observed the complete lack of unity in the Pre-Parliament to the proposed new German National Assembly, Michael arrived in Berlin via Cologne on 21 April 1848. Then a highly cloak-and-dagger situation quickly developed – a situation that could well have ended in tragedy.

The Russian Minister in Berlin, no doubt already well briefed by Kiselev from Paris, pointed out to the Prussian Government that Bakunin, the well-known Russian agitator, was passing through Prussia on his way to incite the Poles in Posen to revolution. The Prussian Government, however, all too conscious of their own insecure position and possible overthrow, were bending over backwards to be as liberal and broad-minded as possible, hoping thereby to keep revolution at bay. They were already regretting having committed themselves to the creation of a Polish sector and the Polish National Committee was doing everything it could to negotiate as wide a boundary for this area as possible. This was thoroughly embarrassing for the obsequious and favour-currying Polish Government and so the warning from the Russian Minister via Kiselev concerning Michael was regarded somewhat tentatively and the resultant action was necessarily ambiguous. In fact the sequence of events was farcical: on the day after his arrival Michael was arrested and asked to promise not to continue his journey to Posen. But this was not all, for if he agreed to give his word he would be allowed to proceed instead to Breslau where revolutionary Polish propaganda was directed at Austria and Russia rather than Prussia. Michael meekly accepted this for two possible reasons. The first was that he was mainly interested in anti-Russian propaganda, and the second that having been arrested for the first time at such an early stage he had received an unpleasant and frightening shock. As a result his own passport was confiscated and Neglinski's passport was invalidated for Leipzig and Posen. As an added complication the Prussian authorities gave him yet another passport – this time in the name of a Prussian citizen named Simon. Having then paid lip-service to frustrating the political aims of Michael's journey the Prussian police chief reported back to the Russian Minister that the agitator Bakunin had been arrested and deported to Cologne.

Michael broke his journey briefly at Leipzig to see Ruge, who was unsuccessfully trying to become elected as a delegate to the Frankfurt National Assembly. Michael told a highly uneasy Ruge about his hopes for the Slav revolution and then continued on his already incident-packed journey to Breslau. The journey had at least proved that he was considered an international conspirator to be reckoned with. The Prussian authorities had certainly given him that impression and once the shock of the arrest had worn off, Michael felt pleasantly controversial.

Breslau, however, was an anti-climax and he immediately felt a despairing sense of flatness. The atmosphere was sterile. Already the Western German revolutionaries had been defeated in Baden at the end of April, and Herwegh's German Legion, which had come to their aid, had also been worsted. This piece of action was followed by fervid but fruitless discussion. The glorious Second Republic was already being attacked by the workers for its failure to fulfil its promises, and the Frankfurt National Assembly was becoming thoroughly hampered by its own red tape and showed every sign of becoming highly bureaucratic. Meanwhile, at Posen, a break between Poles and Prussians had occurred over the Polish sector. Michael felt that he had arrived too late and that the European revolutions were burning themselves out; their ashes were floating into a desert of mediocrity, conservatism and bureaucracy. Worst of all, this had happened before any revolutionary impetus could be pushed over the Russian border, and the project dearest to Michael's heart, the Polish cause, was disappointingly disorganized. Admittedly Breslau was full of revolutionary Poles, but inactivity, over-discussion, lack of money and general suspicion of Michael (stirred up by the 'Russian agent' rumour that was still effectively in circulation) made life both difficult and stagnant. It was not until May that, after a further rising in Vienna and the near-independence of Hungary, the Slavs in the Austrian Empire began to show positive signs of uniting against their oppressors. This move was of course heartily welcomed by Michael, and when the Czech National Committee (which was now running a provisional government) decided to set up a massive Slav conference in Prague at the end of May, Michael, electrified once more by a project so near to his heart, left Breslau without delay.

The conference, which opened on 3 June, was predictably diffuse, and as usual Michael was disappointed. The worst aspect of the conference was that very few delegates were at all interested in Michael's pan-Slav ideals. Each of the diverse groups of Slavs had its own particular axe to grind and their collective aims could hardly have been more contradictory. In the face of this Michael engineered his few pan-Slav supporters into a secret consortium that, like some earlier dabblings with freemasonry, marked the beginning of a new form of political self-indulgence, for secret societies were to become a major obsession and Michael was to saturate himself in unnecessary intrigue. Basically the initiation of secret societies was a prop as well as a synthetic source of drama, for while Michael needed the perpetual adrenalin of dramatic variation, the old feeling of unwilling insularity drove him to seek companionship in an intimate and clandestine group over which he had ultimate sway.

Michael should have realized from his first-hand experiences at the conference that there was no possibility of pan-Slavism. However, he chose to ignore the signs and as the conference stumbled on its divergent path Michael's pan-Slav ideal remained intact. The anti-German union of the Slavs brought joy to his heart and, as a democrat, he was determined to bring about the greater and, in his view, vitally necessary pan-Slavism. From becoming a supporter of the Poles, Michael became a Slav patriot. This patriotism, however, was governed by the grander motive of triggering off a general European revolution.

In his role as representative of the Northern Section's views to the Southern Section, Michael made a number of speeches. He warned the Czechs against trusting in the Hapsburg Empire, which had no interest in Slav independence. He also warned the Southern Slavs against looking for help to the Tsar and he recommended that all Slavs should unite without Russia (until Russia had won freedom for herself and granted it to Poland) and also against Austria. For, to achieve Slav freedom, the Austrian Empire would have to be destroyed and the Russian revolution would have to be initiated. This ambitious Utopia was a prime example of Michael's determined optimism and his refusal to accept that nationalism and democracy were poor bedfellows.

The views of the conference were expressed in the form of a manifesto that was adopted in Prague on 12 June. It was a mild enough piece of work and obviously Michael's revolutionary idealism had been heavily tempered by the chairman, the Czech historian Palacky. It was hopeful rather than revolutionary in content and contained three main points:

1   That a federation of free peoples should emerge from the reorganization of the Austrian Empire.
2   That the Slavs should be liberated from Turkish domination.
3   That the Slavs in Poland should be liberated from Tsarist oppression.

In fact the tone of the manifesto was farcical in its optimism.

Michael himself wrote three papers for the conference, and all three were later published in the press. The documents, in order of publication, were 'The Foundations of the New Slav Policy', 'The Foundations of the Slav Federation' and 'The Internal Constitution of the Slav Peoples'. In the first paper Michael naively stated that having been the oppressed, the Slavs could never become oppressors – a piece of unusual historical inaccuracy for him to make. The second paper suggested the creation of a central Slav Council whose role would be to legislate between and represent all free Slav peoples. The third paper was more personal and was stamped with Michael's own views: basically he held that if the Slav communities were to have a united goal then they should stand by the 'liberty, equality and fraternity' concepts of the French Revolution. This obviously meant the liberation of the serfs, and the doing away with the aristocracy and with privilege. Michael saw the Slav Council as the central body which would command these principles, but there is no record to indicate that this third paper was even discussed by the conference. Obviously it could never have been accepted by them.

On 12 June, the last day of the conference, rioting broke out in the streets of Prague. The insurrection lasted six days and its instigation had nothing to do with Michael. The insurgents were composed of students and workers and Michael only became involved when the barricades were up in the streets and the insurrection was at its height. However, once he became involved he was involved to the hilt, and when the insurrection was crushed he only escaped arrest by hurrying back to Breslau. The measures used to crush the rising were bloody and effective and it is to Michael's credit that he stayed in Prague long enough to see the surrender of the insurgents.

Already depressed by the failure of the Prague insurrection – and indeed by the greater failure of the French and German revolutions – Michael was further depressed by the deepening of the rumour that he was a Russian agent. The most serious aspect of this was the fact that it was now being voiced outside Polish circles, and the Poles, who were still extremely suspicious of Michael, were furthering its circulation. On 6 July Marx's celebrated journal, the *Neue Rheinische Zeitung*, published a letter from a Paris correspondent commenting that the novelist George Sand had in her possession various papers that proved Michael to be in the pay of the Russian Government. Immediately Michael wrote to George Sand, who denied the possession of any such papers in an open letter to the editor of the *Neue Rheinische Zeitung*, and of course Michael also wrote an angry denial refuting the whole charge. Dutifully the paper printed both denials. It would certainly have been more scrupulous if Marx had double-checked his facts before printing the rumour, but he considered that his conscience was salved by printing the denials. Whether any personal malice was meant against Michael it is difficult to say, but as Marx hardly knew Michael at that time and so far had had little reason to fall out with him it is unlikely that direct malice was the reason behind the publication of the rumour. Many years later, at the height of their quarrel, Michael inferred that this incident did imply direct malice, but at the time they met on several occasions with no sign of any unfriendliness.

Shortly after this incident Michael moved from Breslau to Berlin, where he shared digs with Müller-Strübing, the brilliant but dilettante journalist and arts critic whose political ambitions had already earned him a five-year prison sentence. Michael had already met him during his previous stay in Berlin and was pleased to renew his acquaintance with this civilized man, skilled in the arts of drinking, philosophy and entertaining rich Russian exiles (on whom he presumably lived). He was not respected by the Russians, but on the other hand he was a congenial enough companion in an hour of need, and Michael, in his general state of renewed disillusionment, needed someone like him. But the political and philosophical German company he introduced Michael to was not impressive. The torpidity of that company, the failure of the European revolutionary year, the reactionary bourgeoisie, the continual worry of the tiresome rumours, and once again his personal loneliness, forced Michael to begin a grandiose fantasy which gave relief to his depression. This fantasy – which was to remain with him for the rest of his life – involved secret societies and grand-scale, often imaginary plotting aimed towards a Russian revolution. Obviously the experience of past revolutions had shown that secret underground organizations were essential, but it was with these organizations that Michael was at his most unpractical and his most financially incompetent.

The summer wore painfully on and the Russian Secret Service continued to hound him, though, ironically, it is doubtful if many people believed that Michael was really being observed by Russian agents. The circulation of further rumours implying that Michael had planned an assassination attempt on the Tsar ended in the Prussian Government bowing to pressure from the Russian Legation and first arresting and then extraditing him.

This time Michael's fantasies were being given credence by the authorities and from 23 September until late autumn he lived the life of a political suspect on the run. Providentially, however, he found an oasis of peace in Cöthen in the duchy of Anhalt, a small liberal pocket where political exiles and agitators, many already well-known to Michael, were living unmolested. There the freedom of the countryside and the lack of political pressure reminded him forcibly of Premukhino, and with other political refugees from the European revolutionary arena he walked the mountains, hunting, shooting and living a less feudal but nevertheless similar life to that at Premukhino. But his mind was still concentrated on the possibilities of pan-Slavism and it was while he was in Cöthen that he wrote and had printed one of his most famous works: *Appeal to the Slavs*.

III

The opinions which Michael expressed in the *Appeal to the Slavs* were, of course, heavily influenced by the results of the European insurrections and revolutions of 1848. Throughout the continent the uprisings had been ruthlessly crushed, this time by the bourgeoisie rather than the aristocracy. E. H. Carr comments,

> The revolution of 1848 had been the work of the bourgeoisie. Inspired by the traditional bourgeois watchwords of liberty and equality, it rejected aristocracy, but was prepared to retain monarchy tempered by a constitution which assured the political and economic predominance of the bourgeoisie. It did not demand, and did not desire, the complete overthrow of the existing framework of society. The institution of private property was the bulwark of bourgeois supremacy; and when this bulwark was threatened, the bourgeoisie rallied to its defence as brutally and vindictively as the aristocracy had formerly rallied to the defence of its privileges. The proletariat wished to continue the revolution until every privilege, including that of the bourgeoisie, had been swept away; and this new extension of the conception of revolution turned the bourgeoisie at one stroke into stubborn counter-revolutionaries and defenders of privilege. In the summer and autumn of 1848, consistent radicals like Marx and Bakunin weighed the bourgeoisie in the revolutionary scales and found it wanting.[6]

Unlike Marx, however, Michael still had faith in the Slavs, and the following extract from his *Appeal* reveals what he hoped would be their role in bringing about his ultimate goal.

> Brothers! This is the hour of decision. It is for you to take a stand, openly either for the old world, in ruins, which you would prop up for yet another little while, or for the new world whose radiance has reached you and which belongs to the generations and centuries to come. It is up to you, too, to determine whether the future is to be in your hands or, if you want, once more to sink into impotence, into the night of hopes abandoned, into the inferno of slavery. On the choice you will make hangs the fate of other peoples who long for emancipation. Your decision will inspire them to advance towards their goal with quickened steps, and without drawbacks, or this goal – which will never disappear – will again retreat into a shadowy distance . . .[7]

Michael continues by demanding 'the dissolution of the states of the despots' – i.e. the Prussian, Austrian, Turkish and Russian Emperors – in order to bring about 'dissolution, overturn, and regeneration in the entire North and East of Europe, a free Italy, and, as the last result, the Universal Federation of European Republics'.

The last paragraph of the *Appeal* is perhaps the most revealing and George Woodcock comments that 'in the most significant passage . . . we find a strong influence of Proudhon, but it is a Proudhonianism impregnated with Bakunin's personal mystique of destruction'.[8] Michael stated:

Two great questions have moved to the forefront, as though arising spontaneously, from the very first days of the spring! The social question, on the one hand, and the question of independence of all the nations, the emancipation of the peoples, on the other hand, signifying emancipation within and outside. These were not just some few individuals, nor was it a party. It was the admirable instinct of the masses, which had raised these two questions above all the others and demanded their prompt solution. Everybody had come to the realization that liberty was merely a lie where the great majority of the population is reduced to a miserable existence, where, deprived of education, of leisure, and of bread, it is fated to serve as an underprop for the powerful and the rich. The social revolution, therefore, appears as a natural, necessary corollary of the political revolution. It has likewise been felt that, so long as there may be a single persecuted nation in Europe, the decisive and complete triumph of democracy will not be possible anywhere . . . We must, first, purify our atmosphere and make a complete transformation of our environment, for it corrupts our instincts and our will by constricting our hearts and our minds. The social question thus appears to be first and foremost the question of the complete overturn of society.[9]

The overthrow of society begins as a theme here and continues throughout Michael's later writings. Here are the first portents of anarchy, but nevertheless his rejection of the bourgeois State was linked with the concept of revolutionary dictatorship which was a facet of his entire pan-Slav obsession. Throughout 1848 Michael foresaw an inner conspiratorial core which, in post-revolutionary times, would become a revolutionary hierarchy. Years later he still saw a strong dictatorship as a valid instrument in Slav liberation.

Michael had read the Communist Manifesto (published in February 1848), which of course predicted the overthrow of the bourgeoisie by the proletariat, but for him the proof that a bourgeois revolution was impractical could only be gained by experience. The Prague Conference and its revolutionary aftermath provided that proof. The conference had openly supported nationalism rather than democracy and had then allowed General Windisch-grätz to suppress the insurrection unhindered. Michael was now convinced that the future revolution could not be, under any circumstances, a bourgeois revolution. It must be a proletarian revolution or no revolution at all.

However, Michael certainly read Marx's newspaper *Neue Rheinische Zeitung* – the paper which had printed the rumours that he was a Russian agent – so he must have been familiar with Marx's views even if he did not subscribe to all of them. On the June events in Paris Marx had this to say in the paper:

> The fraternity of the two opposing classes (one of which exploits the other) which in February was inscribed in huge letters upon all the façades of Paris, upon all the prisons and all the barracks . . . this fraternity lasted just so long as the interests of the bourgeoisie could fraternize with the interests of the proletariat. Pedants of the old revolutionary tradition of 1793, socialist systematizers who begged the bourgeoisie to grant favours to the people, and were allowed to preach long sermons . . . needed to lull the proletarian lion to sleep, republicans who wanted the whole of the old bourgeois system, minus the crowned figurehead, legitimists who did not wish to doff their livery but merely to change its cut – these had been the people's allies in the February revolution! Yet what the people hated was not Louis-Philippe but the crowned dominion of a class, capital enthroned.[10]

Thoroughly disillusioned with the bourgeoisie, both Michael Bakunin and Karl Marx now saw in the working classes the perpetrators of the new revolution. However, once again there were radical differences in their views, for at this time Michael assessed the revolutionary potential of the working classes in a very different way from Marx. As far as Michael was concerned the peasantry were the prime factors of a hoped-for revolution, although he accepted that they were often both ignorant and conservative. At Premukhino he had been surrounded by serfs and was therefore much more familiar with the peasantry as a working-class body, while Marx, on the other hand, had always lived in towns and regarded the working-class revolutionary as the factory worker. In fact Marx, determinedly systematic as ever, had divided the working classes into three units. They were

1 The organized urban worker whose revolutionary zeal was of a high calibre;
2 The 'Lumpenproletariat' or 'lower grade' worker who was

unorganized yet could be guided into revolution by the example of the first category or by propaganda;

3 The peasantry, whom Marx saw as counter-revolutionary.

This third grouping was totally against Michael's own feelings, for he saw this third category – as with the oppressed Russian serfs – as an important revolutionary factor, provided the more progressive city workers would abandon their snobbish attitude and involve themselves more with the peasants' problems.

At the end of December 1848 Michael, having completed the *Appeal* and finding nothing else to devote his energies to in the pastoral environment of Cöthen, moved to Leipzig. These were to be his last few months of freedom and once in Saxony he lived in hiding, despite the fact that some of his friends had managed to ascertain from the authorities that he would be left unpersecuted.

Nevertheless, after the tranquillity of Cöthen Michael felt highly insecure. Nervously he moved from place to place, mostly staying with friends, for, as usual, he was totally without funds. The ever-faithful Reichel sent him a little money and he eked out a threadbare existence on this while he arranged for the *Appeal to the Slavs* to be translated into Polish, started an ambitious and never-to-be-completed work on political conditions in Russia and began to organize an international revolutionary committee. This was doomed to early failure. Although two ex-Cöthen refugees, young Germans named D'Ester and Hexamer, were highly enthusiastic, Flocon never acknowledged his copy of the *Appeal*, and the Poles, as usual, were suspicious and uncooperative.

The Czechs, however, showed great interest in the *Appeal*. It was published in the *Slavonic Lime-Tree*, an important patriotic journal, and immediately Michael set out to evangelize in Czech circles just as he had tried to do in Polish circles. His two most notable converts to revolution were the Straka brothers, and Michael despatched Gustav Straka to Prague where he was to ask Sabina (editor of the *Slavonic Lime-Tree*) and Arnold, who was the editor of a leading Czech newspaper, to come to Leipzig to confer about European revolution. Only Arnold arrived (Sabina being a deadly rival of his) and it is difficult to know exactly what he made of Michael, for, convinced by now that congresses and committees were not only a waste of time but were open to censorship, the latter talked grandiosely of a network of secret societies to be set up throughout Bohemia to plot revolution. Arnold, having listened to this for hours, was invited to become an active participant. Instead, he returned to Prague, slightly bemused.

So convincing was Michael's personality, and so hypnotic could he be at times, that Arnold could well have half believed him. In fact, however, the Bohemian secret society ring was entirely a product of Michael's imagination. He conceived the fantasy for simple enough reasons. Revolutionary conferences seemed full of endless talk, and insurrections so far had been appallingly short-lived. Therefore, to gain support, and indeed to keep up his own optimism, it was essential first to invent and then to convince others of the validity of the invention. The fact that he might be found out probably *did* enter his head, but it was a risk he had to take to inspire the confidence of others in the coming revolution. In his later *Confession to the Tsar* Michael summarized his secret society idea, although, with hindsight, it was no doubt considerably better conceived on paper than in actuality.

The structure of the movement was as follows: each grouping was to be made up of three separate and independent societies, each of which had a different name, none of the three being aware of the others' existence. The first society was for the bourgeois, the second for the students and the third for the villagers. Each society consisted of a hierarchy, was committed to total obedience, and was tailor-made for the social group it represented. Members of the societies were to be the experienced or the influential, who would use their powers of persuasion (under strict guidance from the central hierarchy) on the populace. All the societies were organized by a central committee,

> which would have consisted of three, or at most five, members: myself, Arnold, and others whom we should have had to select . . . I hoped in this way to establish and strengthen my influence in Bohemia; and at the same time, without Arnold's knowledge, I authorized a young German student from Vienna, who has since fled from Austria, to organize a society on the same lines among the Germans of Bohemia, in the central committee of which I should not at first have participated openly, though I should have been its secret director. So that if my plan had been carried out, all the chief threads of the movement would have been concentrated in my hands, and I could have been sure that the intended revolution in Bohemia would not stray from the lines I had laid down for it.[11]

Hardly a very democratic statement from a man who was to believe so intrinsically in the leavening of society.

In order to discover what, if anything, Arnold was organizing, Michael sent a young Austrian Pole named Heimberger to Prague on his way back from a trip to Vienna. Heimberger reported back to Michael that Arnold had done precisely nothing and with now predictable crankiness Michael sent Heimberger (who seemed to be totally under his influence) to Prague to create another revolutionary structure and to spy on Arnold.

In March 1849, at the invitation of the naive Heimberger, Michael moved, on an English passport, to Dresden. He was accompanied by the Straka brothers and had shaved off his beard. In Prague, where he stopped off en route, reality suddenly loomed unpleasantly large. Michael's Czech revolutionaries turned out to be more nationalistic than democratic; Arnold disliked Heimberger, Sabina disliked and mistrusted both Arnold and Heimberger, and there was a great deal of talk and very little action. Moreover, the Austrian police knew of Michael's presence and he had to keep on changing his address. Furious and frustrated, he moved on to Dresden and there he made a new friendship.

Michael met Richard Wagner through the editor of a radical weekly named the *Volksblatt*. Wagner at that time was a conductor of the State Opera and his conducting made a great impression on Michael. The friendship between the two men became very deep over the space of a few days and Michael spent a considerable amount of time at the house of Richard Wagner and his wife Minna. Wagner remembered Michael at that period as follows:

> With Bakunin everything was colossal, and of a primitive negative power. He liked to discuss; and lying on the not too comfortable sofa of his friend, Röckel, in whose house he was hiding, he was pleased always to talk with others over various revolutionary problems. In those discussions, Bakunin was usually the victor. It was impossible to refute his logical arguments and radical conclusions. From every word he uttered one could feel the depth of his innermost convictions . . .
>
> His many startling remarks naturally made an extraordinary impression on me. On the other hand, I saw that this all-destroyer was the love-worthiest, most tender-hearted man one could possibly imagine. Noticing once that my eyes could not endure the bright light of the lamp, he shaded it for me with his broad hand for about an hour, although I begged him not to trouble. All the while, he calmly developed his most dangerous theories.
>
> He knew my most secret troubles, about the ever present danger to my ideal desires for art. Nothing was incomprehensible to him; yet he did not wish me to affront him with my art projects. I wanted to explain to him my Nibelung work, but he refused to

listen . . . As regards the music, he always advised me to repeat the same text in various melodies: Struggle and Destruction. The tenor was to urge the need for strife against chaos. The soprano was to do so, and the baritone also.

I remember, even yet, with pleasure, that I once persuaded him to listen to the first act of my 'Flying Dutchman'. He listened most attentively to the music and when I stopped for a moment, exclaimed 'that is wonderfully beautiful'. He loved music and wanted to hear more and more.

More than once Bakunin remained with us to supper. On one of these occasions he exclaimed to my wife: 'A real man must not think beyond the satisfaction of his first needs. The only true and worthy passion for man is love.'

Bakunin longed after the highest ideals of humanity. His nature reflected a strangeness to all the conventionalities of civilization. That is why the impression of my association with him is so mixed. I was repelled by an instinctive fear of him; yet he drew me like a magnet.[12]

Once again Michael had found a follower – another Turgenev, another Herwegh, and this time a humbler follower than most. Michael never professed much of an interest in Turgenev's novels or Herwegh's poetry, but Wagner was luckier, for Michael had a genuine interest in music. Minna Wagner on the other hand had rather more reservations and 'was shocked by the way in which their guest swallowed meat and sausages in enormous chunks, and gulped down brandy by the glass, rejecting wine as a tasteless beverage'.[13]

As the first phase of Michael's strange revolutionary career spun towards disaster his activities redoubled until he was almost always physically exhausted. He spent his time in meetings with the political exiles of various nationalities and he lived with, in turn, Wittig (editor of the *Dresdener Zeitung*), Röckel and Andrzejkowicz, who had translated the *Appeal* into Polish. He appeared in a number of disguises and under a variety of different names, and made another unsuccessful attempt to start an international revolutionary committee. He tried to find Polish money and personnel for his famous projected Bohemian revolution and continued to consort and plot with all manner of people, including tried enthusiasts such as Heimberger and the Strakas. But dominating all these intrigues were his friendship with Wagner, his own poverty, his increasing mental and physical exhaustion, and the mutual jealousies of his associates.

At this time Michael published two important articles in the

Dresdener Zeitung. The first was from his proposed book on Russian political affairs and the second a further appeal to the Czechs.

Strangely enough, Michael had little foreknowledge of the Dresden insurrection, largely because he knew few Saxon democrats and was heavily involved in outside matters. He did come into contact with Dresden affairs at a meeting on 1 May 1849 which was convened to discuss possible Polish assistance in co-ordinating revolution throughout Germany, but when barricades were set up in the street on 3 May Michael was not only caught unawares but was actually leaving Dresden for Malta in company with a wealthy friend, Prince Ghika. If Michael had only gone to Malta it is possible that tragedy could have been averted, but unfortunately a combination of his wealthy friend's sudden inability to pay his fares and the outbreak of the insurrection forced him to stay in Dresden.

The motives and ideals of the Dresden insurrection were of very little interest to Michael and he only became involved because, despite his lack of sympathy with the contenders, he was quite unable to see any revolution occur without himself being a dominant force behind it. Nevertheless, despite the fact that his actions were to end in personal disaster, the insurrection brought out some of his best qualities.

The events at Dresden began when the Saxon Diet approved a federal constitution for Germany, conceived by the Frankfurt National Assembly. But the Saxon king, obviously unable to tolerate the Assembly or its views, dissolved the Diet on 28 April 1849. This action had immediate repercussions: the barricades went up, the Civic Guards joined the insurgents and a raid was made on the arsenal – a raid which resulted in a number of rebel fatalities. These sparked off the revolution. On the night of 3 May the royal family hastily left the country and on 4 May Tzschirner (an accomplished radical and ex-vice-president of the Second Chamber), Heubner and Todt (bourgeois constitutional reformers) headed a provisional government. But these men were not revolutionaries and Michael felt that this was just another dismal bourgeois revolution with the kind of structure that his *Appeal* had so roundly condemned. Moreover, he really had no interest in the unity of Germany or the Frankfurt National Assembly and its constitution. He therefore made no move to interfere and it was not until Wagner persuaded him to go and hear a speech by Tzschirner on 4 May that he felt he could no longer afford to remain aloof from the heady revolutionary atmosphere around him, even if its administration *was* dominated by the bourgeoisie.

Using his slight acquaintanceship with Tzschirner and Todt as a lever, Michael pushed himself into the central revolutionary hierarchy. There he told the three leaders that they must concentrate on organizing a revolutionary army. This would defend the insurrection against detachments of Prussian troops who would be called in to reinforce the depleted Saxon army. The military arrangements at the time were in the hands of a semi-mercenary, a somewhat shady adventurer named Heinze, and Michael was certain he would be quite unable to prevent what would turn out to be a massacre of the ill-organized insurrectionists directly Prussian reinforcements arrived. So positive was he that Tzschirner, Todt and Heubner listened to him with interest and anxiety. Michael argued that it was only the Poles who were experienced in the military aspects of revolution and that Heinze would have to be replaced by a Pole. A day later, after a long search, he returned with two Polish military advisers: Kryzanowski and Heltman.

On the evening of 5 May Prussian troops began to advance on Dresden. Unfortunately Heinze still retained his role as commander-in-chief and inevitably there were constant arguments between him and Michael's military advisers. The arguments went on as the Prussian troops continued to advance, and on 6 May Kryzanowski and Heltman fled. Tzschirner and Todt also became strangely elusive and Heubner was not only left in charge of the provisional government but was also the only official leader available to rally those manning the barricades. However, Michael, now totally embroiled in the spirit of the uprising, showed considerable bravery. Not only did he play the *éminence grise* to Heubner, loyally refusing to desert him despite the fact that it was now obvious that the cause was lost, but he publicly continued to encourage the insurgents themselves in the streets and at the barricades. Legends grew up about Michael in Dresden – and he became a near-mythical figure. One rumour claimed that Michael would place all the treasures from the Dresden museums on the barricades to help keep back the Prussians. Another rumour hinted that he was going to hang the Sistine Madonna itself on the barricades in an attempt to stop the cultured Prussians from firing! He was also said to have set alight the Opera House whose conflagration also burnt out the natural history collection, but although the insurgents certainly did set fire to the Opera House there is no real evidence of Michael's involvement in this. The fire occurred on 6 May, and Michael still remained loyally with Heubner as the Prussian troops relentlessly moved on towards the city. On 8 May Heinze was taken prisoner as fierce fighting took place between the rebels and the Prussian troops. It was a hopelessly unequal struggle and the captured rebels were shot and thrown into the Elbe.

It now became apparent that all was lost in Dresden and the best policy was for the rebels to retreat to Freiberg. Michael and Heubner departed for Freiberg in a carriage and on the way they met Wagner, who told them that the workers of the industrial city of Chemnitz were strongly in support of the insurrection and that great hope of maintaining the revolution lay there. Immediately Michael and Heubner, their optimism rekindled, hurried towards Chemnitz, while Wagner, more prudently, left with his wife in the direction of Switzerland. Pausing at Freiberg, which was Heubner's home town, Michael desperately tried to incite Born – the leader of the Arbeiter Verbrüderung, which was the very first of the German worker organizations – to action by persuading him to take the remaining insurrectionists to Bohemia, there to start a new revolution. But Born was against the idea. He had lost too many men and he knew that further revolution was useless and would only result in more brutal suppression. Heubner was also becoming doubtful as to the wisdom of prolonging the struggle. He, like Born, was anxious to dissolve the small revolutionary army before it met with more disastrously heavy casualties, and he told Michael that whilst he admired his courage he was fearful of his ideas. Michael, however, replied, 'If the people have been brought so far that they revolt, we must go with them to the end. If we meet with death, honour at least is saved. If this is not the case, then no person will, in future, have any faith in such undertakings.'[14] Fighting words if somewhat idealistic, and there is no doubt that Michael would have carried them out had not the drama been suddenly terminated. On the night of 9 May Michael, Heubner and another insurrectionist named Martin arrived at Chemnitz and, exhausted, retired for the night to a hotel. They were puzzled, for there was little hint of revolution amongst the industrial workers of Chemnitz and although there is no doubt that Wagner had spoken in good if naive faith the presence of the three revolutionaries in the town was a source of embarrassment to the authorities. In the early morning of 10 May Michael, Heubner and Martin, physically and mentally exhausted, slept heavily, paying no heed to security. A few hours later they were rudely interrupted from sleep by the local authorities and arrested in the name of the Government of Saxony.

IV

The Dresden uprising confirmed for Michael yet again that the bourgeoisie were useless as a revolutionary factor and that the workers, despite his experience at Chemnitz, were the new revolutionaries. His own involvement in the insurrection had been impressive. With no possibility of personal gain and no real feeling for this particular cause, he had loyally supported Heubner to the end. Even Marx later said, in a letter dated 2 October 1852 to the *New York Daily Tribune*, that

> In Dresden the battle in the streets went on for four days. The shopkeepers of Dresden, organized into 'community guards', not only refused to fight, but many of them supported the troops against the insurrectionists. Almost all of the rebels were workers from the surrounding factories. In the Russian refugee Michael Bakunin they found a capable and cool-headed leader.[15]

Michael's years of imprisonment had now begun. For several weeks he was shunted from prison to prison, but, totally exhausted, he saw the entire process through a heavy veil of weariness. On the afternoon of 10 May, under heavy escort, the prisoners were taken back to Dresden where they were incarcerated for fourteen days in the old city prison. From there they were transferred to the cavalry barracks and then for further security they were taken, separately and once again under heavy guard, to Königstein – Saxony's maximum-security fortress. Throughout they were treated as dangerous political prisoners.

Michael arrived in Königstein on 29 August 1849, and once there was treated with some consideration. Escape was impossible, but his room was clean and warm and had a window, he was taken for walks in the grounds under heavy guard, he could have as many books and cigars as he liked, and he was allowed to write and receive letters. He was given money by Herzen, Herwegh's wife Emma and of course the ever-loyal Adolf and Matilda Reichel. He had a lawyer, named Franz Otto, who looked after him with great efficiency and it was he who administered the incoming donations from Michael's friends as well as those from some of his political friends in Cöthen and Leipzig.

Michael obviously found the liberal flavour of the tight security surrounding him totally frustrating – although no doubt at the same time flattering. He had become a dangerous revolutionary and he could see all around him the living proof of this in the wariness of the Saxon authorities. But the novelty soon wore off and two specific fears quickly replaced it. The first was that he might be handed over to Russia where he was sure he would be executed. The second was that here, at Königstein fortress, he was completely cut off from all news of outside events. Michael was only allowed to see back numbers of the newspapers and slowly, now his physical tiredness had gone, a black and destructive gloom descended over him. All that was left was his pursuit of knowledge and this continued, for it provided escapism. He studied English grammar, mathematics and French history, and also read some classics.

Meanwhile the investigations into his revolutionary activities had been extremely thorough: each detail had been scrutinized and each incident analysed. The whole made a particularly damning picture of organized revolutionary activity, and compromising corres- pondence only served further to establish that the result of his im- pending trial was very unlikely to be favourable. The only elusive and nerve-stretching question was just what kind of sentence the Government of Saxony would impose on him. Michael was asked to supply his own written defence but he felt so apathetic and exhausted after the questioning that he was unable to face up to such an arduous and worthless task. Instead Otto, having asked the court for an extension of time, supplied one for him. He completed it on 26 November and its basic argument was that Michael, not being a Saxon subject, could not therefore be guilty of treason against Saxony. Because of this his sentence under Saxon law, if he were to be found guilty, should not exceed four years' imprisonment. But legal technicalities of this kind had little chance of success, and on 14 January 1850 Michael, Heubner and Röckel (who had been arrested separately) were found guilty and were all, pending the right of appeal, sentenced to death.

V

Michael did not immediately react to his sentence, for, like every- thing else that he found unpalatable, he put it in a locked compart- ment at the back of his mind where it stayed. Just in case it should accidentally emerge in periods of depression he distracted himself by drafting a long document which started out as a political confession and ended up as a political statement of intent. The confession, written to Otto as a guide to his appeal, took up a large proportion of Michael's time and was of no use to Otto. The document analysed Russian history from Peter the Great onwards, predicted that revolution would come from the peasants, and commented bitterly on the tyrannical alliance of Russia and Austria. He then returned to the tone of his *Appeal to the Slavs* by preaching the necessary destruction of the Austrian Empire and of Tsardom – two vital steps towards the freedom of the oppressed masses in Europe. Otto, studiously avoiding having anything to do with Michael's document, put in the same appeal as his original defence. It was dismissed and with no more room for appeal the sentence remained as it stood.

The failure of the appeal was no shock to Michael and still he showed no reaction to the death sentence, for he had been told that it was unlikely to be carried out. However, there was always the unpleasant possibility that he might be handed over to the Russian authorities – a possibility that Michael found difficult to put into a memory compartment and forget. Even when two of his female spiritual compatriots, Johanna Pescantini and Matilda Reichel, wrote comforting letters and sent him gifts he was comparatively unmoved. The meaning of such past relationships was very pale to him now.

In fact Michael's worst fears about being handed over to Russia began to look as if they were going to come true when not only Russia but Austria asked the Saxon authorities to hand over their celebrated prisoner. The Saxons, uneasy about making decisions over Michael's future, or alternatively keeping such a top-security risk in prison, settled down to decide which was more in their interests – to give Michael to Russia or to Austria. However, the two powers, each bending over backwards to be courteous towards the other, were anxious not to fall out over such a trifling issue and the Tsar took the initiative by telling the Saxon Government to hand Michael over to Austria first. He then graciously asked Austria if they would mind passing Michael on to Russia when they considered he had been sufficiently punished for his misdeeds within their domain.

On the night of 12 June 1850, therefore, Michael was woken up and driven to the Saxon frontier where he was to be taken on to Austria. No one had informed him of this decision, so he thought that he was being taken to a place of execution. In fact the Saxon king had, a few days previously, commuted the death sentences on Michael, Heubner and Röckel to life imprisonment. At that moment, however, he was not to know that, and it is difficult to gauge how despairing his thoughts must have been as he was driven through the night, believing himself to have only a few more hours in which to live.

VI

On the evening of 14 June 1850 Michael arrived in Prague and was taken to the old monastery of St George at Hradčin. There were some familiar faces in his block – Gustav and Arnold Straka. Once again all three were held in high-security conditions and there were continuous checks on the precautions taken to keep in the political prisoners. The myth of Michael Bakunin had become a far greater danger to the authorities than the reality. Being under martial law he was no longer allowed a lawyer; neither was he allowed to write or receive letters. However, such was his charm and pathetic bear-like state of gloom that the officer in charge of his case, Captain-Auditor Franz, wrote his correspondence for him and administered the money which was still being sent by his friends. Twenty-five thalers from Herwegh was spent on mathematics books, as Michael was still obsessed with abstraction and the escapist attainment of knowledge. Herzen, Otto and some democratic friends sent him more money, which was desperately needed for personal require-ments, such as clothes and food. Michael spent nine months at Hradčin; they were months that passed in a kind of gloomy dream. He wrote nothing, so we are unable to define his exact state of mind, but clearly the fear that he might be returned to Russia had become numbed to an apathetic state in which distraction was the only answer. On 13 March 1851, however, there was a new security scare concerning a possible rescue operation. Although there was little foundation to the rumours, Michael was transferred to the grim fortress at Olmütz in Moravia. Here he was fettered and chained to the wall of his cell, and although his food was increased his physical condition began to deteriorate badly.

Between 15 and 18 April 1851 the now bemused Michael was heavily cross-examined. The Austrian authorities, aware of the Tsar's desire to have him handed over to Russia when he had received punishment from the Austrian Government, obviously felt it was time they took some action. It soon became obvious to Michael that little could be gained from silence, particularly as most of his insurrectionist friends had already been arrested and had confessed. As a result he answered questions openly on his revolutionary activities in Prague and Dresden, and his relationship with Czech revolutionaries. Unfortunately, in his *Appeal to the Slavs* Michael had advocated the complete destruction of the Austrian Empire, and on this basis he was condemned by his own writings so there could be no question of any defence – even a defence on technical points such as Otto had managed to put forward in Saxony. However, rather curiously, Michael came to be regarded by the Austrian authorities as a faded and courageous old revolutionary who deserved pity, and the president of the court stated generously that throughout his interrogation Michael had behaved with 'courage and decision, but with perfect propriety'.

Michael had now been in prison, in Saxony and Austria, for two years – two years which would have broken anyone who lacked his iron constitution. He had retreated into a totally interior life and hardly seemed to know what was going on around him – an ironic travesty of his former Fichtean ideology with its talk of the 'interior life' only being real, and the 'outside life' being totally unreal. He hardly ever spoke and, chained as he was, he became prematurely aged – a wrecked giant who had given up all hope.

On 15 May 1851 an Austrian Military Court was convened to try Michael Bakunin. It was an open and shut case and Captain-Auditor Franz's report merely encapsulated Michael's own confession. He was found guilty of high treason and sentenced to death. A few hours later the death sentence was commuted to life imprisonment, but Michael's worst fears were about to be realized, for it was now revealed that he was to be returned to Russia. He was taken by train and road via Cracow to the Russian border, where he arrived in the early morning of 17 May. A reception committee of Russian Cossacks and policemen were there to welcome him.

In the chilly small hours of the morning Michael's Austrian fetters were changed for heavier Russian ones and he was back on Russian soil; six days later, on 23 May, Michael and his entourage arrived in Petersburg where he was taken straight to the fortress of Peter and Paul.

PART FOUR

Prison and Exile: 1851–61

I

Years later, Peter Kropotkin recorded his impressions of the dour fortress of Peter and Paul, in which he himself was a prisoner. It had not changed very much from the time that Michael had entered it. Kropotkin wrote,

> . . . a sensation of horror is felt by the inhabitants of St Petersburg as they perceive on the other side of the Neva, opposite the Imperial palace, the grey bastions of the fortress; and gloomy are their thoughts as the northern wind brings across the river the discordant sound of the fortress-bells which every hour ring their melancholy tune. Tradition associates the sight and the name of the fortress with suffering and oppressions. Thousands – nay, scores of thousands of people, chiefly Little Russians, died there, as they laid the foundations of the bastions on the low, marshy island Jäni-saari. No remembrance of glorious defence is associated with it; nothing but memories of suffering inflicted upon the foes of Autocracy.

> It was there that Peter I tortured and mutilated the enemies of the Imperial rule which he tried to force upon Russia. There he ordered the death of his son Alexis – if he did not kill him with his own hands, as some historians say. There, too, during the reign of the Empresses, the omnipotent courtiers sent their personal rivals, leaving it an open question in so many families whether their relatives had been drowned in the Neva or remained buried alive in some stone cellar. There the heroes of the first and only

attempt at revolution in St Petersburg, the Decembrists, were confined – some of them, like Batenkoff, remaining there for twelve whole years. There Karakozoff was tortured and hanged – almost a corpse, hardly showing any signs of life when he was brought to the scaffold. And since that time a whole generation of men and women, inspired with love for their oppressed people, and with ideas of liberty filtrating in from the West, or nursed by old popular traditions, have been detained there, some of them disappearing within the fortress for ever, others ending their life on its glacis, or within its walls, on the gallows; while hundreds have left those mute walls for secret transportation to the confines of the snow-deserts of Siberia . . .[1]

But at this stage Nicholas I had no intention of despatching Michael to Siberia; instead he remained in the fortress for two months before he was interviewed by any high official. The layout of the fortress, which covered over three hundred acres, was as below:[2]

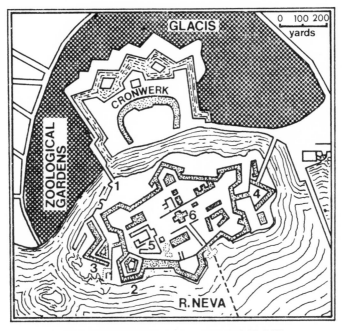

PLAN OF THE FORTRESS OF ST. PETER AND ST. PAUL

1. Courtine of Catherine
2. Trubetskoi Bastion
3. Trubetskoi Ravelin
4. Alexeyevskiy Ravelin
5. The Mint
6. Cathedral

It is not clear in which part of the fortress Michael was imprisoned, but Kropotkin, who was imprisoned in the Trubetskoi bastion in 1873, has given a vivid description of his own cell which must have been similar to Michael's.

There is not much light in them. The window, which is an embrasure, is nearly of the same size as the windows in other prisons. But the wells occupy the interior enclosure of the bastion (that is, the *reduct*), and the high wall of the bastion faces the windows of the cells at a distance of fifteen to twenty feet. Besides, the walls of the reduct, which have to resist shells, are nearly five feet thick, and the light is intercepted by a double frame with small apertures, and by an iron grate. Finally, everybody knows that the St Petersburg sky is anything but bright ... The floor of the cells is covered with a painted felt, and the walls are double, so to say; that is, they are covered also with felt, and, at a distance of five inches from the wall, there is an iron-wire net, covered with rough linen and with yellow printed paper. This arrangement is made to prevent the prisoners speaking with one another by means of taps on the wall. The silence in these felt-covered cells is that of a grave. I know cells in other prisons. Outer life and the life of the prison reach one by thousands of sounds and words exchanged here and there. Although in a cell, one still feels oneself a part of the world. The fortress is a grave. You never hear a sound, excepting that of a sentry continually creeping like a hunter from one door to another, to look through the 'Judas' into the cells. You are never alone, as an eye is continually kept upon you, and still you are always alone. If you address a word to the warder who brings you your dress for walking in the yard, if you ask him what is the weather, he never answers ... The absolute silence is interrupted only by the bells of the clock, which play each quarter of an hour a *Gospodi pomilui*, each hour the canticle *Kol slaven nash Gospod v Sionye*, and each twelve hours *God save the Tsar* in addition to all this. The cacophony of the discordant bells is horrible during rapid changes of temperature, and I do not wonder that nervous persons consider these bells as one of the plagues of the fortress.

The cells are heated from the corridor outside by means of large stoves, and the temperature is kept exceedingly high, in order to prevent moisture from appearing on the walls. To keep up such a temperature, the stoves are very soon shut, whilst the coal is still blazing, so that the prisoner is usually asphyxiated with oxide of carbon. Like all Russians, I was accustomed to keep a high temperature, of 61° to 64° Fahrenheit, in my room. But I could not support the high temperature of the fortress, and still less the asphyxiating gases; and, after a long struggle, I obtained that my stove should not be shut up very hot. I was warned that the walls would be immediately covered with moisture; and, indeed, they soon were dripping in the corners of the vault; even the painted paper of the front wall was as wet as if water were continually poured on it. But, as there was no other choice than between dripping walls and extenuation by a bath-like temperature, I chose the former, not without some inconvenience for the lungs, and not without acquiring rheumatism.[3]

Meanwhile, at Premukhino, the members of the Bakunin family had undergone a number of radical changes in their circumstances. Sadly, it was Tatyana who had suffered most. Her frustrated love for Turgenev, although now controlled, was still a subject of pain and she desperately missed and continuously worried about Michael, becoming more and more lonely as a result. She had adopted the traditional role of the spinster in the family, carefully looked after her parents (particularly Alexander who had gone completely blind), and, like her aunts, found solace in devout religion. For the last four years, however, owing to a decline in her health, Tatyana had lived in the Crimea, staying part of the time with Paul. Paul had taken after Michael in the sense that he was regarded in his own circle of friends as a radical and a full-blooded Hegelian. But he never extended these ideas into action as Michael had and his career in the civil service at Simferopol was highly orthodox. As to the others: Varvara had returned to Dyakov, Alexandra had married a cavalry officer, Nicholas was also married and ran an estate near Premukhino, Ilya was farming in Kazan, Alexis was still at Premukhino and Alexander had become involved with Natalie Beyer. Natalie, who was now thirty-five, had hardly changed in personality but her sister Alexandra, who had so openly declared her love for Michael, was dead.

Michael's steadfast acceptance of his terrible fate was becoming a consistent pattern, but it must have stretched his nerves unbearably not to have any idea of how long the sentence would last or indeed if he would be incarcerated in the fortress of Peter and Paul for life. However, in July 1851 Count Orlov, principal adviser to Nicholas I, visited his cell and asked him to write a full confession, not as a criminal, but as if he were telling all, quite openly, to a spiritual father. After this surprising statement Orlov went on to point out that Michael had no need to fear for his life, as there was no death penalty in Russia. Michael was at first bewildered by this new and strange turn of events, then flattered and enthusiastic. Immediately, and with a feeling of elation, he began to write, and between July and September produced a confession of approximately thirty thousand words.

The confession was an extraordinary document. Extremely articulate and very clear, it gave a full account of his insurrectionary activities from the time when he left Russia in 1840 until the time of his arrest in Dresden in May 1849. It included almost everything he had done and was surprisingly without exaggeration. Although it was written to gain the sympathy of Nicholas I it was not entirely hypocritical. In fact Michael's ambiguity of purpose is difficult to understand. On the one hand he prostrated himself penitently before Nicholas, to whom he wrote as to a stern father confessor, claiming that what he had done was a crime against Russia, but on the other he refused to name his associates and implied that, although penitent, he had not lost his revolutionary zeal. Playing entirely on Nicholas's dislike of the German nation, Michael included a paranoid yet calculated attack on the German race, as people, as politicians, as philosophers, as a culture and, above all, as persecutors of the Slavs, but he then went on to exude Slav patriotism, to propagandize Slav liberation, and to enthuse over the creation of one great free Slav State. Glossing over his earlier advocation of Nicholas's overthrow by stressing his ardent passion for the united and free Slav State, Michael firmly stated that

In Russia I wanted a republic, but what kind of republic? Not a parliamentary one!! I believe that in Russia, more than anywhere else, a strong dictatorial power will be indispensable, but one which would concern itself solely with raising the standard of living and education of the peasant masses; a power free in direction and spirit but without parliamentary privileges; free to print books expressing the ideas of the people, hallowed by their Soviets, strengthened by their free activity, and unconstricted by anything or anyone.[4]

Of his plans for Bohemia, Michael said,

In Bohemia I wanted a decisive radical revolution which would overthrow everything and turn everything upside down, so that after our victory the Austrian Government would not find anything in its old place . . . I wanted to expel the whole nobility, the whole of the hostile clergy, after confiscating without exception all landed estates. I wanted to distribute part of these among the landless peasants in order to incite them to revolution, and to use the rest as a source of additional financing for the revolution. I wanted to destroy all castles, to burn all files of documents in all of Bohemia without exception, including all administrative, legal and governmental papers, and to proclaim all mortgages paid, as well as all other debts not exceeding a certain sum, e.g., one or two thousand gulden. In short, the revolution I planned was terrible and unprecedented, although directed more against things than against people.

But my plans did not stop there. I wanted to transform all Bohemia into a revolutionary camp, to create a force there capable not only of defending the revolution within the country, but also of taking the offensive outside Bohemia.[5]

He rose to further heights of tactlessness by attacking Russia's lack of free public thinking and by praising the revolutionary workers in France in 1848, but he counterbalanced this by such statements as

It is hard for me, Czar of mine, an erring, estranged, misled son, to tell you he has had the insolence to think of the tendency and the spirit of your rule. It is hard for me because I stand before you like a condemned criminal. It is painful to my self-love. It is ringing in my ears as if you, my Czar, said: 'The boy babbles of things he does not understand.'[6]

It would be wrong to say that Michael's confession to Nicholas I was entirely hypocritical – a piece of carefully worded propaganda to try and persuade Nicholas to let him out of the fortress. The key to the real truth lies in Michael's own deep love of Russia and his strange love–hate relationship with Tsardom. Although he resented the Tsar's dictatorial censorship and imperial rule he still subconsciously regarded him as the father-figure of Russia, thus turning what could have been a hopefully placating document into a real confession to an unconsciously loved autocratic father. It was Russia and freedom that he had at heart and although he was at odds with Nicholas over it – and indeed over the whole problem of Slav domination – he had half blundered into a surprisingly honest and uncalculated confession.

Having completed the main part of the document, Michael then made two pleas to Nicholas. The first was that he should be allowed to follow the normal Russian penal tradition and be transferred from prison to Siberia; the second that, as he had not heard from his family since he was in Paris in 1845, he should be allowed to see them for the last time before being despatched to Siberia. Signed 'the repentant sinner, Michael Bakunin', the confession was duly set before Nicholas, who took a surprisingly lenient view of its criticisms of himself and the State. He was flattered at Michael's penitence and the way he praised him. He was also delighted by the anti-German material and the comments on the general decadence of the West. Heavily annotated, he passed it on to the heir to the throne, Alexander, for his opinion. But in spite of his liberal reaction to Michael's confession, Nicholas would not immediately acquiesce to the two pleas contained in it. He decided to compromise, however, by leaving Michael in prison but allowing members of his family to visit him.

II

Meanwhile Tatyana returned to Premukhino from the Crimea in the summer of 1851, nursing the aftermath of a romantic and impossible love she had entertained for a musician named Serov. Three months later Alexander Bakunin and Tatyana received news that Michael was in the fortress of Peter and Paul and that they had permission to visit him there. Alexander, who was too old and blind to make the long journey, nominated Paul to accompany an over-joyed Tatyana to Petersburg. The nomination was accepted and in October 1851 Paul and Tatyana visited Michael in prison. There then followed a correspondence between Michael and his parents.

Michael's letter to his father was as penitent and as humbly repentant as his confession to the Tsar. He even wrote to Varvara telling her that he should never have been so unpleasant to Dyakov. It is once again unlikely that this was all hypocrisy, written merely so that he could be seen to be repentant by the censor who scrutinized his letters home. There was a genuineness to Michael's confession – and yet a permanence to his revolutionary attitude, however many times he humbly apologized for it.

To Tatyana and Paul, Michael had not radically changed, but despite his mountainous appearance his health was obviously extremely poor. However, the reunion with his family and their frequent correspondence and visits brought the memory of Premukhino joyfully alive once more. It seemed to him that he was now privileged to re-enter a secret world that he had thought was closed to him.

During the autumn and winter of 1851 Michael's treatment in the prison improved. He was permitted to read Russian newspapers and a French review, and was able to receive warmer clothes from Premukhino. In July 1852 Tatyana was able to visit him and in February 1854 she visited him again, this time accompanied by Paul. It was noticeable that during this period Michael's health had begun to deteriorate seriously until

> he was attacked by piles and scurvy, disorders consequent on prison diet and on the total absence of that movement which was essential to his powerful and restless frame; and his teeth began to fall out. Continuous headaches, shortness of breath, and noises in the ear like the sound of boiling water, were among the symptoms of which he complains.[7]

The change obviously shocked Tatyana and Paul but they were powerless to help him.

In February 1854 Tatyana and Paul were permitted to see Michael several times during their week's stay in Petersburg and he passed them three notes which they managed to smuggle out. These first uncensored and frank missives clearly indicate how Michael's mental depression was increasing in his captivity. In the first note, written in French, he stressed the anguish of being buried alive and condemned to a life of utter uselessness, pointing out how frustrating it was to sense coming revolutionary activity and be able to do nothing about it, to have unrealized ideas, to be unable to show love for anyone – and to have a cause that could not be fulfilled. He then said,

> Shut up the greatest genius in such a prison as mine, and you will see that after some years a Napoleon would become stupid and Jesus Christ himself wicked. As for me, who am neither great like Napoleon nor infinitely good like Jesus Christ, I shall need much less time to become altogether brutish.[8]

The other notes were more carping. The first accused Tatyana of not doing enough to plead for him or to fight the authorities for his release. The second was self-accusatory, condemning himself for treating Tatyana in such a way, particularly when he could see how despair had taken its physical toll of her too.

In March 1854 the Crimean War was just about to begin and the Russian authorities thought that the British navy might attack Petersburg. For this reason Michael was transferred from the fortress of Peter and Paul to the Schlüsselberg prison on the shores of Lake Ladoga.

In December 1854 Alexander Bakunin, now eighty-eight years old, totally enfeebled and completely blind, died. His death brought about an amazing transformation in his wife – the anonymous and cold Varvara. For this woman, who had spent half her married life breeding and bringing up the ten Bakunin children and the rest of it caring for her elderly, ailing husband, suddenly had a new lease of life. She was sixty-two, and a few months after Alexander's death she travelled, in the company of Alexis, to Schlüsselberg, to visit Michael. With her husband dead, Varvara had achieved a new and positive personality and the sight of Michael's physical condition stirred even her pallid emotions. She determined to secure his release or at least his transference from Schlüsselberg.

In February 1855 Nicholas I himself died and was succeeded by Alexander II. Therefore when Varvara and Alexis arrived at Schlüsselberg in March 1855 the time was ripe for a more liberal official approach to Michael's sentence. Moreover, five of Michael's brothers were now in the army and his first cousin, Ekaterina Bakunin, had recently done exemplary and distinguished work as a nurse on the Crimean front, so it should have appeared to Alexander II that the Bakunin family were remarkably loyal in their service to the Tsar and to Russia, with the exception of the one black sheep currently incarcerated in Schlüsselberg.

Immediately after Varvara had seen Michael for the first time she petitioned Alexander II in the most dramatic and forceful terms. She put forward the unlikely proposition that Michael might be allowed to fight with his brothers at the Russian front and die honourably 'or earn with his blood the right to be called my son'. Unfortunately this valiant petition made little impact on Alexander II and it is quite possible that having read Michael's Confession he felt that he was a highly unlikely subject to stand at the Russian front and there meet an honourable death.

Almost a year passed before Varvara was able to visit Schlüsselberg again, and during this period Michael's physical condition deteriorated still further. Varvara's next visit was in January 1856 and petitioning on a much more modest basis she asked Alexander II if at least some sort of therapy could be produced in the form of a carpenter's bench to prevent Michael's further deterioration. But Alexander saw no reason to relieve Michael's sufferings, so in August 1856 Varvara petitioned Prince Dolgorukov, who was now principal adviser to Alexander II in place of Count Orlov. Once again Varvara wrote her petition most dramatically, pointing out that if

Michael failed to behave well as a result of being released, she would guarantee the right of the Russian authorities to kill her other five sons. But even this dramatic offer seemed to fall on stony ground and in November 1856 she tried yet again with a petition to the minister of foreign affairs, Prince Gorchakov. Michael, having had his hopes raised and dashed three times already, was now in a critical state of mental torment and even half-heartedly suggested to Alexis that poison should be smuggled to him to prevent further mental and physical suffering.

When all seemed lost the fourth petition to Gorchakov partially succeeded. In February 1857 Michael was asked to petition the Tsar himself, the authorities making it clear that if he went the right way about it and used the correct wording he would be given an objective reading. The great problem, however, was the secret formula for the wording – wording that must secure Alexander II's clemency. Michael was terrified lest he should fail to achieve the right tone, but strangely he found he was able to write quite fluently and the document he wrote was quite different from the Confession. Michael chastized himself severely for his past errors and reaffirmed his total loyalty to Tsardom and to Russia. As to the future, he wrote that he only had one wish and that was 'To draw my last breath in freedom, to look upon the clear sky and the fresh meadows, to see the house of my father, to prostrate myself at his grave, to devote the remnant of my days to my mother, who has worn herself out for me, and to prepare myself worthily for death'.[9] Michael was now forty-two years old.

On 21 February 1857 Michael was told that Alexander II had given him the choice of being permanently banished to Siberia or staying in Schlüsselberg. He immediately elected for Siberia and asked, as the last favour of one about to be permanently exiled, to be allowed to spend twenty-four hours en route at Premukhino, where he would take farewell of his family. On 8 March he was taken to the railway station at Petersburg and there, in the company of a colonel and two policemen, conducted to a special coach that was placed at the back of a goods train that was going to Tver. And on 9 March, still accompanied by the colonel and two policemen, he arrived romantically in a sleigh at Premukhino.

Once again it is difficult to estimate just how sincere Michael was when he wrote his petition to Alexander II. But this document is very different from the honestly written ambiguities of the Confession, for Michael was now a totally desperate man. His great capacity for living would hardly allow him to lose the chance of going to Siberia, so it is obvious that he grasped the straw and wrote the most emotive and grandiose apology and plea. It is unlikely that Alexander II believed in these dramatic verbal gestures, but like Nicholas I he may well have approved of some of the sentiments contained in Michael's Confession and was therefore loath to see the prematurely aged revolutionary rot in prison at Petersburg.

III

On the way to Siberia Michael was allowed his visit to Premukhino, but sadly he found that communication with his family was now impossible. However, once in Siberia he began to recover from his long period of imprisonment. Gradually the old vitality began to burn again in the shell that had silently wandered through Premukhino. First of all it was just a flicker – just a hint of the old Michael – and the first indications of its presence showed themselves when he arrived at Omsk, the capital of Western Siberia. Here he gave two letters to his guards to take back to Petersburg. The first, addressed to Prince Dolgorukov, obsequiously thanked him for his help in the most glowing terms. The second, addressed to his mother, gloomily pointed out that the money she had given him for the journey had not been sufficient. It was with this letter that the flicker of the old Michael began to return and from then on the flicker became a slow-burning flame.

The second sign of restoration was that Michael somehow persuaded the authorities to allow him to settle, on the grounds of ill-health, in the town of Tomsk itself, rather than the remote and bleak region in the Tomsk province assigned to him. There Michael's vitality began to return even more strongly when he found that the Siberian exiles were a fascinating and welcoming group. They were, in the main, brilliant men and were highly respected in Siberian society. In fact it was a chillier, gloomier, but more stimulating version of the atmosphere in Cöthen.

Despite the congenial company, however, Michael was extremely frustrated at not being able to leave Tomsk. At the same time he realized that the allowance Varvara was making him from Premukhino would not continue indefinitely, nor was it sufficient for his purposes. Tantalizingly enough, gold had been discovered on the Lena River and was being prospected heavily. Various deposits had been opened up, and Siberia was in the grip of a gold fever. As a result Michael became even more frustrated and was desperately anxious to get to the Lena as soon as possible and begin prospecting.

With this in mind he immediately petitioned Prince Dolgorukov, pointing out that if he were able to leave Tomsk and to travel around Siberia he would be able to fend for himself and would not have to rely on his family for money. But Prince Dolgorukov refused to comply with this request – possibly because he was more perceptive than Michael gave him credit for – and Michael was forced to seek other distraction in Tomsk.

In order to supplement his income he taught French to the two daughters of a Polish merchant named Ksaweri Kwiatkowski and towards the end of 1857 he proposed to and was accepted by the eighteen-year-old Antonia.

This decision is not inexplicable. There is no doubt that his appalling experiences in prison in Saxony, in Austria and later in Russia had not only very obviously totally intensified his already entrenched personal loneliness, but had also heightened his need for someone, not only to admire him as in his previous relationships with women, but to be beside him at all times to maintain his ego and give him companionship and comfort. This is a harsh assessment but undoubtedly a true one, for as has already been made clear Michael was not interested in women sexually in the slightest degree. His deepest friendships had always been with men, although in most cases even they had played the role of intelligent disciples. Women he had used as sounding-boards, and in return they had showered him with love and desire. This Michael had always been able to counter with a high-minded spiritual idealism, within which the unpalatable and dreaded sexual intercourse was sunk without trace. The break-up of Michael's relationships with women usually came about because their physical desire for him broke through the game of spiritual love they were playing (Natalie Beyer being a particularly good example of this) and Michael, sensing danger, hastily retreated. However, in his present condition the unpalatableness of physical contact with a woman was dwarfed by his desperate need for companionship.

Antonia fulfilled neither the role of the intelligent disciple nor that of the spiritual lover. She was very ordinary, completely unintellectual and very dependent. She had few ideas of her own and her conception of marriage was to settle down with her man, serve his needs and bear his children. Although the unemancipated Antonia did not know that she would never have the opportunity to do the latter, Michael's magnetism convinced her that, at the extraordinarily young age of eighteen, she would be able to make him domestically content. It was this subservient loyalty that Michael most needed after his harrowing years in prison. He married Antonia, as it were, on the rebound and although he was often kind to her, she was in no way to figure in his political ideology or to be of the slightest importance to him except on the domestic front. An intelligent woman would not have been able to last a month on these terms, but Antonia, who began by genuinely loving Michael, and ended by accepting him as a fixture in her life that she was fond of, was well satisfied with her role.

Antonia and Michael were married in the summer of 1858 and Michael, having turned down the offer of a clerk's position in Eastern Siberia as beneath his contempt, was at first romantically ecstatic about the union and vowed to guard his subservient child-bride as he might have guarded a pet animal.

In the late autumn of 1858 Michael made one of the strangest friendships of his career. General Nicholas Muraviev was Michael's second cousin and had been the Governor of Eastern Siberia for about ten years. He was extremely popular with the Tsar for acquiring extra territory for Russia by a treaty with the Chinese Government and also for opening up a major trade outlet by establishing the port of Nikolaevsk. He was a liberal and could afford to treat some of the Siberian exiles, with many of whose views he privately sympathized, as his protégés. He had already tried to achieve Michael's release from Siberia but had so far failed, despite his strong influence in Tsarist circles, and when Muraviev and Michael finally met a friendship developed – a strange friendship between two extreme opposites.

Michael and Muraviev did in fact have some characteristics in common. They were both immensely strong-willed, highly intelligent and ambitious and although Michael was hardly in agreement with Muraviev's imperialism, outwardly at least they shared the same liberal views. Liberalization, under the aegis of the insecure and all too anxious to please Alexander II, was in fashion, and such questions as the liberation of the serfs and the redistribution of land were being theoretically and therefore safely discussed. Slav patriotism had been increased by the Crimean War: the West, having gained control of Constantinople, had effectively removed what could have been the capital of any proposed Slav federation. Austria, having quickly backed out of the war when she was most needed, was now hated by all Russian patriots. Muraviev, too much in love with power ever to put his theories into practice, loved to sit on the fence, setting up highly imperialistic Russian projects on the one hand and consorting and gaining credibility with exiles and revolutionaries on the other. Unfortunately, Michael was taken in – or appeared to be taken in – by Muraviev's all too safe liberalism, for the familiar reason of his desperate need for intellectual stimulation and also because he liked to mingle with those in high positions. However, he seriously overstepped himself when he defended Muraviev after he had been attacked in a magazine called *The Bell* that Alexander Herzen was now producing in London and smuggling into Russia. Michael's hot defence of Muraviev and his actions served as a stepping-stone to the extraordinary decision he took over Muraviev's hypothetical future role in Russian history.

In Michael's confession to Nicholas I he had urged the Tsar to lead a revolutionary pan-Slav federation which would regenerate Europe. Nicholas had never taken up the offer and now, naively and with seemingly no realization of Muraviev's hypocrisy, Michael arbitrarily decided that the leader of the revolutionary pan-Slav federation should be Muraviev. Michael believed, and indeed told Herzen, that Muraviev had a healthy contempt, like himself, for the Austrians. He also, amazingly enough, believed that Muraviev would lead the Slavs into a military attack on not just the Austrians but the Turks as well, and that when he was victorious his political credo would involve no parliament but a temporary and very tough dictatorship that would hold together the new Russia. But despite the fact that these were dreams, and extremely self-deluding dreams at that, they were at least another step in Michael's own political thinking. He no longer had any faith in democracy, which had been replaced in his mind by revolutionary dictatorship and pan-Slavism.

During the next two years revolutionary ideology became superseded by an overpowering desire to leave Siberia, but depressingly this possibility seemed remote.

In the spring of 1859, with the help of Muraviev's influence, Michael was employed by the Amur Company, an organization devoted to the development of trade in the new Eastern province. Because of this, Michael and Antonia were able to move to Irkutsk. Throughout the summer and autumn Michael worked for the Amur Company but although he was able to travel about Eastern Siberia, he soon found that his interest in commercial travelling was non-existent. He therefore resigned his post, but fortunately, owing to Muraviev's influence, the President of the company felt obliged to keep Michael in the company's employ without asking him to work. As a result Michael and Antonia lived on 2,000 roubles a year from the winter of 1859 until the early spring of 1861.

During this period Varvara Bakunin made two further attempts to achieve her son's pardon and Muraviev petitioned Dolgorukov on Michael's behalf. Still nothing happened. Then early in 1861 Muraviev retired. His successor was a General Korsakov who, once again, by a fortunate coincidence, was related to Michael, his cousin having recently married Paul Bakunin. At this point Michael began to plan his escape from Siberia.

IV

Michael knew that his only chance of escape lay in making his way from Irkutsk to the mouth of the Amur and somehow boarding a boat. Money was an essential factor for the escape and to facilitate this he wrote an anguished letter to Premukhino, cunningly pointing out that he had developed a bad conscience about his employer who had been paying him for doing nothing for such a long time that he was now desperate to pay him back. There is little doubt that once Michael received the sum, the President of the Amur Company was unlikely to see any of it. Unfortunately for Michael the plan was a shade too clever, for his brothers (to whom the letter was addressed in the hope that they would regard the loan as an advance on Michael's share of the Premukhino estates) simply sent the money direct to Michael's employer.

Dismayed by this awkward turn of events Michael, desperate to escape, even lowered himself to write to the unsympathetic Katkov (another illustration of his amazing ability to insulate himself against humiliation). In this instance his abasement was to no avail as Katkov did not attempt to reply, and eventually, finding that he was unable to acquire money for nothing, Michael was forced to resume work as a commercial traveller.

It was not until the late spring of 1861 that an advance of 1000 roubles and a salary were forthcoming from a Siberian merchant who wanted him to make a business trip to the mouth of the River Amur. Michael knew that this was the only chance he would get and he seized it eagerly. On 5 June 1861 he set out with a letter addressed to the captains of all ships on the Amur, signed by Korsakov and requesting a free passage for him. A stern warning accompanied the letter to the effect that it was essential for Michael to return by the time navigation closed for the winter on the Amur and its tributaries.

Michael set off on his escape route alone, leaving Antonia behind with her family. He had no fear that she might give him away, for Michael knew the strength of Antonia's feelings towards him, but he seemed to have no compunction in leaving her with the loose promise that he would send for her once he was in Europe. There is no record of Antonia's reaction, but there is little doubt that she must have been heartbroken. Equally there is little doubt that she and her family were forced to settle all Michael's debts.

Michael's escape route was highly complicated and showed great initiative. By 2 July 1861 he had arrived at Nikolaevsk, the new port at the mouth of the Amur. He had come via a number of other towns on the Amur, where in his commercial traveller's role he had acquired more money from various merchants who wanted business transacted either en route or at Nikolaevsk. At Nikolaevsk Michael managed to board the *Strelok* with the permission of the Governor of the Maritime Province's Chief of Staff, a man named Afanasiev whom Michael found he could manipulate. The *Strelok*, a government ship, sailed for Kastri with Michael as a passenger – a passenger who was meant to return from Kastri overland to Irkutsk. By chance, however, the *Strelok* took in tow the *Vickery* – an American sailing ship – and Michael managed to transfer himself to it quite easily as the captain of the *Strelok* had no idea that he was not allowed to travel so far afield. On 4 August Michael arrived in Hakodate, a Japanese port, and on 24 August he reached Yokohama, having convinced the Russian consul at Hakodate that he would be returning to Russia via Shanghai and Peking.

Once in Yokohama Michael knew that he was free. The tension left him and a new future was suddenly and miraculously opened to him. On 17 September 1861 he embarked on the *Carrington*, a ship bound for San Francisco, but at the last minute disaster nearly struck as he boarded the ship and was asked by the captain to join in a dinner party he had arranged for an 'honoured guest'. The 'honoured guest' turned out to be the Russian Consul-General.

Meanwhile, in the harbour, a Russian fleet under the command of Admiral Popov was preparing to set sail for Nikolaevsk. Michael, realizing that unless he played his cards right he would be returning with them, brazened it out with the Consul-General by telling him that he had received official permission to go on a pleasure trip. The Consul-General casually enquired whether Michael was going to return with the Russian fleet to Nikolaevsk. Michael replied that he was not, as he wanted to see a little more of the country. The Consul-General seemed satisfied with the explanation and the dinner party ended in a general spirit of bonhomie. The next day the *Carrington* weighed anchor and steamed out of the harbour. Michael watched the Russian fleet slip away on their bow. It had been a very narrow shave but at last he was safe.

On the journey from Yokohama to San Francisco Michael made friends with a young English clergyman called Koe, whose diary of shipboard life makes amusing reading as regards Michael's activities. Professor Carr relates that

> Koe found Bakunin 'more like a friend than anyone I have met for a long time'; and his diary preserves many illuminating glimpses of the voyage. During the long idle days across the Pacific, Bakunin told the story of his life and imprisonments, declared that his two 'great objects' were Slav confederation and the destruction of Austria, sang Russian songs and interested himself in a budding love-affair between a returning missionary from China and an American lady passenger. As befitted Koe's cloth, they talked much of religion. Bakunin condemned the 'rabid atheism' of his friend Herzen, and foresaw 'great discussions' on the subject when they met in London. He sympathized with Protestantism, and even thought that his wife, who, being a Pole, was a Roman Catholic, might 'under gentle treatment' be converted to it. (This was tactfully consoling to the young clergyman, who also contemplated marriage with a Catholic lady.) Finally, a few days before reaching port, a still more delicate subject was broached. 'I find,' wrote Koe in his diary of October 10th, 'I shall have to lend him the money to reach New York – some $250.'[10]

Michael arrived in San Francisco on 14 October 1861 and wrote the following letter to Herzen on 15 October.

> Friends, – I have succeeded in escaping from Siberia, and after long wanderings on the Amur, on the shores of the Gulf of Tartary and across Japan, I arrived to-day in San Francisco.
> Friends, I long to come to you with my whole being, and as soon as I arrive I shall set to work; I shall work with you on the Polish–Slavonic question, which has been my *idée fixe* since 1846 and was in practice my speciality in 1848 and 1849.
> The destruction, the complete destruction, of the Austrian empire will be my last word; I don't say deed: that would be too ambitious; to promote it I am ready to become a drummer-boy or even a scoundrel, and if I should succeed in advancing it by one hair's-breadth I shall be satisfied. And beyond that there appears the glorious, free Slav Federation, the one way out for Russia, the Ukraine, Poland, and the Slavonic peoples generally . . .[11]

Michael predictably concluded the letter by asking Herzen to send some money to New York. From San Francisco Michael travelled to

Panama and then to New York where he arrived on 18 November. He stayed in America for a few weeks during which he made some acquaintances and discovered that Americans seemed highly sympathetic to the Russian people.

Michael finally left New York on 14 December 1861 and arrived in Liverpool on 27 December. At once he set out for London and Herzen, for it was only in his company that Michael knew he could start again his practical revolutionary work. He journeyed to London with eager expectation, leaving behind him in Russia the beginning of what was to be a two-and-a-half-year enquiry into his escape. He also left Antonia patiently and uncritically awaiting news of him. But for the moment, as far as Michael was concerned, the past was behind him and he gave little thought to her. Michael Bakunin at forty-eight was now a veteran revolutionary, but at present he had little idea of what had been happening in Europe over the ten years of his enforced and harrowing exile. Nevertheless, despite the fact that his captors had succeeded in breaking him physically, his mind was as active and as challenging as before. A revolutionary phoenix had risen from the fortress of Peter and Paul – a phoenix that was eager to drink the heady wine of European revolution. It was unfortunate that the barrel had run dry.

PART FIVE

Second Wind: 1861–3

***

I

The life of Alexander Herzen had been inundated by tragedy during Michael's exile. His wife had died in childbirth after a long, tempestuous and passionate love affair with Herwegh. The ensuing scenes between Herwegh and Herzen had developed into a major European scandal, and now Herzen and Natalie Ogarev, second wife of the now highly self-indulgent Nicholas Ogarev, were lovers. But the complications of Herzen's domestic affairs certainly did not overshadow his political life and in no way affected his tolerance of Michael's arrival and all the time and expense he knew it would involve. Herzen later recalled their reunion as follows:

Into our work, into our closed shop of two, a new element had entered, or rather an old element, perhaps a risen shade of the 'forties, and most of all of 1848. Bakunin was just the same; he had grown older in body only, his spirit was as young and enthusiastic as in the days of the all-night arguments with Khomyakov in Moscow. He was just as devoted to one idea, just as capable of being carried away by it, and seeing in everything the fulfilment of his desires and ideals, and even more ready for every experience, every sacrifice, feeling that he had not so much life before him, and that consequently he must make haste and not let slip a single chance. He was fretted by prolonged study, by the weighing of pros and cons and, confident and theoretical as ever, he longed for any action if only it were in the midst of the storms of revolution, in the midst of destruction and danger. Now, too, as in the article signed 'Jules Elizard', he repeated: '*Die Lust der Zerstörung ist eine schaffende Lust.*' The fantasies and ideals with which he was imprisoned in Königstein in 1849 he had preserved, and had carried them complete across Japan and California in 1861. Even his language recalled the finer articles of *La Réforme* and *La Vrai République*, the striking speeches in *La Constituante* and at Blanqui's Club. The spirit of the parties of that period, their exclusiveness, their personal sympathies and antipathies, above all their faith in the second coming of the revolution – it was all here.

Strong characters, if not destroyed at once by prison and exile, are preserved by them in an extraordinary way; they come out of them as though out of a faint and go on with what they were about when they lost consciousness. The Decembrists came back from being buried alive in the snows of Siberia more youthful than the young people who met them, who had been trampled down while still in the ear. While two generations of Frenchmen changed several times, turned red and white by turns, advancing with the flood and borne back by the ebb, Barbès and Blanqui remained steady beacons, recalling from behind prison bars and distant foreign lands the old ideals in all their purity . . .

The European reaction did not exist for Bakunin, the bitter years from 1848 to 1858 did not exist for him either; of them he had but a brief, far-away, faint knowledge. He had read about them in Siberia, just as he had read at Kaydanov about the Punic Wars and of the fall of the Roman Empire. Like a man who has returned after the plague, he heard who had died, and sighed for them all; but he had not sat by the bedside of the dying, had not hoped that they would be saved, had not followed them to the grave. The events of 1848, on the contrary, were all about him, near to his heart, vivid and in detail; the conversations with Caussidière, the speeches of the Slavs at the Prague Conference, discussions with Arago or Ruge – to Bakunin all these were affairs of yesterday; they were all still ringing in his ears and flashing before his eyes.[1]

Immediately Michael began to cross-examine Herzen and Ogarev about what had been happening politically in Europe.

'Only in Poland there are some demonstrations,' said Herzen; 'but perhaps the Poles will come to their senses and understand that a rising is out of the question when the Tsar has just freed the serfs. Clouds are gathering, but we must hope that they will disperse.'

'And in Italy?'
'All quiet.'
'And in Austria?'
'All quiet.'
'And in Turkey?'
'All quiet everywhere, and nothing in prospect.'
'Then what are we to do?' said Bakunin in amazement. 'Must
we go to Persia or India to stir things up? It's enough to drive
one mad; I cannot sit and do nothing.'[2]

Michael, unlike Herzen, had not seen the collapse of the European
revolutionary dream and did not realize that Alexander II, having
liberated the serfs, was now regarded as an ardent reformer. He was
amazed that the Austrian Empire was still intact and deeply grieved
that his idyll of pan-Slav federation was now a totally forgotten
issue. Michael had emerged as if from a deep sleep – a nine-year
sleep during which all rebellion in Europe had petered out. Moreover, he had no money and it became necessary for Herzen to give
him an allowance, as did Botkin and Turgenev in Paris and many
other friends in varying degrees. Michael accepted the money
happily as if it were his due and only paid lip-service to Herzen's
tactful suggestion that by selling his life story and in particular the
tale of his escape from Russia to the *Revue des Deux Mondes* he would
be able to earn his own income. But Michael could not be bothered
to document the tale of his escape and instead he began to make
contacts amongst the Polish and Russian communities in London.
Herzen recalls,

In London he first of all set about *revolutionizing The Bell*,* and
in 1862 advanced against us almost all that in 1847 he had
advanced against Belinsky. Propaganda was not enough; there
ought to be immediate action; centres and committees ought to
be organized; to have people closely and remotely associated with
us was not enough, we ought to have 'dedicated and half-dedicated
brethren', organizations on the spot – a Slavonic organization,
a Polish organization. Bakunin thought us too moderate, unable
to take advantage of the situation of the moment, insufficiently
fond of resolute measures. He did not lose heart, however, but
was convinced that in a short time he would set us on the right
path. While awaiting our conversion Bakunin gathered about
him a regular circle of Slavs. Among them there were Czechs,

* The journal edited by Herzen and Ogarev.

from the writer Fritsch to a musician who was called Naperstok; Serbs who were simply called after their father's names, Ioanovic, Danilovic, Petrovic; there were Wallachians who did duty for Slavs, with the everlasting 'esco' at the end of their names; finally, there was a Bulgarian who had been a doctor in the Turkish army, and there were Poles of every diocese – the Bonapartist, the Mieroslawski, the Czartoryszki: democrats without socialist ideas but with a tinge of the officer; socialists, catholics, anarchists, aristocrats and men who were simply soldiers, ready to fight anywhere in North or South America . . . and by preference in Poland.

With them Bakunin made up for his nine years' silence and solitude. He argued, lectured, made arrangements, shouted, decided, directed, organized and encouraged all day long, all night long, for days and nights together. In the brief minutes he had free he rushed to his writing-table, cleared a little space from cigarette-ash, and set to work to write five, ten, fifteen letters to Semipalatinsk and Arad, to Belgrade and Tsargrad, to Bessarabia, Moldavia and Belokrinitsa. In the middle of a letter he would fling aside the pen and bring up to date the views of some old-fashioned Dalmatian, then, without finishing his exhortation, snatch up the pen and go on writing. This, however, was made easier for him by the fact that he was writing and talking about one and the same thing. His activity, his laziness, his appetite, and everything else, like his gigantic stature and the everlasting sweat he was in, everything, in fact, was on a superhuman scale, as he was himself; and he was himself a giant with his leonine head and tousled mane . . .

There was something childlike, simple and free from malice about him, and this gave him an unusual charm and attracted to him both the weak and the strong, repelling none but the affected *petit bourgeois*. His striking personality, the eccentric and powerful appearance he made everywhere, in a coterie of young people in Moscow, in a lecture-room at Berlin University, among Weitling's Communists and Caussidière's Montagnards, his speeches in Prague, his command at Dresden, his trial, imprisonment, sentence to death, torture in Austria and surrender to Russia – where he vanished behind the fearful walls of the Alexeyevsky ravelin – make of him one of those individualists whom neither the contemporary world nor history can pass by.

That he ever came to marry, I can only put down to the boredom of Siberia. He had piously preserved all the habits and customs of his fatherland, that is of student-life in Moscow: heaps of tobacco lay on his table like stores of forage, cigar-ash covered his papers, together with half-finished glasses of tea; from morning onwards clouds of smoke hung about the room from a regular suite of smokers, who smoked as though they were racing each other, hurriedly blowing it out and drawing it in – as only Russians and Slavs do smoke, in fact. Many a time I enjoyed the amazement, accompanied by a certain horror and perplexity, of the landlady's servant, Grace, when at dead of night she brought boiling water and a fifth basin of sugar into this hotbed of Slav emancipation.[3]

Herzen had always had an ambivalent attitude to Michael. On the one hand he treated him in an avuncular manner and on the other he treated him with headmasterly censoriousness. Michael's attitude to money irritated him considerably, particularly as he was such a regular contributor to the Bakunin funds. At last, however, Herzen managed to transfer Michael from his own house into lodgings, first at Grove Terrace, St John's Wood, and later at 10 Paddington Green.

It was from Paddington Green that in a supplement to *The Bell* Michael wrote his first public piece for thirteen years. Entitled *To My Russian, Polish and Other Slav Friends*, the article appeared on 15 February 1862 and was basically a return to the original concepts of his revolutionary plans of 1848–9 which had now been hurriedly adapted for the situation in the 1860s. Michael pointed out that he was going to dedicate his revolutionary energies to gaining total liberation and independence for all Slavic countries, including of course a continuous fight for Russian and Polish freedom.

The pamphlet establishes Michael as one of the forerunners of Russian populism. In it he also advised students to leave the universities and go to the people.

So, young friends, leave this dying world – these universities, academies and schools in which you are locked, and where you are permanently separated from the people. *Go to the people.* This is your field, your life, your science. *Learn from the people how best to serve their cause.* Remember, friends, that educated youth must be neither the teacher, the paternalistic benefactor, nor the dictatorial leader of the people, but only the midwife for their self-liberation, inspiring them to increase their power by acting together and co-ordinating their efforts.[4]

The article implied that *The Bell* entirely supported this policy and there was a chance at this stage that Michael might have joined Herzen and Ogarev as an editor of the journal. However, their opinions and aims were in fact very different and the joint editorship was not to last long. When Michael presented a second instalment of the article in March 1862 Herzen killed the piece in proof. Michael was furious but, mindful of Herzen's usefulness, merely wrote him a tactful letter, suggesting that they should still maintain their relationship as associates but remain independent of each other's views. George Woodcock comments on the marked difference in their motivation.

It seemed natural at first that he should take his place beside Herzen in directing the propaganda for a liberal Russia which was being conducted through *The Bell*. But differences of personality and opinion soon divided them. Herzen in his own way was near to the anarchism which Bakunin was now approaching; he detested the State, despised Western democracies, and saw the salvation of Europe in the Russian peasant and his communal way of living. But he had not Bakunin's burning faith in violence and destruction, and temperamentally he was too pessimistic to expect anything more revolutionary in Russia than a constitutional government. He also distrusted the Poles and their particular brand of expansive nationalism. Consequently the partnership lasted uneasily for a few months, and then Bakunin withdrew to concentrate on his own grandiose plans.[5]

Although by now Michael could hardly have failed to realize that he had become very much out of touch with the true political situation, it was nevertheless taking him some time to adjust to the radical changes that had taken place in Russia under Alexander II and to the death of revolutionary activity in Europe after 1848. The serfs had been liberated in the spring of 1861 but whilst this amazing reform satisfied some of the Russian radicals it encouraged others to press for further concessions. These groups founded secret societies in Petersburg such as 'Young Russia', and student disturbances were sufficiently developed to bring about the closure of the university.

In the spring of 1862 destructive fires broke out in Petersburg. As a result Herzen as joint editor of *The Bell* soon found himself in the unenviable position of being considered a catalyst to the nihilistic events that had occurred in Russia ever since the loss of the Crimean War. Unflattered by the apparently far-reaching influence of *The Bell*, Herzen protested that he was in no way nihilistic and certainly not a supporter of 'Young Russia'. He hurriedly denounced the organization, thus losing circulation for *The Bell* amongst the radicals whilst still failing to placate the conservatives. Predictably, as Herzen was not sufficiently full-blooded to step out of the middle path, he was condemned by both sides. In his memoirs he commented miserably,

Just as the *colonel rioos* had been the drum-major of our success, so the unmurderous Charlotte Corday was the prophetess of our collapse in public opinion – on both sides, too. At the same time as the reactionaries lifted their heads and called us monsters and incendiaries, some of the young people bade us farewell, as though we had fallen by the wayside. The former we despised, the latter we pitied, and we waited sadly for the rough waves of life to destroy those who made too far out to sea, for we knew that only some of them would get back and make fast to the shore.

The slander grew and was quickly caught up by the press and spread over the whole of Russia. It was only then that the denunciatory era of our journalism began. I remember vividly the amazement of people who were simple and honourable, not in the least revolutionaries, before the printed denunciations – it was something quite new to them. The literature of disclosures quickly shifted its weapon and was twisted at once into a literature of police perquisitions and calumniation by informers.

There was a revolution in society itself. Some were sobered by the emancipation of the peasants; others were simply tired by political agitation; they wished for the former repose; they were satiated before a meal which had cost them so much trouble.

It cannot be denied: our breath is short and our endurance is long!

Seven years of liberalism had exhausted the whole reserve of radical aspirations. All that had been amassed and compressed in the mind since 1825 was expended in raptures of joy, in the foretaste of the good things to come. After the truncated emancipation of the peasants people with weak nerves thought that Russia had gone too far, was going too quickly.

At the same time the *radical* party, young, and for that very reason full of theories, began to announce its intentions more and more impulsively, frightening a society that was already frightened even before this. It set forth as its ostensible aim such extreme outcomes, that liberals and the champions of gradual progress crossed themselves and spat, and ran away stopping their ears, to hide under the old, filthy but familiar blanket of the police. The headlong haste of the students and the landowners' want of practice in listening to other people could not help bringing them to blows.

The force of public opinion, hardly called to life, manifested itself as a savage conservatism. It declared its participation in public affairs by elbowing the government into the debauchery of terror and persecution.

Our position became more and more difficult. We could not stand up for the filth of reaction, but our *locus standi* outside it was lost. Like the knights-errant in the stories who have lost their way, we were hesitating at a cross-roads. Go to the right, and you will lose your horse, but you will be safe yourself; go to the left, and your horse will be safe but you will perish; go forward, and every-one will abandon you; go back – that was impossible: for us the road in that direction was overgrown with grass. If only a sorcerer or hermit would appear and relieve us of the burden of irresolu-tion . . .[6]

While Katkov attacked Herzen in the official press and Herzen gloomily maintained the middle-of-the-road position that he knew was hopeless, Ogarev moved towards the Left and Michael predict-ably threw himself into this revolutionary upsurge with all the vigour of the 'forties.

Meanwhile the relationship between Herzen and Michael had grown worse despite their resolutions of mutual tolerance. Through-out the summer of 1862 they quarrelled over their different stand-points, were reconciled and then quarrelled again. At one stage Herzen, in frustrated anger, suggested that it would be better for both of them if Michael made Paris his headquarters and not London, to which Michael replied with a long and sincerely written apology for his radical ebullience. The apology was accepted, but there was no question of either of them working together in the future.

Michael completely disagreed with Herzen's method of using *The Bell* to propagandize his views. The peasants in Russia were largely illiterate, and propaganda of this kind would not influence them. Nevertheless he remembered that in 1848 open revolutionary organization had been a dismal failure, so he returned to his former occupation of setting up a network of secret societies, not only throughout Bohemia, but now in Russia as well. Once again these clandestine activities became not only an obsession, but an obsession that bordered on farce. Requiring a large staff of agents, Michael seized on every Russian visitor to London he came across and attempted to recruit them. Owing to the 1862 International Exhibition, there were a large number of Russians in London and those who met Michael and whom he tried to press into his service were either horrified, bemused, unwilling or placating. Only a few were genuinely for the revolutionary cause.

A very amusing if ironic anecdote gives insight into the current state of Michael's frustrated activism – activism that was now, once again, cocooning itself in fantasy.

A former Russian officer who was held to be both chivalrous and trustworthy arrived in London. Eventually the ex-officer was taken to meet Michael, who stated firmly that he was sure that he would like to do something for the common cause. Politely, if somewhat warily, the ex-officer agreed and immediately Michael asked him to take a letter to Jassy. Slightly stunned, the ex-officer agreed, but stated that there was a money problem for such a long journey. Michael, however, said that Herzen would be only too delighted to provide the necessary travelling expenses. When he had reached Jassy, the new emissary would be able to travel on to the Caucasus, where he could be a trustworthy contact. The dumbfounded ex-officer left Michael to await developments and Michael contacted Herzen over the travelling expenses. Herzen, however, was far from co-operative. He told Michael in no uncertain terms that, as usual, he was being impractical and was merely using the shy young man as a means of satisfying one of his own whims. Herzen went on to refuse point-blank to finance such a fantasy. Michael accepted the rebuttal with good humour and Herzen records that he then sat down to a hearty meal (naturally at Orsett House) which he ate with relish.

Unfortunately anyone who carried a message back to Russia from Michael's revolutionary front in London was likely to be seized by the Russian Secret Police, so to 'protect' the unfortunate agents Michael devised an elaborate and totally useless series of secret codes. Their naivety was almost unbelievable: pseudonyms such as 'private gentleman' or 'Baron Tiesenhausen' (Herzen), 'Brykalov' (Michael), 'Junior' (Herzen's son) and 'the poet' or 'Kosterov' (Ogarev) abounded, code letters were sent with the code enclosed or would begin conventionally and then break into code with the most obvious reference to the change of style. Lost in his usual secret-society fantasies, Michael spun a dreamlike revolutionary web which was totally impractical.

However, the game was becoming a deadly one, as the Russian authorities began to suppress any revolutionary propaganda or activity with growing severity. Herzen, Ogarev and Michael were denounced as public enemies of Russia along with *The Bell*, they were spied upon at their meetings by a Russian police spy, and, as a result, on 5 July 1862 one of Michael's unfortunate messengers was arrested on the Russian frontier with letters of support from Michael, Herzen and Ogarev to revolutionary sympathizers in Russia. In particular, there were letters from Herzen and Ogarev to Nicholas Serno-Solovievich, the head of the Land and Liberty secret society (one of the most important in existence), and as a result Serno-Solovievich was also arrested. Other recipients of Michael's curious correspondence were also seized and the chain even spiralled back to Turgenev. In 1863, much to his dismay, the latter was asked to go to Petersburg. There he was questioned for his association with dangerous political exiles such as Michael Bakunin. Turgenev desperately denied any involvement with him and was cleared. Meanwhile the Russian secret police were building up a very interesting dossier as Michael's naive code and agent system was further cracked and more and more of his postmen were arrested. What had started as a typically amateurish conspiracy on Michael's part had escalated into a witch-hunt.

Despite these disastrous activities, Michael's reputation and his escape from Siberia had given him a romantic, near-heroic reputation amongst Londoners. However, apart from a brief connection with a delegation of working men, the interest of a radical weekly and the monotonous but mortifying revival of the rumour that he was a Russian spy, Michael had little or no contact with English politics (which he obviously despised) or the English people (whose class-system he thought almost as bad as the Russian). England was a base – that was all – and he had no interest in its citizens or its way of government. Besides, he hardly spoke the language and indeed found it quite irrelevant to get to know it in any depth.

The Russian-agent rumour was sufficiently persistent to convince Herzen that Marx was again behind it. Michael, however, did not agree. The rumour appeared most forcibly in the *Free Press* and the *Morning Advertiser*, and Michael indignantly denied the allegations in letters to both these papers. Eventually it died down again, having provided the only significant contact Michael was to have with the English or the English press.

Foreign exiles were another matter, and the most notable of these whom he met in London was Napoleon III's cousin, Prince Jerome Bonaparte. Most of the time, however, he associated with Russians and Poles and devoted himself to the destruction of the Austrian Empire and to Slav freedom.

This was in fact an extremely difficult cause to promote, for the Austrian Emperor was securely established on his throne and the

Slavs seemed to be loyal to him. However, Adolf Straka had emigrated to England and told Michael that Joseph Frič was in charge of Czech national propaganda in Europe and that Frič's brother, Vyacheslav, was in Prague. Michael, of course, saw Vyacheslav Frič as an agent – a super-agent, perhaps – and with this in mind he wrote him a long letter outlining his pan-Slav ideals in the hope that Vyacheslav would try to re-create a revolutionary movement in Bohemia. Unfortunately the letter failed to reach him.

Meanwhile Michael became more and more anti-German in his outlook and this racial bias, already documented in his Confession to Nicholas I, made him reject any attempted reconciliation of the Slavs and the Germans. He even decided that the aristocratic leaders of the Czech national movement were heavily German-influenced and would have to be removed. The hoped-for national revolution should be based on co-operation between the educated youth and the people, and when this revolution had succeeded a pan-Slav federation which included Russia should be fought for.

A common hatred of Austria also united Michael and Mazzini, the highly popular extremist Italian leader, whom Michael liked and respected, feeling that he had discovered a powerful ally in enlisting Italy's help for the Polish cause.

However, despite his revolutionary enthusiasm, quite suddenly, in the spring of 1862, Michael remembered that he had a wife, and that he needed her with him again. He was still desperately lonely. He felt that he must have certain items of familiar furniture around him and with the lack of contact with his family and Premukhino Antonia's presence was even more essential. Michael therefore wrote to Natalie Bakunin, pleading for her assistance in sending Antonia to Europe, and in June 1862 he wrote to Antonia herself, saying,

> My heart is aching for you. Day and night I dream only of you. As soon as you join me, we will go together to Italy. There it will be cheerful and gayer, and there will be plenty of work. Don't be afraid, my heart, you shall have a servant-girl and there will be enough to live on – only come.[7]

Antonia had become a symbol – a reminder of the old 'spiritual' love that he had so much enjoyed – but Michael's family and his friends, particularly Turgenev and Herzen, could only disapprove of the strange marriage that he had committed himself to under such stressful conditions. Even Antonia was wary of undertaking the difficult journey to an insecure future, but so obsessed with the symbol of Antonia did Michael become that in September 1862, by borrowing from his friends in time-honoured style, he raised some funds for her journey and forced his family to accept Antonia at Premukhino for a short visit and to provide the rest.

At Premukhino there had again been changes. Varvara was dead and Nicholas and Alexis had spent some months in the fortress of Peter and Paul for voicing their displeasure at the current condition of the liberated serfs. Black-sheep Alexander was already in Europe and had in fact visited Michael in London during January 1862. Unfortunately they did not understand one another. The remaining members of the family did not seem to be able to take the risk of contacting him. Natalie Bakunin was now Michael's only means of communication with his family.

In the meantime Michael briefly met Bishop Paphnutius of the Old Believers. The bishop had travelled to London from Russia in an attempt to link his religious dissenters with the Russian political exiles. Michael, hoping that he might be able to use the Old Believers to stir up rebellion amongst the Russian peasantry, tried hard with the bishop, but the meetings proved fruitless and instead he turned his attention to an ex-Russian serf named Martyanov.

Martyanov had actually arrived at Herzen's home in the autumn of 1861. He had managed to buy his own freedom but had been cheated over this by his master. Infuriated at getting no recompense from the Russian authorities, Martyanov had come to Europe hoping to arouse sympathy for his case. To Michael and even to Herzen Martyanov was remarkable in that unlike their other associates he was a genuine Russian peasant who had been a serf. Predictably, therefore, just as Antonia had become Michael's symbol of longed-for spiritual love, Martyanov became a symbol of the Russian peasants whom Michael saw as his prospective revolutionaries.

In April 1862 Martyanov, now roused to represent the Russian people as a whole, sent Alexander II a complaining letter (which was reprinted in *The Bell*). The letter, although loyal to the dynasty of the Tsar, urged Alexander to become more of a spiritual father than a despot. Martyanov ended by suggesting that Alexander should take an immediate step in the direction of spiritual paternalism by convening a Russian National Assembly. Michael was delighted with Martyanov's somewhat naive but courageous approach, while Herzen looked on patronizingly, for he was intellectually remote from a person like Martyanov. Professor Carr says of Michael at this stage,

It was part of that inherent simplicity which distinguished Bakunin from every radical and revolutionary of the time.

Herzen idealized the Russian people, Marx the proletariat. But it is impossible to imagine Herzen borrowing his ideas from a farm labourer or Marx from a factory hand. Only Bakunin, the aristocrat, was sufficiently free from class-consciousness to be perfectly unconstrained in his relations with a former serf, and to find it as natural that he should be influenced by him.[8]

Michael, now extremely friendly with Martyanov, immediately set to work to implement the letter by collecting signatures to petition the Tsar on the founding of a Russian National Assembly. He then wrote an article, grudgingly published later by Herzen in *The Bell*, called 'The People's Cause: Romanov, Pugachev, or Pestel?' which set out the three alternatives Michael had in mind concerning revolution in Russia. They were as follows:

1 A bloodless revolution brought about by Alexander II himself;

2 A peasant uprising, as led by Pugachev in the reign of Catherine the Great;

3 A revolution of the intelligentsia, as led by Pestel in December 1825.

This idea of a revolutionary dictatorship which was being offered to Alexander II was not inconsistent with Michael's thinking (he had suggested as much to both Nicholas I and Muraviev) but Herzen and Ogarev were amazed. Herzen was in favour of constitutional democracy and it was clear to him that Michael's plans did not include this at all. Moreover, Herzen was quite unable to see how Michael could possibly be influenced by anyone as crudely naive as Martyanov. He summarized the article as 'a medley of Bakuninist demagogy' while Ogarev called it 'confused Tsarism'. Naturally enough, however, Martyanov approved of it.

Meanwhile the secret society Land and Liberty (the name was taken from an article by Ogarev in *The Bell* – 'What do the people need? It is very simple. The people need Land and Liberty') was rapidly expanding throughout Russia, despite the arrest and subsequent imprisonment of its founder, Serno-Solovievich. Michael, having convinced himself that the Central European Slavs were a lost cause and that the Old Believers and Martyanov were probably the same, now enthusiastically embraced the cause of Land and Liberty and tried to urge an extremely unwilling Herzen (half-committed as he was to Land and Liberty through Ogarev's involvement with it) to use *The Bell* to back the society. Michael recommended that a new system of agents should be set up and the network should spread to the furthermost corners of Russia. However,

Herzen was once again too middle-of-the-road to plunge into such a venture without giving it an inordinate amount of thought, and before he had finally committed himself Michael had switched his attentions to the situation now arising in Poland.

As a result of the liberal changes taking place in Russia under Alexander II, the fate of Russian Poland came under review when the Russian authorities began to think of a possible 'administrative autonomy' for the area. Meanwhile the Poles themselves were divided into two opposing groups:

1   The Central National Committee which wanted:
    (a) freedom from Russian domination, and
    (b) freedom from the domination of the Polish landlords.
    They were supported by both radicals and revolutionaries in Russia.

2   The Committee of the Szlachta (the aristocracy) who wanted freedom from Russian domination so that they could reign supreme themselves. The Russian authorities were prepared to co-operate with them but the Szlachta tended to be too demanding. They wanted not only Poland restored to them, but also territories which had originally belonged to Poland in the days when she stretched into greater areas of Eastern Europe. The Russian authorities, however, had no intention of returning these lands, but only of giving autonomy to a far more limited area.

In May 1862 Alexander II made his brother, Grand-Duke Constantine, who was known to be a liberal, Regent of Poland, while the post of Civil Governor was given to the pro-Russian aristocrat Marquis Wielopolski. However, the new system of government frustrated both committees, assassination-attempts were made on both the Regent and the Civil Governor, and revolution looked as if it would break out at any moment.

Michael disapproved of the Szlachta, but as he was in favour of a 'Peasant' Poland he did not necessarily agree with all the demands of the Central National Committee. Nevertheless he welcomed the rising heat of the coming revolution and had many meetings, in London and for a brief period in Paris, with various emissaries and representatives of the Polish cause, introducing them in many cases to the at first sceptical and then cautiously enthusiastic Herzen. Some of these, like the Russian officer Potebnya – who pointed out that the dissatisfied Russian troops in Poland would join the revolutionaries – were impressive because of their evident sincerity, but others, like the power-crazy Polish general Mieroslawski, were much more dubious. General Mieroslawski, already a veteran revolutionary, closely resembled Michael in temperament. He was passionately in favour of restoring the original Polish frontiers and consequently despised the National Committee. He relates that Michael promised to publish a manifesto on the day of the revolution ordering the Russian armies in Poland to retreat behind the Dnieper but this is not mentioned in Bakunin's account of their meeting.

Michael had openly proffered his support for the coming Polish revolution at a banquet given by Prince Jerome Bonaparte in July, but it was not until September that Michael was visited by anyone of importance from the National Committee. In September three representatives of the Central National Committee – Padlewski, Milovicz and Giller – came to London to raise support amongst the Polish émigrés and their associates. Naturally they contacted Michael, who took them to meet Herzen. Herzen had already prepared a statement of intent to read to the three representatives but although Michael agreed with it in principle he was sure that it would not please the others. He was right in this. A letter from the Central Committee was then read by Milovicz which had as its basic policy 'the recognition of the right of the peasantry to the land tilled by them, and the complete self-determination of every people, the right to determine its own destiny'. Milovicz pointed out that his letter was much more positive than Herzen's. As a result Herzen rather hesitantly agreed to some changes and, as a point of principle, asked the Poles for some changes in their own document. (Later Michael felt annoyed and upset, feeling that the logically-minded Herzen had remained cold and unenthusiastic throughout the interview.) Herzen recalled that, after the acrimonious inquest,

> Bakunin waved his hand in despair and went off to Ogarev's room. I looked mournfully after him. I saw that he was in the middle of his revolutionary debauch, and that there would be no bringing him to reason now. With his seven-league boots he was striding over seas and mountains, over years and generations. Beyond the insurrection in Warsaw he was already seeing his 'Glorious and Slav Federation' of which the Poles spoke with something between horror and repulsion; he already saw the red flag of 'Land and Freedom' waving on the Urals and the Volga, in the Ukraine and the Caucasus, possibly on the Winter Palace and the Peter-Paul fortress, and was in haste to smooth away all difficulties somehow, to conceal contradictions, not to fill up the gullies but to fling a skeleton bridge across them.[9]

A further interview between the Polish representatives and

Herzen and Michael produced more terminological difficulties but eventually a manifesto was approved, signed and sent to the press. Obviously Giller and his companions overrated the importance and the influence of the Herzen organization, both at home and abroad. Herzen, for his part, realized that a revolutionary network *was* slowly forming in Russia but so delicate was it at this stage that any tremor might destroy it. On this basis Herzen warned the Polish representatives that their rising could well be premature. Michael tried to interrupt him but Herzen continued by rightly defending his close analysis of the wording of the manifesto, pointing out that from the point of view of the Russian people, land and provincial freedom were essential revolutionary ingredients and if these words were not seen on Polish revolutionary banners the possible Russian revolution would be set back for years. Giller, however, assured Herzen that the Polish revolution would not disappoint him in that respect.

The autumn and winter of 1862 were dominated by the grumblings of the impending Polish revolution. Michael, meanwhile, fell out with the pretentious Mieroslawski over Michael's involvement with the National Committee. This started an egotistical and rather uninteresting battle between Michael and Mieroslawski which was still being waged five years later.

In December Michael entered into a farcical correspondence with an anonymous letter-writer who signed himself 'Abracadabra' and described himself as a Russian-born Pole, an ex-Siberian exile and now a Polish revolutionary sympathizer living in Paris. 'Abracadabra' warned Michael of Mieroslawski's manipulations and went on to ask for news of the Polish cause. Michael, intrigued and flattered, kept up an eager correspondence with the mysterious 'Abracadabra' and, as usual, naively told him as much as he knew about Polish affairs. Luckily his information was not of any great importance, for 'Abracadabra' was a Russian secret police spy – a fact that Michael never discovered.

In January 1863 Sleptsov, a friend of Serno-Solovievich, the imprisoned founder of Land and Liberty, arrived in London and asked Herzen and Ogarev to become 'agents' of the society in London. Herzen described his dilemma in his memoirs.

The plenipotentiary was full of the importance of his mission and invited us to become the *agents* of the League of Land and Freedom. I declined this, to the extreme surprise not only of Bakunin but even of Ogarev. I said that I did not like this hackneyed French term. The plenipotentiary was treating us as the *Commissaires* of the Convention of 1793 treated the generals in the distant armies. I did not like that either.

'And are there many of you?' I asked him.

'That is hard to say: some hundreds in Petersburg and three thousand in the provinces.'

'Do you believe it?' I asked Ogarev afterwards. He did not answer. 'Do you believe it?' I asked Bakunin.

'Of course; but,' he added, '*well, if there are not as many now there soon will be!*' and he burst into a roar of laughter.

'That is another matter.'

'The essence of it all is the giving support to feeble beginnings; if they were strong they would not need us,' observed Ogarev, who was always dissatisfied with my scepticism on these occasions.

'Then they ought to come to us frankly admitting their weakness and asking for friendly help instead of proposing the stupid job of being agents.'

'That is youth,' Bakunin commented, and he went off to Sweden.

And after him Potebnya went off too. With heartfelt sorrow I said good-bye to him. I did not doubt for one second that he was going straight to destruction.

A few days before Bakunin's departure Martyanov came in, paler than usual, gloomier than usual; he sat down in a corner and said nothing. He was pining for Russia and brooding over the thought of returning home. A discussion of the Polish rebellion sprang up. Martyanov listened in silence, then got up, preparing to go, and suddenly stopped in front of me, and said gloomily:

'You must not be angry with me, Olexander Ivanovich; that may be so or it may not, but, anyway, you have done for *The Bell*. What business had you to meddle in Polish affairs? The Poles may be in the right, but their cause is for their gentry, not for you. You have not spared us, God forgive you, Olexander Ivanovich; you will remember what I say. I shall not see it myself; I am going home. There is nothing for me to do here.'

'You are not going to Russia, and *The Bell* is not ruined,' I answered him.

He went out without another word, leaving me heavily weighed down by this second prediction and by a dim consciousness that a blunder had been made.

Martyanov did as he had said; he returned home in the spring of 1863 and went to die in penal servitude, exiled by his 'People's Tsar' for his love for Russia and his trust in him.

Towards the end of 1863 the circulation of *The Bell* dropped from two thousand or two thousand five hundred to five hundred, and never again rose above one thousand copies. The Charlotte Corday from Orlov and the Daniel from the peasants had been right.[10]

Herzen's cold reception of the young Russian revolutionary and his disbelief of Sleptsov's confident claim that there were large numbers of members of Land and Liberty in Russia embarrassed the kindly Ogarev and annoyed the perpetually optimistic Michael. But Herzen, although basically right about the society's grandiose claims, eventually, under the pressure of both Michael and Ogarev, agreed to be the chief representative abroad and gloomily began to prepare a manifesto concerning the birth of the ex-Russian branch of Land and Liberty which was to be published in *The Bell* on 1 March 1863. Under the pressure of his two compatriots Alexander Herzen had unwillingly committed himself to revolution.

Rumours of an imminent uprising in Poland increased at the beginning of the new year and Michael wrote a letter, which accompanied a long epistle of Ogarev's, to the Russian officers who were committed to take part in it.

Friends and Brothers, – The lines written by our friend Nikolay Platonovich Ogarev are full of true and boundless devotion to the great cause of our national and indeed pan-Slav emancipation. One cannot but agree with him that the premature and partial rising of Poland threatens to interrupt the general steady advance of the Slav, and especially of the Russian, progressive movement. It must be owned that in the present temper of Russia and of all Europe there is too little hope of success for such a rebellion, and that the defeat of the progressive party in Poland will inevitably be followed by the temporary triumph of the tsarist despotism in Russia. But on the other hand, the condition of the Poles is so insufferable that they will hardly be patient for long.

The government itself by its infamous measures of cruel and systematic oppression is provoking them, it seems, to a rebellion, the postponement of which would be for that very reason as necessary for Poland as it is essential for Russia. To defer it till a much later date would undoubtedly be the salvation of them as well as of us. You ought to devote all your efforts to bring this about, without, however, failing to respect their sacred rights and their national dignity. Exhort them as far as you can and so far as circumstances permit, but yet lose no time, be active in propaganda and organization, that you may be ready for the decisive moment;

and when, driven beyond the utmost limit of possible patience, our unhappy Polish brothers rise, do you rise too, not against them but for them; rise up in the name of Russian honour, in the name of Slav duty, in the name of the Russian people, with the cry, 'Land and Freedom'; and if you are doomed to perish, your very death will serve the common cause . . . and God knows! Perhaps in opposition to every calculation of cold prudence your heroic exploit may unexpectedly be crowned with success . . .

As for myself, whatever may await you, success or destruction, I hope that it may be granted to me to share your fate.

Good-bye – and perhaps till we meet again soon.

M. Bakunin.[11]

In the end the Polish revolution was precipitated by the Russian authorities themselves. They decided to bring the situation to a head and triggered off the insurrection by ordering conscription for the Russian army in Poland.

Accordingly, on 15 January 1863 a selective levy was ordered upon the urban proletariat, the main body of dissatisfied people upon whom the revolutionaries were undoubtedly relying for most of their forces. Immediately the National General Committee was forced into starting the revolution and on the night of 22 January the barracks of the Russian garrison in Poland were attacked. This attack automatically ruled out the possibility that the Russian officers would join the insurrection. Nevertheless, terrorist activities and guerrilla fighting started up all over Poland and the exiles in Europe, whether they were cynical or optimistic, were thrown into a fever-pitch of excitement. Nothing like it had occurred since 1848 and immediately Michael was desperate to get to Poland and to lend them his support. Soon, with the aid of a false passport and the backing of a rich Polish Count, he was ready to make the difficult journey to Poland, but the Poles were suspicious of this exiled Russian, no doubt having heard the unfortunate rumours of his being a Russian agent.

Michael wrote letter after letter to the General Committee, offering to stir up peasant revolts in the Ukraine and Lithuania, to recruit a Russian legion of deserters from the Russian army, and agitate against the Russian Government itself as a diversionary measure, but they firmly requested that he should remain in London. He eventually realized that neither he nor his services were required, but to an optimistic nature like Michael's this was far from being a deterrent and he made arrangements to sail to Copenhagen. He incurred further suspicion and scepticism by giving the London representative of the National General Committee one of his extraordinary codes so that he could correspond with him, but all he received in response was a recipe for invisible ink. Even this mockery did not deter him, and he asked the committee to provide a representative to meet him in Copenhagen to discuss how his abilities could best be utilized.

On 21 February 1863 Michael left London for Copenhagen. At that time the revolution appeared to be holding its ground, and there were rumours of the possibilities of intervention by both France and Great Britain in support of the Polish revolutionaries.

Once in Copenhagen Michael waited in vain for contact from the National General Committee and slowly began to realize that no such contact would be forthcoming. Facing up to this prospect, he evolved an alternative plan of travelling to Stockholm, there to organize Swedish patriots into beginning an insurrection in Finland (a Russian territory) which would aid the Polish revolution. After a few days he decided to wait no longer for contact from the National General Committee and boarded a ship for Sweden.

In Sweden, Michael made a number of friends, opened up routes for Land and Liberty across Finland, arranged for the distribution of *The Bell* and had discussions with members of all the Polish parties. Michael assured everyone that a peasant revolution was about to break out in Russia and his assurances held conviction as he really did believe in the potential of the revolutionary movement. At the same time he was making his final arrangements to enter Poland and Lithuania and lead the peasant revolt himself.

Meanwhile a Polish Legion, about two hundred strong, had been recruited in Paris to aid the rebels. There was one Russian amongst them; the rest were Hungarians, Frenchmen, Poles and various other nationalities. Their aim was to sail to the Baltic and disembark on the Lithuanian coast. In charge of the expedition was a certain Colonel Lapinski, who was, to say the least, something of a rough diamond.

When Michael had been in Sweden for a week, the legion, in great and slightly melodramatic secrecy, arrived in London on 14 February 1863. This was the first of many mistakes. The armaments were not ready, open drilling was done in Woolwich – which soon banished any secrecy the legion had hitherto enjoyed – *The Globe* published an article about it and news of the proposed expedition soon came to the ears of the Russian ambassador. He lost no time in informing the British authorities that a ship called the *Gypsy Queen* was about to carry arms and legionnaires to support a revolution against a power friendly to Great Britain. The British Government, anxious to prevent a diplomatic incident, sent representatives to board a ship called the *Ward Jackson* (the name *Gypsy Queen* was a mistake on the part of the Russian ambassador) at Gravesend and temporarily refused the ship clearance papers while a full-scale investigation was made. But this in no way cast a shadow over the expedition and Herzen vividly, and very cynically, describes the hilarious start to the legion's campaign:

> Cwerczakiewicz and Demontowicz informed all who were taking part in the expedition that they were to assemble at ten o'clock on such and such a railway platform to go to Hull by a special train provided by the shipping company. And so by ten o'clock the future warriors were beginning to assemble. Among them were Italians and a few Frenchmen; poor, brave men, sick of their portion in homeless wandering, and men who were true lovers of Poland. And ten o'clock passed and eleven o'clock, but there was no train. Little by little rumours of a long journey began to be disseminated among the homes from which our heroes had mysteriously left, and at twelve o'clock the future warriors were joined on the platform by a flock of women, inconsolable Didos deserted by their fierce adorers, and fierce landladies who had not been paid, probably in order to avoid publicity. Unkempt and unclean, they clamoured, they wanted to complain to the police . . . some of them had children . . . all the children yelled and all the mothers yelled. The English stood around and looked wonderingly at the picture of 'the Exodus'. In vain older members of the party inquired whether the special train would soon come in, and showed their tickets. The railway officials had never heard of any such train. The scene was becoming noisier and noisier . . . when suddenly a courier from the chiefs galloped up to tell the waiting warriors that they had all gone mad, that the departure was at ten o'clock in the evening, not in the morning, and that this was so obvious that they had not even written it down. The poor warriors went off with their bags and their wallets to their deserted Didos and mollified landladies.
>
> At ten o'clock in the evening they left. The English even gave them three cheers.[12]

For a brief period at least, matters proceeded more efficiently. Captain Weatherby was persuaded to weigh anchor and, without clearance papers, the *Ward Jackson* sailed from Gravesend to Southend.* Two highly irate customs officers were still on board

---

* Herzen was incorrect when he mentioned Hull as the departure port.

but they were unceremoniously off-loaded at Southend. Then, with the legion on board, the *Ward Jackson* very quickly made off, leaving the British Foreign Office to explain to the Russian ambassador in the politest possible terms that the ship was no longer around to be detained.

Meanwhile, in Stockholm, Michael was pleased to find that he was at last appreciated, being continuously acclaimed as a famous Russian revolutionary. However, in London he was viewed far more cynically and, fearing his indiscretion, it was not until the *Ward Jackson* had actually left Southend that Michael received a cable from Herzen and Cwerczakiewicz asking him to join the expedition when it reached Helsingborg. Michael, furious at not being told before, was mollified by the hope of action at last and quickly set off for Helsingborg. (It is interesting to note that when action finally came, Michael, despite all the cynicism and suspicion that was currently attached to him, was asked to participate.)

Michael, taking with him a Pole named Kalinka, arrived at Helsingborg on 26 March 1863. Immediately there was friction on both sides. Michael did not think highly of the Polish volunteers and they were irritated by the arrival of Kalinka who belonged to the Szlachta rather than the National Committee. Moreover, Weatherby, once the romance of the piratical situation had worn off, began to worry about fines and his own future welfare. There were other drawbacks to the voyage as well, for owing to a mild winter the Russian port of Reval was ice-free and Russian cruisers might well be able to intercept the *Ward Jackson* in the Baltic. Undaunted, Michael wrote to Paris asking for an armed cruiser, and although he never received a reply his reputation amongst members of the expedition was immensely enhanced.

On 28 March the *Ward Jackson* sailed for the island of Gothland on the Swedish side of the Baltic, but at this stage the situation became completely out of hand. The plan had been to sail from Gothland to the Lithuanian coast, but Captain Weatherby, who had become more and more uneasy, was now convinced that he was sailing into disaster. So strong was this feeling, in fact, that on the excuse of picking up fresh supplies of drinking water he put in to Copenhagen and confided his problems to the British minister there, Sir Augustus Paget. As a result Weatherby stated that he would not captain the *Ward Jackson* again until all Poles had left the ship and the crew immediately went ashore in the wake of their captain. Directly Michael had heard this news, he also went to Paget and was received politely. Michael told Paget that Weatherby was in Russian pay but the minister could not accept this and, although he agreed that Weatherby had behaved villainously (from Michael's point of view anyway), he was quite unable to force him to continue with the voyage. He did suggest, however, that Michael should have a word with the *Ward Jackson*'s agents in Copenhagen.

On being appealed to, the agents eventually supplied a Dutch crew for the *Ward Jackson* and the ship sailed for Malmo, where it arrived on 30 March. There the glorious legionnaires were given an effusive welcome but unfortunately this was the last happy event in the sad history of the *Ward Jackson*, for while Michael and the legionnaires were celebrating with the locals the Swedish authorities seized the ship and its cargo.

For two months the shattered adventurers contemplated their ill-fortune in Malmo, although many of the brave legionnaires left for home. In the end Michael himself left for Stockholm, where during the summer of 1863 a row of massive proportions developed amongst the expedition's leaders as to who was to blame for its inglorious and ludicrous failure. While they were thus engaged, the surviving members of the expedition chartered a Danish ship named *Emelia*, and after some subterfuge sailed into the Baltic. They attempted to land on the Prussian coast from where they planned to trek to the Lithuanian border, but at this point further and final disaster struck the expedition. The boats in which they were to row ashore were not seaworthy and many of the occupants of the first landing-craft were drowned. As a result the morale of the expedition, already low, completely collapsed and the entire project was abandoned.

In June 1863 the Polish insurrection, fated from the start yet an amazingly vigorous enterprise, was finally suppressed by the Russians. Disappointing though this was, Michael had already begun to fall out of sympathy with this, his favourite obsession. No longer could he regard Polish nationalism as a force for revolution, for it was obvious that the Poles were not true revolutionaries and that territorial gain was high on their list of priorities. Certainly they were prepared to use the support of Russian radicals, but only in pursuit of their own ends. Once again Michael was forced to remove his political blinkers and to admit to himself his own self-deceit. Once again he had blinded himself to a situation whose reality had been all too apparent to inactivists like Herzen, while it had required a sledgehammer of experience to force Michael to accept it.

In February 1863, as Michael was preparing to leave Sweden, Antonia had crossed the Russian border, after signing a declaration that she would never return. She arrived humbly in London in

April, overawed and miserably anxious to join her husband, and Herzen was forced to provide lodging for her. Michael was always to remember with bitterness the fact that Herzen was particularly cool towards Antonia at this juncture, but no doubt Herzen saw her as a nuisance-like appendage that was likely to sap Michael's most productive quality – his energy. Herzen considered that Michael's energy, often so damaging during tricky negotiation or periods of political inactivity, was of vital use in a crisis and should not be impeded. In fact Herzen was so apathetic about her that he omitted to cable Michael that Antonia had arrived in London – another factor that was always to anger Michael in the future. However, Michael discovered that Antonia was in London when he left the *Ward Jackson*, and he cabled Herzen that she should be sent out to Stockholm. Wearily Antonia arrived in Stockholm on 8 April 1863. Michael, meanwhile, although pleased to see her, was preoccupied. His enthusiasm for the pan-Slav ideal was on the wane and he was looking towards Finland as a possible starting-point for the hoped-for Russian revolution.

At that time Sweden was an excellent base for Michael's activities. Not only was it closely involved with the Finnish problem – Finland having been seized from Sweden by Russia in 1809 – but in Sweden Michael had become a famous figure. The Russian revolutionary famed for his colourful escape from Russia was respected in Stockholm far more than in London and although the Swedes were in no way revolution-minded, they were, without doubt, far too near to Russia for comfort. The radicals had watched the Polish insurrection hopefully and had been dismayed when it was crushed, and despite the qualms of Sweden's Conservative Government, who wished at all times to maintain cordial relations with Russia and Austria, the Swedish radical leader Blanche personally admired Michael and what he stood for. Nevertheless, if Michael saw in Finland another Poland he was once again deliberately ignoring the real facts, for the liberal views of Alexander II had in fact given new hope to the Finnish bourgeoisie and they were anxious to please Alexander in the expectation that the constitution might be returned to them. Therefore, despite the interest of Charles XV of Sweden and the poet Emil von Quanten, who was Charles's private secretary and a firm advocate of Swedish–Finnish union with the King taking the additional title of Grand Duke of Finland, Michael's schemes showed little sign of bearing fruit.

Rather belatedly the Russian minister in Sweden, Count Dashkov, suddenly discovered that the visiting Canadian Professor Henri Soulié was, in fact, the dangerous Russian agitator, Michael Bakunin. Immediately Dashkov asked the Swedish authorities to expel Michael, but Sweden's democracy would not allow this; as a sop the Swedish authorities assured Dashkov that they would research full details of Michael's career and lay them before the Swedish public so that they could judge for themselves the validity of this Russian exile who was rapidly becoming a Swedish folk-hero.

In May 1863 a critical official survey of Michael's activities appeared in the *Posttidningen*. This was countered by an outraged radical press together with articles by Michael in the *Aftonbladet* vigorously defending himself. The Russian authorities, seeing that Michael's fame was being increased by the controversy, had the idea of destroying him by trying to publish some of the ambiguities of his Confession to the Tsar. This plan, however, was never carried out and on 28 May 1863 a banquet was organized in Michael's honour by a number of Swedish radicals. At the banquet was Herzen's son Sasha, who had been sent to Sweden to join Michael in order to begin a political career. Michael was pleased to have Sasha under his wing, for he saw him not only as a good sounding-board but also, owing to his father, a more liberal revolutionary figure than himself and therefore more acceptable to the unrevolutionary Swedes. The banquet was attended by a wide cross-section of bourgeois Swedish society and after Blanche had proposed the toast of 'young Russia and Michael Bakunin', Michael replied, in French, by thanking Sweden for her 'noble hospitality'. He added that, with the exception of Great Britain, no country had given such generous hospitality to political refugees as Sweden. Michael went on to point out that the Russian Government had encouraged the peasants to rebel against the Polish landowners and that he and his associates were not anti-monarchists, nor indeed were they fully fledged revolutionaries in that sense. All they demanded was the liberty of oppressed peoples, and that could be brought about within a monarchistic or a republican framework. He then described the 'patriotic, conservative, liberal and democratic' basis of Land and Liberty and went into a somewhat ambitious account of its growing Russian membership. Not only, according to Michael, was the Russian membership immense, but Land and Liberty was rapidly forming its own State-within-a-State administration. Already an alliance had been formed with the Warsaw Central Committee. Michael concluded by proposing a toast to Swedish patriotism and Scandinavian union.

This incredible speech, aimed as it was at the bourgeois audience at the banquet, with its wild exaggerations, over-elaborations and identification of the secret society with constitutional monarchy, was followed by Sasha Herzen speaking of his father's work in London, of Ogarev and of *The Bell*.

Ironically, shortly after this speech a series of catastrophes began once again to sabotage Michael's beliefs and to make him realize that Scandinavia was no longer a suitable retreat. First of all Michael and Sasha had a serious, if ludicrous, quarrel over which of the two was the official representative of Land and Liberty in Stockholm. The quarrel was violent and protracted and did nothing to enhance the reputation of either party. Moreover the crushing of the Polish insurrection, the appeasement of the Finns by Alexander II, the disintegration of Land and Liberty, a row with von Quanten and failing finance all began very clearly to indicate that it was time for Michael to move on. But where could he go? There were so many countries now to which he could not return either for fear of being arrested or because of the quarrels, rancour and bad feeling that he had left behind him. In the end he decided that Italy was the most attractive proposition. Revolution was in the air there and Italy was a country that was cheap to live in. Once again Michael prepared to make one of his innumerable fresh starts.

Michael and Antonia left Stockholm for Italy via London on 8 October 1863. They were seen off by a deputation of relieved Swedes and Poles, and the Russian press, as a send-off, reprinted the statement of a highly obscure Pole that Herzen and his friends had been responsible for misinforming Polish circles about the size and stature of the organization Land and Liberty. This apparently had given the Poles an ill-founded sense of security, pushing them into a totally ill-conceived rebellion. Despite the obviousness of this propaganda, Herzen, with the liberal reputation of *The Bell* collapsed around him, was furiously angry. His own weakness in sitting so austerely on the fence had finally wrecked his career and *The Bell*, once widely read in Russia as the voice of progressive liberalism, was dismissed as the propaganda of traitors. In his rage and self-contempt Herzen looked round for someone to blame.

There was no need to look very far: Michael was everyone's scapegoat. Years of tolerance to Michael's erratic behaviour were stripped away as Herzen angrily planned to print a statement in *The Bell* completely dissociating himself from Michael. Michael, however, still genuinely respected Herzen, though he shrewdly summed him up as follows:

> Herzen has presented, and continues to present, the Russian cause magnificently before the public of Europe. [Michael is ignoring the fact that the circulation of *The Bell* had dropped to

approximately five hundred copies, so that it was unlikely to be commanding much attention at that time.] But in matters of domestic policy he is an inveterate sceptic, and his influence on them is not merely not encouraging, but demoralizing. He is, first and foremost, a writer of genius; and he combines all the brilliant qualities with the vices of his profession. When liberty has been established in Russia, or when it begins to be established, he will be, beyond question, a powerful journalist, perhaps an orator, a statesman, even an administrator. But he decidedly has not in him the stuff of which revolutionary leaders are made.[13]

Michael and Antonia stayed in London for a few weeks before travelling, via Brussels and Paris, to Italy. Fortunately Herzen was away and Michael found a sympathizer in Ogarev. Indeed Ogarev even went so far as to write to Herzen asking for clemency for the return of the prodigal. His intervention seemed to have done some good, for when, in December, Michael met Herzen in Paris, Herzen's mood was mild. Michael was penitent over his mistakes and Herzen held back the torrent of abuse he would dearly have loved to pour over Michael's head. They parted amicably, at least on the surface.

Michael and Antonia then departed for Switzerland and spent Christmas with Sleptsov at Vevey. Later Michael visited his old friends the Vogts in Berne and converted them to the Polish cause, and on 11 January 1864 Michael and Antonia finally arrived in Italy.

PART SIX

International Revolution: 1863–9

I

Michael Bakunin lived in Italy from 1864 to 1867 and it was during this period that he finally rejected nationalism and formulated his creed of revolutionary anarchism. At first, however, he was content to settle in Florence and regain some of the energy he had expended on the Polish uprising. Meanwhile an underlying discontent amongst Italian intellectuals, who were dissatisfied with Mazzini's republican nationalist movement, 'reflected the abiding, inarticulate resᶜntment of the Italian poor, to whom political liberation had brought very little relief'.[1] Here was a promising revolutionary situation for Michael when he felt ready to exploit it.

Bourgeois in the main, with a small unorganized working-class population, Florence was far from being an important political centre and the Bakunins led a very ordinary life, albeit filling their rather bourgeois home with an ever-increasing, ever-shifting population of strange visitors. This period of calm lasted for approximately a year during which Sasha Herzen arrived, was reconciled to Michael and became a regular caller at the Bakunin house. Michael also worked out methods of smuggling copies of *The Bell* from Italy into Russia and took up Freemasonry again, though more out of fascination for the secret-society atmosphere than for any lasting respect for its aims. However, the Freemasons did influence Michael in one important respect: partly owing to their influence he became an atheist.

Michael's attitude to God in the past had been to ignore institutionalized religion and orthodoxy, but to maintain that religion was a necessity. He had often stressed his own personal belief in God. In 1849, for instance, he had written, 'You are mistaken if you think that I do nòt believe in God . . . I seek God in man, in human freedom, and now I seek God in revolution.' However, the Church's repressive attitude towards the masons moved him towards atheism, until in the 1870s his views had hardened beyond any possibility of change.

At the beginning of the autumn of 1864 Michael grew restless and returned to Stockholm, the scene of earlier hopes and disasters. He stayed only a few weeks, however, for no one showed much interest in him. Nevertheless he made good use of his time, for he was able to obtain a loan from his brothers at Premukhino, claiming that his journalism for certain Swedish newspapers would, without doubt, pay off the debt. Inevitably only one article appeared in the Swedish press.

On his way back to Italy Michael stayed in London for a fortnight. He paid a duty call on Herzen and had a meeting with Marx. In fact Marx, curious to see again the subject of so much discussion, made the first approach and called on Michael on 3 November 1864. It was their first meeting for sixteen years.

Marx's main preoccupation at this time was the founding of the International Working Men's Association. This organization came into being somewhat unexpectedly, for although there had been a number of attempts at co-ordinating the interests of workers throughout the world very little had in fact been achieved. This was largely because only a minority were radical enough to start secret co-ordinating committees, and the committees if started were largely repressed by the governments involved. Moreover, greater economic prosperity had given workers more individualistic ambitions and of course there was the inevitable problem of co-ordinating the interests of different nationalities.

In 1863, however, a large exhibition of modern industry was held in London and a number of French workers came to visit it. A preliminary meeting was held between the English unions and the French workers, and as a result a further meeting was proposed in which attempts would be made to start an organization which should not only hold discussions but also achieve economic and political co-operation. The end-result of this could then be the much-dreamt-of international democratic revolution. This meeting, attended by radicals from a number of different countries, resolved to constitute an international federation of working men whose aim was to destroy the current system and to replace it with a system where the workers would control industry themselves. This obviously involved the sharing of all profits and would be the first step towards abolishing private property.

Marx was selected as a representative of the London German workers on the executive committee and at the next meeting took the chair. He immediately strengthened the vague constitution, making it far more militant, and pledged the movement to overthrow the capitalist regimes and to try and enter democratic parliaments.

The International expanded very quickly and Marx remained undisputed leader. He was now in his late forties and despite his strength of will and intellect looked physically older than his years. Three of his six children were dead, largely owing to the severe poverty in which they had been living in Soho, and Engels's allowance to him had been severely curtailed by the European economic crisis which had begun in 1857. Ironically the crisis had been welcomed as a force for rebellion from the International's point of view, but it was financially restrictive for Marx himself. With journalism tailing off and the unpaid activities of the International increasing, Marx was in a serious financial position.

Michael later described his 1864 meeting with Marx as follows:

At that time I had a little note from Marx, in which he asked me whether he could come to see me the next day. I answered in the affirmative, and he came. We had an explanation. He said that he had never said or done anything against me; that, on the contrary, he had always been my true friend, and had retained great respect for me. I knew that he was lying, but I really no longer bore any grudge against him. The renewal of the acquaintanceship interested me, moreover, in another connection. I knew that he had taken a great part in the foundation of the International. I had read the manifesto written by him in the name of the provisional General Council, a manifesto which was weighty, earnest and profound, like everything that came from his pen when he was not engaged in personal polemic. In a word, we parted, outwardly, on the best of terms, although I did not return his visit.[2]

Marx, on the other hand, wrote to Engels,

Bakunin wishes to be remembered to you. He has left for Italy today. I saw him yesterday evening once more, for the first time after sixteen years. He said that after the failure in Poland he should, in future, confine himself to participation in the Socialist

Movement. On the whole he is one of the few persons whom I find not to have retrogressed after sixteen years, but to have developed further . . . [3]

Michael was excited by his interview with Marx and on his way back from London to Florence he stopped in Paris, with a view to forming a secret revolutionary society which he termed 'The Brotherhood'. Unlike Marx and Herzen, who both believed in as much publicity as possible for a revolution, Michael was as usual most concerned that all societies and alliances should be formed in the depths of secrecy. In Florence he gathered around him a number of dissatisfied Italian intellectuals who were prepared to plot and plan with him, optimistically ignoring not just the paranoia of the secrecy itself but the dubious number of supposed members of the organization. A young professor named Gubernatis relates how he himself became involved.

> Bakunin got up from his seat, came over to me, pressed my hand and asked me with an air of mystery whether I was a Mason. I replied that I was not and did not want to be, having a distaste for secret societies . . . Bakunin answered that I was right, that he himself did not attach much importance to Freemasonry, but that it served him as a means of approach to something else. Then he asked me whether I was a Mazzinist and a republican. I replied that it was not in my character to follow a single man, however great, and that I might well be a republican, but never a Mazzinist, though I recognized that Mazzini had performed a great service to the cause of freedom; that a republic in itself seemed to me an empty phrase . . . What was required now was freedom, what was required now was a transformation of society in which all would be equal not merely in law, but in such questions as the distribution of bread, which is not at present uniform for all, since some enjoy a superfluity while others are in want. At this point Bakunin pressed my hand warmly and exclaimed: 'Well, you are our man; we are working for that. You must join our work . . . The reactionaries act in concert, the supporters of freedom are scattered, divided, and at variance; it is essential to bring about a secret agreement between them on an international scale.'[4]

Gubernatis naively surrendered his government appointment in order to work for the so-called 'Brotherhood'. However, despite his naivety he genuinely wanted to work, and he soon saw with cynicism that there was far more talk than action with the 'Brotherhood'. Moreover, he could not fail to notice that while Michael was eager to collect any donations of a financial nature some of it found its way into his own pocket instead of being sent to the suffering Poles. Gubernatis tried to make Michael dissolve the society, on the basis that it was utterly and completely useless, but in any case its activities came to an abrupt end when Michael and Antonia left Florence in May 1865.

II

The Bakunins spent the summer of 1865 at Sorrento in order to see Michael's favourite brother Paul and his wife Natalie – the sister-in-law whom Michael had never met, yet so often corresponded with. Sadly, the meeting was not a great success. Paul and Michael had grown too far apart and the encounter only reawoke Michael's interest in the past, and his often-thought-about, but scarcely begun memoirs.

In October 1865 they moved to Naples, despite the fact that their only contact there was an ex-governess who had been employed by Herzen in London and now ran an English school in Naples. They incongruously became fond of the elderly spinster, although she was of little financial or political use, and when she died they were sincerely upset.

Michael found Naples completely reactionary but in the winter of 1865 he had the good fortune to meet his first willing financial backer – the Princess Obolensky. She was an extraordinary woman. A high-ranking Russian aristocrat, she lived in Naples to avoid her husband and, for excitement, supported European revolutionaries of all kinds who flocked around her like bees round a honey jar. Michael soon became a favourite with her. She found him captivating and his reputation added to her adventurous and scandalous prestige, whilst her generous gifts were soon keeping him in funds and adding to his ambitions.

The Neapolitans were naturally prone to intrigue and the dissatisfied nationalists who surrounded Princess Obolensky were obvious, if bourgeois material with which Michael could found yet another secret society. Called the International Brotherhood, the society was a true Bakuninesque work of art and was divided into two groups which were organized in the following complex manner:

a. The International Family. This was to be the administrative umbrella of the Brotherhood and was to have two methods of operation. The first was to organize propaganda within the framework of the law; the second was to plot revolution outside it. Ironically, despite his growing anarchism Michael imposed upon the administrative section of the Brotherhood total discipline, with himself as disciplinarian.

b. The National Families. These were even more complicated, as each had its own executive committee to which all members had to be obedient. The committees were directed by a Central International Directorate.

The National Families were composed of the following categories of members:

i. Those who were prepared to plot and to initiate revolution;

ii. Honorary members who had a private fortune (like Princess Obolensky) and could be vicariously sympathetic without getting themselves into trouble.

Both types of members were naturally required to swear an oath of allegiance to the Brotherhood which was taken melodramatically upon a dagger. Anyone who broke this oath was liable to be hunted down and summarily dealt with.

In fact members of the Brotherhood were extremely scarce despite Michael's grandiose claims to the contrary, but the Brotherhood is significant in that its formation and aims show a definite change in Michael's political thinking.

It was widely held in radical circles that when Napoleon III died a new series of rebellions would break out in Europe. Quite rightly Michael reasoned that it was vital to avoid the mistakes of 1848 and because of this he organized the International Brotherhood to initiate revolutionary consciousness which, despite the growth of the labour movements, was still conspicuously lacking. In Italy, particularly, revolutionary consciousness had been drowned in nationalism and Michael now realized that nationalism was in fact counter-revolutionary. He therefore considered that such organizations as the International Brotherhood were 'indispensable to the success of the Social Revolution; that the Revolution must simultaneously destroy the old order and take on a federalist and anarchistic direction'.[5]

Three documents written by Michael at this time – 'The International Family', 'The Revolutionary Catechism' and 'The National Catechism' – reveal the new direction of these aims and in fact provide the basis of the anarchist movement.

The function of 'The Revolutionary Catechism' was to outline, for the benefit of the members of the International Brotherhood, a practical programme of action for revolution and the fundamental principles on which it was based. As was to be expected, much of the Catechism was concerned with the overthrow of existing beliefs. For instance it rejected religion and the existing political and economic structures in the following terms:

II   Replacing the cult of God by *respect and love of humanity*, we proclaim *human reason* as the only criterion of truth; *human conscience* as the basis of justice; *individual and collective freedom* as the only source of order in society.

VII   *Absolute rejection of every authority including that which sacrifices freedom for the convenience of the state*. Primitive society had no conception of freedom; and as society evolved, *before* the full awakening of human rationality and freedom, it passed through a stage controlled by human and divine authority. The political and economic structure of society must now be reorganized on the basis of freedom. Henceforth, *order in society must result from the greatest possible realization of individual liberty, as well as of liberty on all levels of social organization*.

IX   *Political organization*. It is impossible to determine a concrete, universal and obligatory norm for the internal development and political organization of every nation. The life of each nation is subordinated to a plethora of different historical, geographical and economic conditions, making it impossible to establish a model of organization equally valid for all. Any such attempt would be absolutely impractical. It would smother the richness and spontaneity of life which flourishes only in infinite diversity and, what is more, contradict the most fundamental principles of freedom. However, without certain *absolutely essential conditions* the practical realization of freedom will be for ever impossible. These conditions are:

A   *The abolition of all State religions and all privileged Churches, including those partially maintained or supported by State subsidies*. Absolute liberty of every religion to build temples to their gods, and to pay and support their priests.

B   The Churches considered as religious corporations must never enjoy the *same* political rights accorded to the productive associations; nor can they be entrusted with the education of children; for they exist merely to negate morality and liberty and to profit from the lucrative practice of witchcraft.

C *Abolition of monarchy; establishment of a commonwealth.*

D *Abolition of classes, ranks, and privileges; absolute equality of political rights for all men and women; universal suffrage.*

E *Abolition,* dissolution, and moral, political, and economic dismantling of the *all-pervasive, regimented, centralized State,* the alter ego of the Church, and as such, the permanent cause of the impoverishment, brutalization and enslavement of the multitude. This naturally entails the following: *Abolition of all State universities:* public education must be administered only by the communes and free associations. *Abolition of the State judiciary:* all judges must be elected by the people. *Abolition of all criminal, civil and legal codes now administered in Europe:* because the code of liberty can be created only by *liberty itself. Abolition of banks and all other institutions of State credit. Abolition of all centralized administration of the bureaucracy, of all permanent armies and State police.*[6]

On a more positive note the Catechism recommended:

F Immediate direct election of all judicial and civil functionaries as well as representatives (national, provincial and communal delegates) by the universal suffrage of both sexes.

G *The internal reorganization* of each country on the basis of the *absolute freedom of individuals, of the productive associations and of the communes.* Necessity of recognizing the *right of secession: every individual, every association, every commune, every region, every nation has the absolute right to self-determination, to associate or not to associate, to ally themselves with whomever they wish and repudiate their alliances without regard to so-called historical rights* [rights consecrated by legal precedent] *or the convenience of their neighbours.* Once the right to secede is established, secession will no longer be necessary. With the dissolution of a 'unity' imposed by violence, the units of society will be drawn to unite by their powerful mutual attraction and by inherent necessities. Consecrated by liberty, these new federations of communes, provinces, regions and nations will then be truly strong, productive and indissoluble.

H *Individual rights.*

    1 The rights of every man and woman, from birth to

168

adulthood, to complete upkeep, clothes, food, shelter, care, guidance, education (public schools, primary, secondary, higher education, artistic, industrial and scientific), all at the expense of society.

2 The equal right of adolescents, while freely choosing their careers, to be helped and to the greatest possible extent supported by society. After this, society will exercise no authority or supervision over them except to respect, and if necessary defend, their freedom and their rights.

3 The freedom of adults of both sexes must be absolute and complete, freedom to come and go, to voice all opinions, to be lazy or active, moral or immoral, in short, to dispose of one's person or possessions as one pleases, being accountable to no one. Freedom to live, be it honestly, by one's own labour, even at the expense of individuals who *voluntarily* tolerate one's exploitation.

4 Unlimited freedom of propaganda, speech, press, public or private assembly, with no other restraint than the natural salutary power of public opinion. Absolute freedom to organize associations even for allegedly immoral purposes including even those associations which advocate the undermining (or destruction) of individual and public freedom.[7]

Showing an unexpected understanding of the frailty of human nature Michael states firmly:

6 Society cannot, however, leave itself completely defenceless against vicious and parasitic individuals. Work must be the basis of all political rights. The units of society, each within its own jurisdiction, can deprive all such anti-social adults of political rights (except the old, the sick, and those dependent on private or public subsidy) and will be obliged to restore their political rights as soon as they begin to live by their own labour.

7 The liberty of every human being is inalienable and society will never require any individual to surrender his liberty or to sign contracts with other individuals except on the basis of the most complete

equality and reciprocity. Society cannot forcibly prevent any man or woman so devoid of personal dignity as to place him- or herself in voluntary servitude to another individual; but it can justly treat such persons as parasites, not entitled to the enjoyment of political liberty, though only *for the duration of their servitude.*

8 Persons losing their political rights will also lose custody of their children. Persons who violate voluntary agreements, steal, inflict bodily harm, or, above all, violate the freedom of any individual, native or foreigner, will be penalized according to the laws of society.

10 Individuals condemned by the laws of any and every association (commune, province, region or nation) reserve the right to escape punishment by declaring that they wish to resign from that association. But in this case, the association will have the equal right to expel them and declare them outside its guarantee and protection.[8]

Michael recognized that while he had expressed true anarchistic principles by advocating the overthrow of the existing order he had not in fact outlined an anarchistic Utopia, free from any organization or restriction. He explains:

I   *Rights of association* [*federalism*]. The co-operative workers' associations are a new fact in history. At this time we can only speculate about, but not determine, the immense development that they will doubtlessly exhibit in the new political and social conditions of the future. It is possible and even very likely that they will some day transcend the limits of towns, provinces, and even states. They may entirely reconstitute society, dividing it not into nations but into different industrial groups, organized not according to the needs of politics but to those of production. But this is for the future.[9]

Naturally great emphasis is laid on social equality and it is made clear that in order to bring this about the right of inheritance will be abolished. Collective labour and communal living are advocated, as is 'free marriage'.

'The National Catechism' was written as a general guide for

individual countries. It points out that 'The national catechisms of different countries may differ on secondary points, but there are certain fundamental points which must be accepted by the national organizations of all countries as the basis of their respective catechisms'.[10]

These points range from a detailed analysis of the future structure of society to an equally detailed account of how the revolution is to be brought about, and while Michael fully accepted that the revolution would be extremely violent he wisely insisted that it should not be followed by a brutal aftermath.

'The National Catechism' ends on a characteristic note:

10 In order to prepare for this revolution it will be necessary to conspire and to organize a strong secret association co-ordinated by an international nucleus.[11]

III

It was now becoming clear that Michael would be unable to settle in any one country for long. He would be enthusiastic at first but then grow restless, or the authorities would grow restless with him. This time a combination of the removal of Herzen, Ogarev and *The Bell* to Geneva, the circulation of some scurrilous rumours about Michael's alleged subversion and forging of bank-notes and, most important, the departure of Princess Obolensky to Switzerland, made Michael anxious to leave Italy. Moreover, in September 1867 there was to be a Congress in Geneva designed to discuss 'the maintenance of liberty, justice and peace'. It was an excellent excuse to leave the narrow confines of Italy for yet another new environment.

While they were in Italy Antonia had taken a lover. This was predictable enough, for although Antonia may well have been intellectually dull, physically she was quite normal. Although she was very fond of Michael she must have realized by now that to hope for any physical involvement with him was unrealistic. Therefore to prevent a sexually starved and childless future Antonia became involved, somewhat ironically, with one of Michael's leading associates in the International Brotherhood – an Italian named Carlo Gambuzzi. Michael appeared to be quite unaffected by their relationship; perhaps he realized that it was inevitable. Jealousy, therefore, was irrelevant and as Michael plunged even further into his political work Antonia's relationship with Gambuzzi became stronger. It also became more public. Yet Antonia had no wish to humiliate Michael, and indeed as their barren marriage progressed Antonia gradually took over the role of a colourless, sometimes reprimanding mother to a colourful, wayward and never properly understood child.

Michael's tolerance of Antonia's affair with Gambuzzi was in fact yet another example of his liberated attitude towards women. In the past he had always directed his bitterest tirades against the despotism of the patriarchal family, the domination of husband over wife, and the economic, social and sexual subjugation of women. Thus in many ways he was a pioneer of women's emancipation. As far as Antonia was concerned, Michael felt that she should be free to have sex with whom she pleased, and Gambuzzi remained his close and dedicated friend and follower.

Michael left Naples for Geneva in August 1867. When he arrived he was disappointed to find that only Ogarev was in residence. As Herzen was, by now, living openly with Ogarev's second wife Natalie, Ogarev himself, his epilepsy made considerably worse by his alcoholism, had 'rescued' a prostitute called Mary Sutherland and her son, and had taken them in to live with him. *The Bell* had by now ceased publication and Herzen, having left a lukewarm invitation for Michael to use his flat and a small loan of 100 francs, was living in Nice. He did not return to Geneva for the Congress.

The Geneva Congress was due to open on 9 September 1867, and as he prepared for it Michael entered what was to be by far the most influential phase of his life. The conference was liberal rather than revolutionary in tone but despite its bourgeois concept and largely bourgeois personnel Michael thought it could serve a useful purpose. It certainly marked a further change in Michael's attitude, for instead of keeping his activities secret he now expressed his opinions openly.

About 6000 attended the conference, although about half of these in fact came from Geneva itself. A President was elected and an Executive Committee, whose Russian representatives were Michael and Ogarev. As in Sweden, Michael's reputation was legendary and

As with heavy, awkward gait he mounted the steps leading to the platform where the Bureau [the Executive Committee] sat, dressed as carelessly as ever in a sort of grey blouse, beneath which was visible not a shirt, but a flannel vest, the cry passed from mouth to mouth: 'Bakunin!' Garibaldi, who was in the chair, stood up, advanced a few steps, and embraced him. This solemn meeting of two old and tried warriors of revolution produced an astonishing impression . . . Everyone rose, and there was prolonged and enthusiastic clapping of hands.[12]

The conference had been convened partly with a view to analysing the possibilities of peace among nations and establishing a United States of Europe, and partly with a view to preventing war breaking out between Prussia and France over Luxembourg – a war that would involve all of Europe. On the first day of the conference, however, Garibaldi began by attacking the Pope and by advocating the real God of Protestantism – thereby annoying all atheists and Catholics present. Then James Guillaume, later to become a great friend of Michael's and at that time a Swiss representative of the International Working Men's Association, introduced a socialist note into the proceedings by indicating the provisos of the International's participation in the Geneva Congress, i.e., that it must be clearly understood that the International stood for the emancipation of the working classes and their subsequent release from the exploitation of capitalists.

Despite the expression of these two unexpectedly extreme points of view, the first two days of the assembly were days of enthusiasm. Michael, speaking in French, was extremely well received and a later résumé of his speech written by himself (the original account was not accurate) indicated that he began with a condemnation of the Russian Empire, declared that it could only be saved by a combination of socialism and federalism, and went on to attack the folly of nationalism and the use of international arbitration to settle international disputes, and to recommend the destruction of the centralized States. 'We must desire their destruction in order that, on the ruins of these forced unions organized from above by right of authority and conquest, there may arise free unions organized from below by the free federation of communes into provinces, of provinces into the nation, and of nations into the United States of Europe.'[13]

On the third day of the conference Garibaldi left, enthusiasm waned and criticism began. Religious believers in league with conservatives battled with atheists and socialists. Eventually it was voted that a League of Peace and Freedom should be formed. The rest of the resolutions were platitudes and the grand closing banquet was an occasion for argument and disillusion. Michael, blinkered as usual to reality, optimistically ignored the basic failures of the conference and felt certain that he could convert the new League to federalism, socialism and atheism.

IV

Michael was appointed to the central committee of the League of Peace and Freedom, and as the meetings were to be held in Berne and the generous Princess Obolensky was now living in nearby Vevey Michael and Antonia could conveniently move to Vevey to join her. However, although the Princess was still comfortably off, her husband, tired of her so-called scandalous activities, had ensured that she was not going to live in such splendour on his money by substantially cutting her allowance – though in fact she was wealthy enough in her own right not to let this make too great a difference to her life-style. Michael spent the winter of 1867 and the spring of 1868 among a new group that now surrounded the Princess – a group which was mainly composed of a number of young Russian political exiles who had fled after their involvement in the Petersburg fires and the Polish insurrection. Michael considered them to be promising material for the International Brotherhood.

Meanwhile his main preoccupation was with the central committee of the League of Peace and Freedom, which was constituted as follows:

Left Wing	Bakunin and Zhukovsky (Russians)
	Mroczkowski and Zagorski (Poles)
Bourgeois Majority	Swiss, Italian and French representatives.

Michael produced a basic policy which he thought the League should adopt. It was called 'Federalism, Socialism and Anti-Theologism', and although written with great enthusiasm it was not finished, as was the case with so much of Michael's work. In the policy document Michael expanded theories he had put forward in the Catechism, demanding that individual countries must be reconstituted so that a United States of Europe could be created as a prelude to complete international federalism. He also completely rejected all his former ideas of harnessing nationalism to revolution, recognizing yet again that those who supported nationalistic principles were rarely concerned with the welfare of the people.

12 The League will recognize *nationality* as a natural fact which

has an incontestable right to a free existence and development, but not as a principle, since every principle should have the power of universality, while nationality, a fact of exclusionist tendency, separates. The so-called *principle of nationality*, such as has been declared in our time by the Governments of France, Russia, Prussia, and even by many German, Polish, Italian and Hungarian patriots, is a mere derivative notion born of the reaction against the spirit of revolution. It is aristocratic to the point of despising the folk dialects spoken by illiterate peoples. It implicitly denies the liberty of provinces and the true autonomy of communes. Its support, in all countries, does not come from the masses, whose real interests it sacrifices to the so-called public good, which is always the good of the privileged classes. It expresses nothing but the alleged historic rights and ambitions of States. The right of nationality can therefore never be considered by the League except as a natural consequence of the supreme principle of liberty; it ceases to be a right as soon as it takes a stand either against liberty or even outside liberty.[14]

He stated wisely that while unity must be the ultimate goal of Man it was essential that this unity should be based on complete freedom and not be brought about by any form of pressure.

13 Unity is the great goal towards which humanity moves irresistibly. But it becomes fatal, destructive of the intelligence, the dignity, the well-being of individuals and peoples whenever it is formed without regard to liberty, either by violent means or under the authority of any theological, metaphysical, political or even economic idea. That patriotism which tends towards unity without regard to liberty is an evil patriotism, always disastrous to the popular and real interests of the country it claims to exalt and serve. Often, without wishing to be so, it is a friend of reaction – an enemy of the revolution, i.e., the emancipation of nations and men. The League can recognize only one unity, that which is freely constituted by the federation of autonomous parts within the whole, so that the whole, ceasing to be the negation of private rights and interests, ceasing to be the graveyard where all local prosperities are buried, becomes the confirmation and the source of all these autonomies and all these prosperities. The League will therefore vigorously attack any religious, political or economic organization which is not

thoroughly penetrated by this great principle of freedom; lacking that, there is no intelligence, no justice, no prosperity, no humanity.[15]

In the second part of the document Michael discussed his views on socialism in some detail. Inevitably he was heavily influenced by Proudhon on this subject, laying stress on freedom and equality of opportunity for all, which could only be brought about by the abolition of the law of inheritance.

Although Michael succeeded in persuading the committee to abandon religion he failed at this stage to persuade them to adopt any suggested social change for the working class. They also refused to change the bourgeois tone of the League by adding to its title the words 'democratic and republican'. However, by the time the committee met again in the early summer of 1868 Michael had improved his position and was able to prevail upon the committee to accept the following programme for the League's next annual conference in September:

The League recognizes that it is absolutely essential not to separate the three fundamental aspects of the social problem: the religious question, the political question and the economic question. It therefore affirms –

1   that religion, being a matter for the individual conscience, must be eliminated from political institutions and from the domain of public instruction, in order that the Church may not be able to fetter the free development of society;

2   that the United States of Europe cannot be organized in any other form than that of popular institutions united by means of federation and having as their basic principle the equality of personal rights, and the autonomy of communes and provinces in the regulation of their own interests;

3   that the present economic system requires a radical change if we wish to achieve that equitable division of wealth, labour, leisure and education, which is a fundamental condition of the liberation of the working classes and the elimination of the proletariat.[16]

It was at this stage that Michael's thoughts probably first focused on the International. He had shown no real interest in it at the Geneva Congress and did not even react when he was sent a personal copy of *Das Kapital*. However, some of his own adherents belonged to the International and on looking again at its manifesto Michael came to the conclusion that he fully agreed with many of its aims. In the summer of 1868 he therefore joined its Geneva section.

It was not long before Michael evolved the idea of allying the League to the International. He shrewdly calculated that as prime mover of the League he would be in a parallel position to Marx. He therefore presented the idea at the next meeting of the central committee.

As a result the committee asked representatives of the International to attend the second annual conference of the League. However, the congress of the International, meeting in September 1868, despite vigorous canvassing by Michael, sent an official refusal to the central committee of the League, pointing out that there was no need for the League to exist, as the International was already operating successfully in the field they intended to cover.

This icy reply was not only a severe disappointment to Michael but it put him in an extremely embarrassing position, for Marx had managed to prove conclusively that the League was redundant. His colleagues were furious and Michael, realizing that his reputation was at stake, stated firmly that he would send the International a stinging rebuke from the forthcoming conference of the League. What he did not realize was that this was the beginning of a massive trial of strength between himself and Karl Marx.

V

On 21 September 1868 the League assembled in Berne for its second conference. On the third day Michael proposed the motion that was so near to his heart, conscious that anything he said now could either make or break his political career. It read as follows:

> Considering that the question which presses itself most urgently on our attention is that of the economic and social equalization of classes and individuals, the Congress declares that, without this equalization, that is to say, without justice, freedom and peace are unobtainable. Consequently, the Congress puts on its agenda the study of practical methods of settling this question.[17]

The motion was accompanied by two speeches, both of which threw the conference, again predominantly bourgeois in tone, into a state of considerable apprehension. In the first speech Michael vehemently pressed the claims of the workers, but in the second, which resulted from a suggestion by a delegate that he was a communist, he expressed himself very clearly on the subject that was ultimately to differentiate his principles so totally from Marx's:

> Because I demand the economic and social equalization of classes and individuals, because, with the Workers' Congress of Brussels, I have declared myself in favour of collective property, I have been reproached with being a Communist. What difference, I have been asked, is there between Communism and Collectivism? . . .
>
> Communism I abhor, because it is the negation of liberty, and without liberty I cannot imagine anything truly human. I detest Communism because it concentrates all the strength of Society in the State, and squanders that strength in its service; because it places all property in the hands of the State, whereas my principle is the abolition of the State itself, the radical extirpation of the principle of authority and tutelage, which has enslaved, oppressed, exploited and depraved mankind under the pretexts of moralizing and civilizing man. I want the organization of society and the distribution of property to proceed from below, by the free voice of society itself; not downwards from above, by the dictate of authority. I desire the abolition of personal hereditary property, which is merely an institution of the State, and a consequence of State principles. In this sense I am a Collectivist, not a Communist.[18]

Although Michael's resolution was supported by the Russian and Polish delegates, most of the Italians and the American delegate, it was rejected by everybody else. In the face of this defeat Michael obviously had to resign and at the end of the conference he sent in a statement to this effect signed by a number of his followers who were also leaving the League. Now his eyes were on the International, but despite his singular lack of success in uniting the International and the League he had no intention of joining the International as an ordinary member. For this reason he needed to form his remaining supporters into a specific organization which he would head.

With this in mind Michael immediately founded the International Alliance of the Socialist Democracy, explaining his reasons for doing so in terms that must have considerably irritated the leaders of the International.

> The socialist minority opposition at the Berne Congress of the League of Peace and Freedom [25 September 1868] resigned from the League when it officially rejected the fundamental principle of

all workers' organizations – the economic and social equality of all mankind, through the abolition of classes. Belonging to different nationalities, the minority accepted the proposal of several of its members to constitute a new organization: the International Alliance of the Socialist Democracy, which, while being wholly integrated into the great International Working Men's Association, would fulfil a special function: the study of political and philosophical questions, insofar as they are relevant to the achievement of the full and genuine equality of humanity.

Convinced that this kind of an organization is essential because it will enable the sincere democratic socialists of Europe and America, on the basis of ideological clarity, to achieve unity of purpose and forge an independent organization fully able to resist and counteract the influence and pressure now being exerted by all false bourgeois socialist factions: therefore, we, together with our friends, are initiating such a movement by organizing the Central Section of the International Alliance of the Socialist Democracy . . .[19]

Michael was quite sure that his new organization was performing a useful function despite the similar motivations of the International. He states positively in a letter to some of his followers,

. . . The International is certainly a splendid organization, undoubtedly the finest . . . creation of the century. The International laid the foundation for the solidarity of the workers of the whole world, outside the world of States and the exploiting, privileged classes. It has achieved even more: it embodies today the first seeds of the organization of the future society, while at the same time inspiring the workers in all lands with the necessary consciousness of their mission and confidence in their own powers. While the International has indeed rendered these great services to the Social Revolution, it is still not sufficiently capable of organizing and directing this Revolution . . .

All serious revolutionists who have actively participated in the International since its foundation in 1864 must from their own experience come to the same conclusion. The International helps prepare the ground for the Revolution but cannot carry it through. It expedites the open and legal struggle of the united workers of the world against the exploiters of labour, the capitalists, the landlords and industrialists but goes no further. Outside of this, its only other useful function is the theoretical propaganda of socialist ideas among the masses, likewise very useful and necessary but still very far from welding the masses into a revolutionary organization . . .

In short, the International is immensely useful in providing the necessary and favourable atmosphere for such an organization, but it is not yet THIS* organization.[20]

In October 1868 Michael and Antonia left Vevey for Geneva, as usual for financial reasons. The wealthy Olga Levashov, who had been contributing towards the Bakunins' expenses in place of Princess Obolensky, had also invested in a Russian journal called *The People's Cause*. Michael was appointed co-editor with her brother-in-law, Nicholas Zhukovsky, and the first edition, expressing many of Michael's views, appeared in September 1868. However, while he was absorbed in the Congress his place was taken by Nicholas Utin, who was thus able to usurp Michael's position. As a result the two men quarrelled violently and Michael, now deprived of Olga Levashov's financial support, left Vevey.

In Geneva Michael managed to persuade some members of the International to join the Central Bureau of the Alliance and exerted every effort to set up the organization on a large scale. However, although its activities spread to France, Spain and Italy its impact was never as far-reaching as Michael would have liked.

Michael was quite determined that the Alliance should join the International 'as an anarchistic body enjoying a certain autonomy . . . and acting as a kind of radical ginger group'.[21] With this in mind, in mid-December 1868 the Executive Committee of the Alliance formally applied for membership to the Executive Committee of the International in London. Becker, one of the members of the International whom Michael had recruited into the Central Bureau, wrote the letter, as he was considered to be the most tactful person to approach Marx. In the letter the following proposals were put forward:

1 That if the Alliance joined the International the Central Bureau of the Alliance should be retained in Geneva and also be permitted to attend the congresses of the International.

2 That Alliance members, whilst also being members of the International, should equally be allowed to hold their own meetings.

3 That the Alliance would suggest ideas to the Executive Committee of the International for the Committee to act upon.

4 That the various branches of the Alliance, while maintaining

* Sam Dolgoff's emphasis.

their own autonomy, should become branches of the International as well.

Marx and Engels could scarcely give the idea credulity and considered it ludicrous yet dangerous. Marx wrote to Engels saying that

> Mr Bakunin is condescending enough to be ready to take the workers' movement under Russian patronage. The thing has been brewing for two months . . . I thought it was still-born and, for the sake of old Becker, meant to let it die a natural death. But the affair has turned out more serious than I supposed; and to pass it over in silence any longer out of respect for old Becker is inadmissible. The Council decided tonight to disavow publicly – in Paris, New York, Germany and Switzerland – this interloping society . . . I am only sorry about it because of old Becker. But our Association cannot commit suicide for his benefit.[22]

Marx, meanwhile, had the announcement of the decision postponed for a week while he did some undercover work. He wrote Alexander Serno-Solovievich a letter that contained the remark 'What is my old friend (I don't know whether he still is my friend) Bakunin doing?' The ruse worked; Serno-Solovievich sent the letter on to Michael, who replied to Marx in the following vein:

> You ask whether I am still your friend. Yes, more than ever, my dear Marx, for I understand better than ever how right you were to walk along the broad road of the economic revolution, to invite us all to follow you, and to denounce all those who wandered off into the byways of nationalist or exclusively political enterprise. I am now doing what you began to do more than twenty years ago. Since I formally and publicly said goodbye to the bourgeois of the Berne Congress, I know no other society, no other milieu than the world of the workers. My fatherland is now the International, whose chief founder you have been. You see, then, dear friend, that I am your pupil – and I am proud to be this. I think I have said enough to make my personal position and feelings clear to you.[23]

It was certainly a generous letter and Otto Ruhle commented that 'This sentimental entrée not only redounded to Bakunin's credit, not only showed his good feeling and his insight, but deserved a better reception from Marx than the biting cynicism and the derogatory insolence which it encountered (cynicism and insolence which were only masks for embarrassment).'[24]

Michael, writing later, however, had this to say of Marx and his circle, which shows that there was more than a degree of calculation in his 'generous' letter to Marx as well as revealing his usual anti-Semitic obsession:

Marx loved his own person much more than he loved his friends and apostles, and no friendship could hold water against the slightest wound to his vanity. He would far more readily forgive infidelity to his philosophical and socialist system . . . Marx will never forgive a slight to his person. You must worship him, make an idol of him, if he is to love you in return; you must at least fear him, if he is to tolerate you. He likes to surround himself with pygmies, with lackeys and flatterers. All the same, there are some remarkable men among his intimates.

In general, however, one may say that in the circle of Marx's intimates there is very little brotherly frankness, but a great deal of machination and diplomacy. There is a sort of tacit struggle, and a compromise between the self-loves of the various persons concerned; and where vanity is at work, there is no longer place for brotherly feeling. Everyone is on his guard, is afraid of being sacrificed, of being annihilated. Marx's circle is a sort of mutual admiration society. Marx is the chief distributor of honours, but is also invariably perfidious and malicious, never frank and open, inciter to the persecution of those whom he suspects, or who have had the misfortune of failing to show all the veneration he expects.

As soon as he has ordered a persecution, there is no limit to the baseness and infamy of the method. Himself a Jew, he had round him in London and in France, and above all in Germany, a number of petty, more or less able, intriguing, mobile, speculative Jews (the sort of Jews you can find all over the place), commercial employees, bank clerks, men of letters, politicians, the correspondents of newspapers of the most various shades of opinion, in a word, literary go-betweens, one foot in the bank, the other in the Socialist Movement, while their rump is in German periodic literature . . . These Jewish men of letters are adepts in the art of cowardly, odious, and perfidious insinuations. They seldom make open accusation, but they insinuate, saying they 'have heard – it is said – it may not be true, but', and then they hurl the most abominable calumnies in your face.[25]

On 22 December 1868 the International formally rejected the Alliance's application on various grounds, ranging from the disorganization that the introduction of another such body would bring to the movement the fact that the Brussels Congress had already clarified that the existence of the International made any other organization with the same aims irrelevant.

In March 1869 the International Brotherhood was dissolved after a meeting in January when its few remaining members condemned Michael for his dictatorial attitudes. Michael wrote them a stinging letter which pointed out how hard he had worked on the organization and how much he deserved to rest a little now. His letter also took the Brotherhood to task for gossiping about the relations between Antonia and Carlo Gambuzzi, who was at this point founding a branch of the Alliance in Italy. The gossip centred upon the birth of Antonia's first child, which had been born in the autumn of 1868. Antonia's daughter could not possibly have been Michael's and was all too clearly Gambuzzi's, but at this stage Michael was far more concerned with his battle with Marx than with the infidelity of his wife with one of his closest associates.

Then in January 1869 Michael's political fortunes suddenly took a turn for the better and he began to attain the powerful position for which he had been waiting so impatiently, and for so long.

PART SEVEN

The Battle with Marx: 1869–70

I

Michael's short-lived period of power owed much to the administrative abilities of James Guillaume, the young Swiss schoolmaster who had presented the resolution from the International to the Geneva Congress in 1867. Like many before him, he became a disciple of Michael's, but unlike most of his predecessors Guillaume not only possessed an orderly mind, but – much as he admired him – refused to allow Michael's brilliant flights of fancy to blunt his critical faculties. Their friendship began in January 1869 when representatives of the thirty sections of the International that were located in French Switzerland met together in Geneva in order to found a local federation which they called the Fédération Romande. Guillaume was the representative for Le Locle, a little town in the Swiss Jura, and by chance he was billeted with the Bakunins during this short visit to Geneva.

Some weeks later, much to Guillaume's delight, Michael came to stay with him at Le Locle. A local banquet, a speech from Michael attacking the bourgeoisie and religion, and a number of discussions with this famous figure, inspired both Guillaume and Le Locle with revolutionary fervour. Guillaume, however, was not disciple enough to agree to joining the Alliance, for he honestly saw no reason to complicate the International with the inclusion of yet another organization. Michael, however, countered this irritatingly common-sense attitude with wild talk of the Brotherhood and its mighty and mysterious network. On a more constructive level he agreed to contribute to the local Le Locle publication, *Progrès*, although later

184

he surprised Guillaume by 'accepting his proposal' to make it the official organ of the Alliance. In fact Guillaume had suggested no such thing and firmly ignored Michael's wilful self-delusion.

At the end of February 1869 the Alliance replied to its rejection by the International by suggesting that the Alliance itself should be dissolved and that its sections should become sections of the International. On 9 March 1869 the General Council of the International agreed to their entry on these terms, for, feeling that he had won and that Michael had at last capitulated, Marx was prepared to relent. He was of course able to take full advantage of the situation by rubbing salt into Michael's wounds, adding that he wanted an exact count of the ex-Alliance followers who would be joining the International, and full details on their various sections. He was convinced that Michael had, as usual, over-inflated the numbers and that there were far fewer than suggested.

On 22 June the Alliance was officially dissolved, and a reconstituted Geneva section, of whose Executive Committee Michael, Perron and Becker were members, was formally admitted to the International on 28 July. Michael had, at last, achieved a position of authority, albeit diminished, within the International.

Throughout the spring and summer of 1869 Michael regularly contributed to the Fédération Romande's journal, *L'Égalité*, and during Perron's absence in July and August he took over as editor, publishing a number of articles on surprisingly wide-ranging subjects. Four of these articles described the policy of the International, and the first, published on 7 August, is concerned with its principles. He also includes a denunciation of the bourgeoisie.

> ... Until now there has never been a true politics of the people, and by the 'people' we mean the lowly classes, the 'rabble', the poorest workers whose toil sustains the world. There has been only the politics of the privileged classes, those who have used the physical prowess of the people to overthrow and replace each other in the never-ending struggle for supremacy. The people have shifted support from one side to the other in the vain hope that in at least one of these political changes ... their century-old poverty and slavery would be lightened. Even the great French Revolution did not basically alter their status. It did away with the nobility only to replace it with the bourgeoisie. The people are no longer *called* serfs. They are proclaimed free men, legally entitled to all the rights of free-born citizens; but they remain poverty-stricken serfs in fact.

And they will remain enslaved as long as the working masses

continue to serve as tools of bourgeois politics, whether conservative or liberal, even if those politics pretend to be revolutionary. For all bourgeois politics whatever the label or colour have only one purpose: to perpetuate domination by the bourgeoisie, and *bourgeois domination is the slavery of the proletariat.*

What was the International to do? It had to separate the working masses from all bourgeois politics and expunge from its programme the political programmes of the bourgeoisie. When the International was first organized, the only institutions exerting major pressure were the Church, the monarchy, the aristocracy and the bourgeoisie. The latter, particularly the liberal bourgeoisie, were undoubtedly more humane than the others, but they too depended upon the exploitation of the masses, and their sole purpose was also to fight their rivals for the privilege of monopolizing the exploitation. The International had first to clear the ground. Since all politics, as far as the emancipation is concerned, is infected with reactionary elements, the International had first to purge itself of all political systems, and then build upon the ruins of the bourgeois social order the new politics of the International.[1]

II

While he was battling to gain entry to the International Michael had formed a relationship that was to bring him both political and personal tragedy.

It was in the spring of 1869 that the highly destructive personality of Sergei Nechayev obtruded into Michael's life. The son of a serf from Ivanovo, he had started work when he was nine years old as an errand boy, later progressing to his grandfather's paint shop and, later still, to the position of office boy. He was sixteen before he learnt to read and write properly and it was not until he was nineteen that he passed an examination qualifying him to teach religion in primary schools. Having obtained a post as teacher in Petersburg, Nechayev attended some lectures at the university and met the revolutionary student circles there. He attended many illegal meetings and eventually his rooms at the school became a meeting-place for revolutionary debate. A poor speaker and debater, Nechayev plotted from the side-lines, seeking recognition from the public of the appalling conditions under which the students lived and at the same time ensuring that the students were aware of the appalling conditions of the peasantry. Furthering his own sense of power, he managed to organize petitions and to make decisions, but once having done this the unpleasant side of his nature began to reveal itself, for when he had once gained their compliance he dominated, bullied and threatened his student disciples. In a sinister way he even hinted that he was the representative of a large revolutionary organization. This young, bullying and somewhat demonic man of the people was an interesting but, at this stage, somewhat incredible figure to the student circles of Petersburg. Realizing this, Nechayev sought to find a means of substantially strengthening his credibility and it was mainly for this reason that, fabricating an ingenious story about his arrest and imprisonment, in March 1869 he 'escaped' across the South Russian border with a false passport, making his way to Geneva. Meanwhile, in Petersburg, Nechayev had become a martyr and a mass meeting was organized to petition his 'release' by the bewildered Russian authorities.

Michael was one of the first people of importance whom Nechayev contacted in Geneva and the latter lost no time in informing him that not only had he just escaped from the fortress of Peter and Paul but he represented a revolutionary movement in Russia, based in Petersburg and currently opening up other revolutionary fronts throughout the country. Michael was completely taken in, or if he did have any doubts he conveniently overlooked them. He was instantly attracted to Nechayev, called him his 'Boy' (in English) and was for a time quite dependent upon him. In many ways Nechayev and Michael were kindred spirits, and in addition Nechayev revived Michael's deep feeling for Russia, and, apparently, brought with him the chance of becoming involved with revolutionary activity within the beloved country itself.

Nechayev, for his part, was a strangely courageous but utterly superficial young man. He desperately wanted acclaim and was clever enough to win it with a mesmeric combination of lies and charm. There was, however, a dangerously destructive side to his personality, and he wanted revolution for revolution's sake. In this he went much further than Michael, who still had a tremendous, if naive, faith in humanity and genuinely wanted to bring about a greatly improved life for everyone. Certainly he believed that the existing order must be destroyed but only as a means of creating a new mode of life. Nechayev on the other hand possessed a ruthless destructiveness that was in no way creative.

However, there was little to choose between Nechayev and Michael when it came to the creation of imaginary organizations. In May 1869 Michael had given Nechayev this extraordinary document: 'The bearer of this is one of the accredited representatives of the Russian section of the World Revolutionary Alliance No. 2771.' Michael signed it himself and sealed it with the words 'European Revolutionary Alliance, Central Committee'. This was pure invention and was never heard of again.

Whether or not Nechayev believed in Michael's fantasies it is difficult to say, but if he did not he must have decided that as Michael's friendship would obviously be useful to him he might as well pretend that he did.

While the Alliance gradually dissolved and the International decided to accept its new members, Michael and Nechayev together wrote eight pamphlets which Nechayev was to take back to Russia: a member of a fictitious revolutionary organization taking messages of hope to an equally fictitious revolutionary organization. Written between April and August 1869 they were:

1 'Some Words to Our Young Brothers in Russia' (signed by Michael);
2 'To the Students of the University, of the Academy and of the Technological Institute' (written as from Moscow and signed by Nechayev);
3 'Publications of the Society "The People's Justice" No. 1, Summer 1869' (two articles again written as from Moscow, signed by 'The Russian Revolutionary Committee');
4 'Honourable Russian Nobility!' (signed 'Descendants of the Rurik and the Party of the Independent Nobility');
5 'How the Revolutionary Question Presents Itself' (unsigned);
6 'Principles of Revolution' (unsigned);
7 'Russian Students';
8 'Revolutionary Catechism' (written by Nechayev in cipher).

Pamphlets 5 and 6 expressed extremely destructive principles, but they were both surpassed by the famous Pamphlet 8, which presents a terrifying picture of the revolutionary. The most extreme parts of the pamphlet read as follows:

1 The revolutionist is a doomed man. He has no personal interests, no affairs, sentiments, attachments, property, not even a name of his own. Everything in him is absorbed by one exclusive interest, one thought, one passion – the revolution . . .
6 Rigorous towards himself, he must also be severe towards others. All tender, softening sentiments of kinship, friendship, love, gratitude, and even honour itself must be snuffed out in him by the one cold passion of the revolutionary cause. For him there is only one satisfaction, consolation and delight –

the success of the revolution. Day and night he must have one thought, one aim – inexorable destruction. Striving coldly and unfalteringly towards this aim, he must be ready to perish himself and to destroy with his own hands everything that hinders its realization . . .

8 A revolutionist may feel friendship or attachment only for those who have proven themselves by their actions to be revolutionists like himself. The measure of friendship, devotion and other obligations towards such a comrade is determined solely by the degree of his usefulness to the cause of the all-destructive revolution . . .

11 When a comrade comes to grief, in deciding the question whether or not to save him, the revolutionist must take into consideration not his personal feelings, but solely the interests of the revolutionary cause. Therefore, he must weigh on the one hand the useful work contributed by the comrade, and, on the other, the expenditure of revolutionary forces necessary to rescue him, and he is to decide according to which side outweighs the other . . .

15 The whole ignoble social system must be divided into several categories. In the first category are those who are condemned to death without delay. The association should draw up a list of persons thus condemned in the order of their relative harmfulness to the success of the cause so that the preceding numbers may be removed before the subsequent ones . . .

22 The Association has no aim other than the complete liberation and happiness of the masses, i.e. of the people who live by manual labour. But, convinced that this liberation and achievement of this happiness is possible only through an all-destroying popular revolution, the Association will by all its means and all its power further the development and extension of those evils and those calamities which must at last exhaust the patience of the people and drive them to a general uprising . . .

25 Therefore, in getting closer to the people, we must first of all join those elements of the masses which, since the foundation of the Moscow State power, have never ceased to protest, not in words alone but in deed as well, against everything which is directly or indirectly connected with the State: against the nobility, the bureaucracy, the clergy, the guilds (meaning the merchants and capitalists in general) and against the parasitic kulak. Let us join hands with the bold world of bandits – the only genuine revolutionists in Russia.

26   To consolidate this world into one invincible, all-destroying force is the sole object of our organization; this is our conspiracy, our task.[2]

Originally the Catechism was not intended for publication and when Nechayev returned to Russia the same year he took it with him in coded form only. Its authorship was originally in doubt, as Michael's style is certainly to be detected, but conclusive evidence has recently been produced* that the work was Nechayev's project alone and that Michael did not have a hand in it.

From the point of view of Michael's political career, the issuing of all these pamphlets was to prove disastrous, as they were an ideal weapon for the Marxists to use against him later. However, he was totally infatuated with Nechayev and thought his dear 'Boy' could do no wrong. Moreover Michael had never been able to foresee the consequences of his actions. Even Ogarev became involved, and Herzen was horrified to learn, when he returned to Geneva in May 1869, that Ogarev had written one of the pamphlets himself. But Herzen was now a sick man and had no energy to try and sort out the disastrous situation, although he disliked and distrusted Nechayev on sight and already knew the weaknesses of Ogarev and Michael.

In fact Michael and Nechayev made full use of Ogarev, knowing that Herzen found it difficult to refuse him anything. The problem, as usual, was money. A fund of £800 had been given to Herzen and Ogarev by a Russian landowner named Bakhmetiev to use in spreading revolutionary propaganda throughout Russia. The money had been given to Herzen and Ogarev jointly, and so far they had managed to keep the sum intact by using the interest only. However, Michael and Nechayev were soon able to convince the alcoholic Ogarev that they should have at least some of the money, and although it took Ogarev some time to convince Herzen, at last, out of sheer weariness, he gave in. Cynically, and unwillingly, Herzen agreed that half the sum should be passed over to Michael and Nechayev.

III

In this busy and stimulating period Michael was heavily involved on yet another front. The Geneva branches of the International had become divided into two major groups:

* By Professor Michael Confino (see page 205).

Right Wing Group: The Geneva-born watchmakers and jewellers (the Fabrika), who, although they wanted improvements in working conditions and general reforms, allied themselves with the bourgeois radicals. They dominated the International in Geneva.

Left Wing Group: The manual workers who had mainly immigrated from Italy or France and who wanted revolution.

Michael of course was anxious to redress the balance and to manoeuvre the revolutionary left wing into domination over the reformist right wing. Michael wrote the following commentary on the two groups:

On the one side, the solid phalanx of the Fabrika, with its phoney bourgeois radicalism [opportunism] whose class-collaborationist leaders hoped to ingratiate themselves with the local politicians, using their control of the Geneva International, as a pawn to win favours and privileges for themselves and promote their political ambitions. On the other side, the weakly organized construction workers, who, because of their deplorable economic and social condition and their pronounced socialistic and revolutionary sentiments almost always supported revolutionary socialist principles.

After the construction workers emerged victorious from their great strike [Spring 1868] thanks to the *generous and energetic help of the Fabrik workers*, these workers, solid citizens of Geneva, joined the Central Section of the International and brought with them their opportunistic bourgeois spirit and ideas. As a result, the Central Section split into two camps . . .

The Genevans [Fabrika] were at first a minority in the Central Sections, but they were well organized, and constituted a compact group, while the construction workers were an uncoordinated assemblage, lacking a common policy. Besides, the Genevans were experienced speakers and skilled political connivers; as against this, the construction workers were defenceless, they had only their socialist-revolutionary instinct. Their will to resistance was further blunted and inhibited by their feeling of *gratefulness* towards the Geneva Fabrik workers for their decisive strike aid [a moral obligation to condone the failings of friends].

For some time, both the construction workers and the Fabrik

workers were more or less equally represented at the monthly meetings of the Central Section. [The central sections consisted of members at large, representing no specific industry, ostensibly promoting the overall aims of the whole International: the trade sections were actually local unions in particular factories and industries, concerned with improving the specific conditions in their respective trades and industries.] But when the construction workers organized their local union branches, they ceased to attend the Central Section meetings, and dropped their membership, because they could not afford to pay dues to both the Central Section and their local unions. Thus, the Central Section fell under the full authoritarian control of the united Fabrik groups.

But the construction workers lost control of their local unions. The locals met only once a month, and then only to deal with financial matters [pay dues, etc.] or to elect their executive committee. Vital matters of principles, tactics and workers' education were not discussed at these meetings, and even worse: the members left everything to their committees. Almost always the same people were re-elected to the committees, which naturally took on a permanent and all-powerful character at the expense of the locals which gradually became altogether impotent. The members of the various committees came to think of themselves as the collective dictators of the Geneva International, brazenly ruling the organization from behind closed doors, without even the formality of consulting the membership. And under the direction of the Fabrik leaders, these same committees joined a secret coalition, a sort of dictatorial government, in flagrant violation of the basic principles and statutes of the whole International.

To save the International from becoming the political tool of the phoney bourgeois radicals, the Geneva Alliance group was determined to put an end to this disastrous situation.[3]

In September 1869 Michael attended the annual Congress of the International which was being held in Basel. This, the fourth Congress, was the starting-point of a final power-struggle between Michael and Marx. As Woodcock says,

In some respects Marx and Bakunin were alike. Both had drunk deep of the heady spring of Hegelianism, and their intoxications were lifelong. Both were autocratic by nature, and lovers of intrigue. Both, despite their faults, were sincerely devoted to the liberation of the oppressed and the poor. But in other ways they differed widely. Bakunin had an expansive generosity of spirit and an openness of mind which were both lacking in Marx, who was vain, vindictive and insufferably pedantic. In his daily life Bakunin was a mixture of the bohemian and the aristocrat, whose ease of manner enabled him to cross all the barriers of class, while Marx remained the unregenerate bourgeois, incapable of establishing genuine personal contact with actual examples of the proletariat he hoped to convert. Undoubtedly, as a human being, Bakunin was the more admirable; the attractiveness of his personality and his power of intuitive insight often gave him the advantage over Marx, despite the fact that in terms of learning and intellectual ability the latter was his superior.

The differences in personality projected themselves in differences of principle. Marx was an authoritarian, Bakunin a libertarian; Marx was a centralist, Bakunin a federalist; Marx advocated political action for the workers and planned to conquer the state; Bakunin opposed political action and sought to destroy the state. Marx stood for what we now call nationalism of the means of production; Bakunin stood for workers' control. The conflict really centred, as it has done ever since between anarchists and Marxists, on the question of the transitional period between existing and future social orders. The Marxists paid tribute to the anarchist ideal by agreeing that the ultimate end of socialism and communism must be the withering away of the State, but they contended that during the period of transition the State must remain in the form of a dictatorship of the proletariat. Bakunin, who had now abandoned his ideas of revolutionary dictatorship, demanded the abolition of the State at the earliest possible moment, even at the risk of temporary chaos, which he regarded as less dangerous than the evils from which no form of government could escape.[4]

With these wide personal and ideological differences it was inevitable that the Basel Congress would be an electric occasion, particularly when the most vital items on the agenda were proposals to abolish the right of inheritance and private property in law – proposals that the right-wing watch-makers were totally opposed to and that Michael was obviously going to champion.

By sheer force of personality Michael had already achieved a majority for abolition within the Geneva sections, although he had not been elected as one of their delegates. This was probably partly because he was already a delegate for Naples and partly because the Geneva sections of the International may have hesitated to appoint such a controversial delegate as Michael.

Marx, as usual, did not attend the Congress in person. This time, however, he was bitterly to regret his own absence and complacency, for his representative at the Congress was not adequate to the task of beating Michael's eloquence – something that Marx himself could probably have done.

The drama began to unfold when the Marxists and the Bakuninists were in total agreement over the abolition of private property in land. After a brilliant speech by Michael in which he took the proposal still further and demanded the abolition of the State, the motion was passed by a vast majority. However, when it came to the debate on the abolition of inheritance Michael was even more enthusiastic, for this had become one of his major obsessions. He had mentioned it in many of his more recent articles and felt strongly that it was a vital step towards equality.

Marx's representative, a German tailor from London named Eccarius, put Marx's point of view in the form of a report from the General Council, and argued that

> inheritance was the effect, not the cause of a social organization based on private property. Its abolition naturally followed, not preceded, that of private property. Indeed to abolish inheritance alone would be tantamount to an admission that private property not acquired by inheritance was right and legitimate. If it was desired to advocate partial measures which might be achieved even under a bourgeois system, it was better to concentrate on such practical reforms as a tax on inheritance or the limitation of testamentary rights than on a purely visionary ideal like the abolition of inheritance.[5]

However, Michael in his turn pointed out that although it was obvious that the right of inheritance was the result of 'acts or facts previously accomplished', nevertheless it was now causing serious effects itself and must therefore be removed 'if one desires an order of things different from the existing one'.

As there was little time to debate the question still further, a vote was taken on Michael's proposal; the result was thirty-two delegates for the motion, twenty-three against and thirteen abstaining, and because of these abstentions the rules of the Congress declared that the resolution was defeated. However, the Congress voted against the report of the General Council so the situation ended in deadlock. This meant that for the first time the General Council of the

International had failed to carry its point, and Michael's status, as he had hoped and dreamed, had suddenly risen to such an extent that he was now a serious challenge to the authority of Marx himself.

Not unnaturally Marx was absolutely furious at the way Michael had undermined the authority of the General Council but he took no direct action at the time. However, by a curious coincidence, shortly before the Basel Congress the old rumour that Michael was an agent of the Russian Government had re-emerged. This time it was reported to have come from a certain Wilhelm Liebknecht, a German Social Democrat who was a friend of Marx. Michael, feeling persecuted, convened a 'court of honour' at the Congress to judge the slander and the 'court' sensibly smoothed the matter over by ruling that it was due to a series of misunderstandings. The public exoneration pleased Michael enormously, but the matter was not to rest there. Moses Hess, who had been another delegate at the Conference, heavily attacked Michael in the French radical newspaper *Le Réveil*, saying that Michael was a Russophil, a leader of Russian communism and was trying to undermine the International, so Michael had some basis for feeling persecuted. Assuming, incorrectly this time, that Marx was behind the attack, Michael took refuge in another anti-Semitic outburst. This unpleasant prejudice had shown itself continuously throughout Michael's life and it appeared again in a long letter to *Le Réveil* which denounced most of the Jewish race, explained that Hess had revived the Russian-agent slander once again – and, after a résumé of his life to date, went into a long digression on Italian politics. He sent the document (entitled 'Confession of Faith of a Russian Social Democrat preceded by a study on the German Jews') to Herzen, who, although annoyed at its prejudiced tone, did manage to persuade the editor of *Le Réveil* (who had no intention of publishing the Bakunin material) at least to publish a defence of Michael by Herzen himself. It was a kind letter and, as the journal further stated that no slur on Michael's 'political honour' had been intended, once again Michael was temporarily appeased.

Herzen, however, wrote Michael a note pointing out that he had 'attacked the pupil Hess and left Marx the master unchallenged', but Michael, to Herzen's irritation, replied,

> For five-and-twenty years Marx has served the cause of Socialism ably, energetically, and loyally, taking the lead of every one in this matter. I should never forgive myself if, out of personal motives, I were to destroy or diminish Marx's beneficial influence.

Still, I may be involved in a struggle against him, not because he has wounded me personally, but because of the State Socialism he advocates.[6]

IV

In October 1869 Michael left Geneva for Lugano. There were two main reasons for yet another move. Antonia was pregnant again and as gossip about her relationship with Gambuzzi was still rife neither she nor Michael wanted to winter in Geneva. At the same time money sources had become scarce and a move to Italian Switzerland would at least reduce their expenditure, as the cost of living was considerably lower there. After staying with the Reichels and Vogts at Berne for a short period Michael arrived in Lugano and discovered that the city had become the headquarters of the Mazzinist party. But neither Mazzini nor his followers had much in common with Michael at this time, and to avoid conflict he travelled on to Locarno.

Meanwhile Nechayev had left Switzerland for Russia, armed with some of the Bakhmetiev fund and a vast number of pamphlets. Before he left, at the end of August 1869, he had assured Michael that the Russian revolution would begin on the ninth anniversary of the liberation of the serfs. Once in Moscow he formed a society and a newspaper called *The People's Retribution*. This was modelled upon the ideas put forward in the 'Revolutionary Catechism', and was based upon the traditional nineteenth-century cell system (groups of five with each member of the group commanded by a chief who was in turn commanded by a central committee). Inevitably, like Michael's societies, *The People's Retribution* was directed by Nechayev alone.

In November 1869 Nechayev's terrorist tactics, however, reached new heights when he was defied by a committee member named Ivanov. In retribution Nechayev induced four students to assist him in the murder of his antagonist. Thinking that a printing-press was hidden in a cave in part of the Petrovsk Academy Park, Ivanov was lured in, attacked, shot in the back of the neck by Nechayev, and then thrown into a pond, suitably weighted down with bricks. Next day Nechayev hurriedly left for Petersburg and a wave of student arrests began when Ivanov's body was discovered. An immediate search began for Nechayev but he managed to elude the authorities, slipping out of Russia as quietly as he had slipped in.

Meanwhile, in Locarno, Michael was working hard on an ironic commission. A Russian publisher wanted Marx's *Das Kapital* translated into Russian and Michael had been asked to do it. He was to receive a fee of 1200 roubles with 300 in advance, and although he found the work both arduous and boring he persevered with it. In mid-December the heavily pregnant Antonia joined him, by which time the publisher's advance had been spent and Michael had to borrow 300 francs from Herzen. It was to be the last loan from Herzen, for in January 1870 he died. Michael miserably struggled on with the translation, hearing nothing but rumours of Nechayev's activities. Then, on 12 January 1870, two days before the birth of Antonia's second daughter, Michael was delighted to hear from Ogarev that Nechayev had arrived in Geneva. 'Boy' was home and Michael's heart surged with love and affection. He wrote straight away, suggesting that he should come to Locarno.

Nechayev was delighted to seek sanctuary in Locarno. He fully realized that because he had committed a criminal rather than a political act the Russian authorities might demand that he should be extradited from Switzerland at any moment. Anxious to justify himself, Nechayev wrote a letter to *Le Progrès*, claiming that he had been betrayed by his comrades and taken to Siberia, embellishing the account with other fantasies of a like nature. Michael, overjoyed at his return, backed him up with even more fictitious details expounded both to *Le Progrès* and in letters to his friends. On 7 February Michael wrote a letter to a French friend that vibrantly sang Nechayev's praises:

How those lads there work! What discipline and what a tight organization they have, and what power lies in such collective activity where all personal feelings are set aside! They have even given up their own names, their personal ambitions, and above all the desire for fame. They have taken upon themselves only the risks, the dangers, and the hardest of privations! But they know what power they represent, and they act accordingly! . . . You have not forgotten my young savage? He has done things! . . . He has suffered terribly. He has been arrested, was beaten half-dead, then released and all that only to start all over again. And they are all of the same calibre. The individual has ceased to count, and his place has been taken by the legion, invisible, unknown, and ubiquitous, always at work, daily dying, and daily being resurrected. They are being arrested by the dozen but the hundreds come forward to replace them. The individual disappears, but the legion is immortal and grows in strength from day to day . . . That is the organization I have dreamed of. I dream of it still, and will continue to dream of it, hoping that I shall live to see it here among ourselves.[7]

An optimistic account indeed of Nechayev's nefarious Russian activities.

Nechayev, regaining confidence amidst the exiles in Switzerland, wrote in February 1870 an amazing letter to Lyubavim, Marx's Russian publisher, telling him that he must allow Michael to give up the translation or he would meet an unpleasant fate. In this masterly fashion he saved Michael from having to repay the advance of 300 roubles. The next step was for both Michael and Nechayev, short once again of funds, to persuade Ogarev, now that Herzen was dead, to part with the remainder of the Bakhmetiev fund. They obtained it with surprising ease: the rest of the money was handed to Ogarev by young Alexander Herzen, from Ogarev to Michael and from Michael to Nechayev – in the presence of many of the remaining Herzen family.

There then followed a farcical attempt to procure some of Natalie Herzen's private fortune for 'revolutionary' purposes. Michael in fact was not as deeply implicated in this as Nechayev but he was by no means blameless. Between them they brought considerable pressure to bear on her, partly in order to gain access to her money and partly to obtain her permission for *The Bell* to be revived under their doubtful management. Natalie, however, despite inheriting her father's revolutionary zeal and genuinely wanting to live a useful rather than an idle life, had also inherited some of his caution. Moreover, she was highly intelligent and was well able to see through any dubious arguments while her strong moral scruples prevented her from accepting that the end could justify the means.

Natalie met Nechayev at the house of Nicholas Ogarev at a time when she was particularly concerned about her father's old friend. The various members of the Herzen family were by now living in either Florence or Paris and Natalie was worried that Ogarev might feel they had abandoned him.

By chance, one of her visits to Ogarev coincided with a visitation from Nechayev himself, masquerading, of course, under an alias. Natalie and 'Mr Volkov' were duly introduced and Natalie subsequently noted in her diary that his appearance was quite remarkable. 'Everything about him was original, pure Russian, but it was his dark eyes, peering out every so often from behind his large, dark spectacles, that were especially striking.'[8]

At this first meeting, Nechayev made no attempt to ingratiate himself with Natalie. Their conversation was brief and Nechayev scarcely looked at her, fixing his gaze for the most part on the floor. However, as soon as he realized that she could be of use to the 'Cause', he exerted himself to enlist her services.

They met two or three days later, again at the home of Nicholas Ogarev. Natalie was discussing her impending visit to Berne with Ogarev, telling him that she would shortly be returning to her sisters in Paris. Nechayev, who was in the room, surprised Natalie by suddenly asking Ogarev whether he had talked to her about the drawings. Ogarev had not and she pressed him to explain. Nechayev somewhat obscurely took over the explanation. It transpired that what he really wanted was some drawings inciting the Russian peasants to violence, but, of course, he was reluctant to put this so boldly. As a result, he made the whole thing so obscure that it was some time before Natalie understood what he really meant. She strongly condemned the scheme, saying the peasants would need to be checked, not roused, if there was a revolution. Nechayev and Natalie began to argue but Ogarev intervened, promising to explain it himself to Natalie when she returned from Berne.

This conversation was typical of most that Nechayev and Natalie had at the time. Nechayev never seemed able to state anything directly and usually expressed himself so tortuously that Natalie had the greatest difficulty in understanding him. She, for her part, genuinely wanted to help, but her logical mind led her to expect straightforward answers to her questions.

Meanwhile the other members of the Herzen family were growing uneasy. They were not at all anxious for Natalie to become involved with Michael and Nechayev. Her brother Sasha urged her to leave for Paris immediately and to remain there with her sisters. He hoped that if she stayed away from Geneva for long enough, Nechayev might move on before she returned. But Natalie was by now extremely curious about the mysterious Cause that Nechayev hinted at and in which Ogarev seemed to be involved, and was reluctant to be sent away. There was something about Nechayev's personality which fascinated even while it repelled.

In fact, Nechayev spent a considerable amount of time and trouble influencing Natalie and, for a while, his efforts were rewarded. Before her departure for Paris he succeeded in convincing her that he was engaged in important revolutionary work; she herself could make a valuable contribution to the Cause if she would only overcome her timorousness and agree to act independently of her family. Playing skilfully on her devotion to Ogarev, Nechayev stressed that if only she would return to Geneva alone, without any other members of her family, she could be of great use to Ogarev, helping him with all the important work with which he was now unable to cope.

This of course was a strong argument. Natalie continuously worried about Ogarev and felt that it was wrong to leave him when he was old and drinking heavily. However, she had no intention of blindly working for Nechayev, without carefully considering the validity of his work. She shrewdly examined various aspects of his Cause and quarrelled with him on many occasions about his lack of scruples.

Nechayev was unmoved by her probing and criticisms, pressing her relentlessly to return to help Ogarev as soon as she could escape the constant surveillance of her family. He described in some detail an occasion on which Ogarev had received a vital telegram requiring immediate action on his part. Instead of acting, Ogarev, he said, fell asleep with the telegram in his hands and he, Nechayev, arriving by chance at the critical moment, had managed to pass on the message to the proper quarter. Nechayev stressed that had he not done so many people might have lost their lives.

Despite herself Natalie was impressed. She wrote in her diary: 'The situation as he described it to me was indeed extremely serious. I believed that something really was going on in Russia, that everything was in ferment, that a storm was brewing, and that something was being prepared for the nineteenth of February 1870. . . .'[9]

In this masterly fashion Nechayev managed to enlist her support. Unknown to the other members of her family, she acted as courier for various 'important' letters which could only be delivered by hand. Moreover, despite strong family opposition, she insisted on returning to Geneva. There she became immersed in helping Ogarev, mainly in a clerical capacity.

Nechayev, however, was not prepared to let matters rest there. Despite the fact that he constantly emphasized the vital nature of Natalie's support and work to the Cause, in reality he required her cooperation for something far more significant: he and Michael had decided that they wanted to start a journal and call it *The Bell*. The reason for the choice of title is of course obvious. *The Bell* had been a very important publication and anyone reviving it would automatically inherit its goodwill. Equally obviously, the Herzen family would strenuously resist the journal's revival by Michael and Nechayev whose views were very different from Herzen's. Ogarev's approval they discounted: his health had by now deteriorated to such an extent that almost anyone could influence him. It was therefore of the utmost importance to both Michael and Nechayev that Natalie should agree.

Nechayev first broached the project to Natalie. He did so in his usual clandestine way, asking Ogarev to send her to him with some important documents which could only be brought by a trusted messenger. In order to comply she had to lie to her family and friends, but, fascinated by his extraordinary personality, his Cause and the role she herself would be required to play in it, she agreed to go. Once with him they argued for hours on various points and then suddenly he brought up the subject of the new *Bell*. Natalie was appalled. She very much disliked the idea herself and knew that her family would never forgive her if she agreed.

On this occasion Nechayev failed to influence Natalie. He had in fact underestimated her. Following her to Geneva, where he was joined by Michael, he continued to bully her. Natalie noted in her diary: 'At the end of every conversation I was more and more convinced that their methods were so repugnant that I could have nothing in common with them. He [Nechayev] was continually trying to prove that these methods were essential. Soon Bakunin arrived and assisted him so well in this that they almost succeeded in driving me completely out of my mind.'[10]

Michael and Nechayev continued to press Natalie on the subject of *The Bell* for some time. At one point they even tried to persuade her to become its editor. In addition to this they tried by every means to persuade her to commit herself to their Cause, even accusing her of being afraid that they were after her money. They stressed that this was not the case and that they had vast capital in Russia. Natalie remained unimpressed and noted in her diary that their protestations were inconsistent and insulting to her intelligence. They generously stated that *they* wanted nothing from her but that *Ogarev* must not be forgotten. Natalie wrote in her diary: 'I was perfectly well aware that if I was helping Ogarev it was because they were putting him to expense – the money was coming from the same source, so why this comedy?'[11] But by now she was under considerable pressure for Ogarev was anxious that she should agree to work with him. It is much to her credit that she was able to view the whole situation objectively and to detect the inconsistencies and lies in their impassioned declarations.

The first issue of the new *Bell* appeared on 2 April 1870. Six weeks later it collapsed from lack of circulation, having used up yet more of the Bakhmetiev fund. Meanwhile, unfortunately for Nechayev, one of the Russian revolutionaries arrived in Geneva. Fully conversant with the true details of Nechayev's recent activities in Russia, he lost no time in making them public. As a result Nechayev's credibility was undermined and the authorities pursued him with increased vigour.

However, despite this change of fortune Nechayev lost none of his personal arrogance. He now felt that he could well dispense with Michael and ignored his requests that he should be paid an allowance out of the Bakhmetiev fund. He had used Michael to gain access to this money and through him had acquired plenty of contacts and considerable influence – and now he had no further need of him. They also quarrelled over *The Bell*, for Nechayev dismissed Michael's advice and assistance, preferring to edit the magazine by himself.

Michael must have been deeply hurt and humiliated by Nechayev's attitude. He had committed himself to the young Russian completely, considering his interests before his own and even following his lead instead of treating him as a disciple, as in his previous relationships. However, it is interesting to note that despite the fantasy-world he and Nechayev had been living in and despite the fact that even his optimistic spirit must have been oppressed at this time, he was still able to express his views rationally. His editorial assistance on the new *Bell* having been rejected, he settled down to write a pamphlet entitled 'The Bears of Berne and the Bear of Petersburg'. Rather pathetically in the circumstances the pamphlet was mainly written in support of Nechayev, for Michael was anxious that he should not be snatched back into Russia by the combined efforts of the Swiss authorities (the Bears) and the Tsar (the Bear). He also defended Princess Obolensky's absolute right to live apart from her husband and he vehemently attacked the Swiss Government for allowing the Princess's husband to take her children back to Russia with him – and for pushing the lady and her lover into seeking sanctuary in London.

The pamphlet also included an extension of Michael's views on the immorality of the State, expressed with all his former lucidity:

The transcendental anti-human immorality of the State is not exclusively caused by those designated to discharge the functions of the State. It would be more correct (to put things in their proper sequence) to emphasize that the State corrupts men. For corruption is the natural and inevitable product of State institutions; it stems from the nature of the State . . . Immorality is the fundamental principle of the State.

The State is the total negation of humanity. It is a restricted collectivity [monopoly] standing outside of and imposing itself over humanity, bending everything to its own advantage – forcing everyone to submit to its dictates . . .[12]

In May Michael presented Nechayev with an ultimatum. First

on the list were his own financial requirements and secondly he insisted that publication of *The Bell* should be resumed – this time under the direction of himself and Ogarev. Nechayev, not wanting an immediate confrontation with Michael, did not resist. He was by now on the run, as that month a young Russian had been arrested by the Swiss police who had mistaken him for Nechayev.

On 2 June Michael wrote Nechayev a letter. It took him eight days to write and was the longest he had ever written. In fact it could more accurately be described as a revolutionary pamphlet. This important document, a copy of which was discovered by Professor Michael Confino in Natalie Herzen's archives at the Bibliothèque Nationale in Paris, makes it clear that it was Nechayev, not Michael, who wrote the 'Revolutionary Catechism'.

Michael began the letter quite gently, addressing Nechayev as 'Dear Friend' and summarizing the reasons for the failure of their campaign. He reproached Nechayev for deceiving him about the strength of the Cause and the number of people involved in it, despite the fact that he himself had a strong tendency to exaggerate the number of his own supporters. At this stage of the letter Michael was still clinging desperately to his faith in Nechayev, hastening to add that he was sure Nechayev was not lying out of self-interest. Nevertheless, 'neither love nor respect can prevent me from telling you frankly that the system of deceit, which is increasingly becoming your sole system, your main weapon and means, is fatal to the cause itself.'[13]

Michael continued by giving a short account of his life, stressing that, as he had been separated from Russia for thirty years, Nechayev was one of the very few serious Russian revolutionaries that he had ever met. This meeting had therefore been very important to him; Michael had felt until then that he had no real knowledge of the Russian revolutionary youth about whom he so often wrote.

Michael then described the main reasons why he had decided in the first place to ally himself with Nechayev. He said that he had been heavily influenced in Nechayev's favour because their revolutionary plans had been identical. In addition to this, he had felt that Nechayev had such a strong personality that he would be able to unite all the different factions behind the one Cause. He went on to describe the revolutionary programme on which they had once been so completely agreed but from which Nechayev had now departed, adding firmly that he would have to sever their connection, 'if your convictions and you, or your friends' departure from it were completely final.'[14]

At this stage the tone of Michael's letter became much more

critical. He began to list some of Nechayev's mistakes and analysed the defects in his character. In addition, he included a passage which proves, without doubt, that he had no hand in the 'Revolutionary Catechism'. 'Do you remember how cross you were when I called you an *Abrek** and your catechism a catechism of *Abreks*? You said that all men should be such . . . you wished, and still wish to make your own selfless cruelty . . . into a rule of common life.'[15]

As if anxious to placate Nechayev, Michael then reverted to emphasizing his abilities and reaffirming his faith in him; but, despite himself, the telling questions arose. Did Nechayev really have an organization or was it as yet unformed? If it did exist, how large was it? Did the Committee itself exist? And so on. Still determinedly friendly, Michael protested that Nechayev should have trusted him and told him the truth; even if the entire Cause existed only in his mind Michael would still have helped.

However, Michael felt impelled to remind Nechayev that as he was forced to exist on other people's money and had already been accused of raising funds under false pretences, he should have some regular form of income. How would he acquire this if all his time was spent working for the Cause? It was essential for Michael not to further discredit himself by 'standing at the head of a secret society about which, as you are aware, I know nothing',[16] but, despite this, he was prepared to do so as he had such faith in Nechayev.

Michael then went on to outline the programme for the revolution in Russia, following this with a complete plan for the administration of the country after the State had been successfully overthrown. He advocated collective dictatorship, explaining clearly and in detail how this could be organized. Then followed another analysis of Nechayev, accusing him of 'having fallen so much in love with Jesuit methods that you have forgotten everything else.'[17]

At this point, Michael moved from the general to the particular. He listed the many dishonest and culpable acts Nechayev had committed, roundly condemning them. He emphasized: 'Your system of blackmailing, entangling and scaring Tata† was extremely repugnant to me. . . .'[18]

Michael admitted that he had also been hurt. He described all the things he had done for Nechayev, acting all the time in good faith, only to find that Nechayev had completely deceived him and used him. Now his credibility had been ruined and he was completely bankrupt. He stated vehemently: 'This is enough, Nechayev

---

* A Caucasian mountaineer banished from his clan, or having made a vow of revenge.
† Natalie Herzen.

– our old relationship and our mutual obligations are at an end. You yourself have destroyed them.'[19]

Somewhat dramatically, Michael declared that he was prepared to make a public confession of his stupidity to try to redeem his reputation. Amazingly, however, he was still reluctant to let Nechayev pass out of his life and promised him an even closer relationship if he could change his attitude.

Michael laid down the personal and general conditions which Nechayev would have to accept if he wished to continue their relationship. The personal conditions inevitably concerned the alleviation of Michael's financial state and the restoration of his damaged reputation, while the general conditions, of course, concerned a new and more honourable attitude to the Cause. Michael listed both sets of conditions at length and closed the letter with a strong plea for Nechayev to accept them. He concluded: 'If you do not accept, my decision is inflexible. I shall have to break all ties with you. . . .'[20]

Michael sent the letter to Nechayev, by this time hiding in the mountains, via Ogarev and Natalie Herzen, with a covering note asking them to make a copy of his letter to Nechayev. Still hopeful that Nechayev could yet be reclaimed, he said: 'The main thing for the moment is to save our erring and confused friend. In spite of all he remains a valuable man. . . .'[21]

The copy of this letter found in the Natalie Herzen archives is proof that his friends faithfully carried out Michael's instructions. Nechayev, however, must have been unmoved by Michael's letter, for far from making any attempt to comply with its conditions he decided to travel quickly to London, which seemed a safer hiding-place. With remarkable calculation Nechayev stole some papers and letters belonging to Michael, Natalie Herzen and Ogarev. He was discovered doing this, but, completely unabashed, he still managed to get away with some highly incriminating evidence which he presumably felt might come in useful for future blackmail.

The logical conclusion of Nechayev's career was fast approaching. In London he managed to produce two issues of a paper called *The Commune*, but during that period Michael wrote various letters of warning to his London associates. An extract from one such letter read,

I have just heard that Nechaev has come to you and that you have given him the addresses of our friends. I can only conclude that both letters in which I and Ogarev warned you arrived too late, and I am not exaggerating when I say this is very serious.

Because all I wrote you about Nechaev was far from exaggerated, yet it does not even approach the reality. Yes, he has betrayed us, and betrayed us even at a time when we gave him everything and stood by him without reservation. Yes, as long ago as last year he stole our letters. Yes, he compromised us by acting in our name without our knowledge and our agreement. Yes, he lied shamelessly to us. I proved it in the presence of Ogarev, Natalie Hertsen and others, and when he could not deny my evidence, do you know what he replied? 'We are very grateful for everything you did for us, but as you did not want to submit to us in every respect because you had, as you said, international obligations, we had to take precautions against you for any contingency. Therefore I felt justified in stealing your letters, and I felt obliged to create discord among you, because it is harmful to us if such a strong bond exists outside our circle.' And Mrochkovsky introduces such a man to a radical English politician! ... I only hope, my friends, and I hope it for your own sake and for your peace of mind, that you believe in me and show him the door.[22]

Later Nechayev went to France and then back to Switzerland, still producing revolutionary propaganda. He also published a Russian translation of the Communist Manifesto as now that he had broken with Michael he came under the influence of Marx, Blanqui and Babeuf. In July 1871 there was a trial of eighty Nechayev disciples in Petersburg and those four associated with him in the murder of Ivanov received comparatively stiff sentences of hard labour. On 14 August 1872 Nechayev, having evaded the authorities for a surprisingly long time, was arrested in Switzerland, and in October 1872 he was taken to Russia where he was tried in Moscow on 8 January 1873. Michael Prawdin describes his appearance as follows:

When the accused was called before the court, he looked, as a newspaper wrote, a small, slight figure between the two gendarmes with drawn swords. But he came in with a swaggering gait, his head held high, though he was deadly pale, his hands in his trouser pockets. He walked straight to the dock, sat down and began to scrutinize those present with an insolent expression. According to the reporter, the defendant with his brown hair combed straight back, the thinnish moustache with the ends drawn up, and a scanty, slightly lighter beard ending in broad side-whiskers, had the appearance of a somewhat foppish plebeian. Particularly remarkable were his narrow, very deep-set eyes, casting restless, furtive glances. His wide forehead and prominent cheekbones made his face look almost square and gave him a vulgar expression.

When the judge asked Nechaev for his particulars, he replied: 'I do not recognize this Court. I am a refugee, I do not recognize the Russian Emperor or the Russian laws . . .' He was interrupted by the judge but continued to speak, raising his voice. Thereupon the judge ordered him to be removed from the Court. Nechaev struggled, broke away from the gendarmes, was seized again and forcibly taken out of the room.[23]

He was eventually imprisoned in solitary confinement in the fortress of Peter and Paul – ironically the place that he pretended to have escaped from so many years ago. Nechayev faced his trial with courage and stood defiantly in front of his accusers. He also faced his prison sentence with great fortitude but eventually died of scurvy at the age of thirty-five. Later the Third Department filed this appraisal of Nechayev's personality:

Nechaev cannot be called an average personality. The deficiency of his original education is continually evident, but it is covered over by an astonishing pertinacity and will-power manifesting themselves in the mass of knowledge that he acquired afterwards. This knowledge and the effort that was necessary to acquire it, have developed in him all the advantages of the self-taught man in the highest degree: energy, habitual self-reliance, complete command of the subjects with which he deals. At the same time they have also developed in him all the disadvantageous traits of the self-taught: contempt for everything that he does not know, complete lack of critical evaluation of his knowledge, envy and relentless hatred of all who have received by their good fortune the education which cost him such an effort, recklessness. He is unable to distinguish sophistry from logic and deliberately ignores any facts which do not accord with his views. He is full of suspicion, contempt and enmity against all who, by their means, their social position or their education enjoy a higher standing. Even if they pursue the same aims, they gain nothing in his eyes. He distrusts their sincerity and finds their activities silly and dilettantist. They are for him an obstacle that must be overcome as quickly as possible. Only men of equal upbringing and of the same views as his are for him real servants of the people and deserve trust and sympathy. All others who stand out of the masses are regarded as enemies of the people, and peaceful, fruitful and manifold development can only ensue after their liquidation. Although he several times rejected violent overthrow, because that would be only a reaction without creating anything positive, he considers violence necessary, because the upper classes must be liquidated at any price. Hatred is for him one of the most important driving forces of social development. Often persons in the position of the author deserve to be respected by their adversaries, but this author does not produce such a feeling of esteem. None of his notes were written with a view to publication, and nevertheless he describes himself as surrounded by privations which he has in fact not suffered. There is no trace of sincerity in the reasons given for this or that action, and one finds no sign of recognition of the right of others to self-defence. On purpose he develops in himself instincts which drive him into blind enmity against the present State order without questioning the justification of these instincts. He finds satisfaction in cherishing his hatred for all higher placed persons. With egotistic pleasure he describes himself as a revolutionary not by conviction but by temperament. He must exercise a seductive influence upon less educated people, particularly upon such who started at the same level but did not reach his standard; but also upon better educated people who are critically disposed towards their own opinion.[24]

Nechayev's activities were viewed with the utmost disgust by the prominent revolutionary figures of the time, including of course Marx himself. Nevertheless, Nechayev was to find acclaim in some quarters. For instance, Bolshevist literature included analyses of Nechayev's personality, his actions and his theories. Students of the Russian Revolution have noticed some similarities between the teachings of Nechayev and those of Lenin. In his book, *The Revolutionary Period of History from 1861 to 1881*, published in Petersburg in 1913, W. W. Glinsky gave the following appraisal of Nechayev's significance:

In the person of Nechaev, the Russian revolutionary movement produced an important figure, whose actions adumbrated many of its chapters, outlined the ways of its development and wrote a prologue to its history. Although later generations of the same revolutionary creed were not satisfied with this prologue and kept it carefully secret, we must, looking back on nearly forty years of the whole revolutionary movement, confess that this movement inaugurated its practical realization precisely with the appearance of Nechaev on the stage, and that the last years of these four decades are in their character much nearer to him than to other personalities of the movement who denounced him for so long.

An even greater tribute was paid to Nechayev by Michael Kovelensky. In his book, *The Russian Revolution in Court Procedures and Memoirs*, published in Moscow in 1923, he had this to say of him:

> What a grandiose figure on the road of the Russian revolution! Tremendous revolutionary energy, gigantic organizational talent, declaration of pitiless war against the whole old world, which is condemned to decline and disappear. Rejection of the supremacy of the old bourgeois morals, which will be replaced by a new ethic of revolution for the success of which all means are justified. . . . With the thundering slogan 'Everything for the revolution!' this super-revolutionary appears before us. With every means at their disposal his subsequent followers in the battle try to renounce him, but the men of 'Land and Freedom' and of 'People's Will' can do nothing else but follow his steps. The stamp of his genius impresses itself upon the whole of the Russian revolutionary movement.

In self-defence Michael pretended that he had destroyed Nechayev, but this went unbelieved. Indeed Michael's relationship with Nechayev, their writings, their plans, the scandal over the Bakhmetiev fund and their eventual quarrel were disastrous for Michael's political career. But Michael had been unable to view Nechayev objectively, for he had been totally infatuated with 'Boy'. He had loved him dearly and that love had completely dulled his perception to the ramifications of their association. However, ultimately he was able to write to Ogarev with endearing shrewdness, 'We were fools, and how Herzen would have had the laugh of us if he had been alive, and how right he would have been to scold us. Well, there is nothing to be done. Let us swallow the bitter pill, and we shall be wiser in future!'[25]

But he was not to know at this stage to what extent the Nechayev episode had delivered him into Marx's hands. Michael was now fifty-six and looked older. Slowly he was crumbling. In July 1870 he returned to Locarno, where he licked his wounds before the beginning of the Franco-Prussian War. On 16 July 1870, he turned his thoughts from the loss of his beloved 'Boy' to revolution again.

PART EIGHT

The Final Disillusionment: 1870–6

I

From the end of the Basel Congress in the autumn of 1869 until the conclusion of the Franco-Prussian War a year later Michael did not give his full attention to the progress of the Alliance, but in some European countries – mainly France, Spain and Italy – owing to the vigorous activity of some of his more able adherents, Bakuninism had become quite well established.

France

Here the International was extremely strong, particularly in Paris. For the most part followers of Proudhon, the French Internationalists were not only opposed to Marxist views but were determined to avoid political agitation. Michael, however, had no contact with this group; the centre of Bakuninist activity at that time was in Lyons, as a result of the efforts of Albert Richard, a loyal supporter of Michael's. Richard saw Michael regularly and had met Nechayev. A Congress of the French International was held at Lyons in March 1870 and although Michael did not go himself he did send a speech.

Spain

In the autumn of 1869 Fanelli, the Italian revolutionary who had first met Bakunin in Naples, pioneered Bakuninism when he founded branches of the International in Barcelona and Madrid. A Spanish Federation was formed in 1870 and all its branches were fully recognized as members of the International. Also a highly secret Social-Democrat Alliance was set up by the two delegates to the

Basel Congress who, having met Michael only briefly, did not realize how dubious his largely mythical organizations were.

Italy

Bakuninist influence was strong in Italy. In 1868 Gambuzzi had founded the Naples branch of the Alliance and in the spring of 1870 Michael had visited Milan and had persuaded some Italian radicals to found a branch of the International there.

However, despite the conspicuous successes in these countries Bakuninism had very little hold in either Germany or England, and in Switzerland Michael's influence, which had reached its peak at the Basel Congress, had begun to wane. This was due to a number of contributory factors.

Firstly, when Michael left Geneva for Locarno the Alliance became apathetic and under the pallid leadership of Perron, Robin (a French political exile) and later Henry Sutherland (the son of Ogarev's mistress), most members fell away. Meanwhile the other sections of the International in Geneva squabbled parochially among themselves. Secondly, Nicholas Utin, who had quarreled violently with Michael over the editorship of *The People's Cause*, somewhat fortuitously arrived in Geneva just as Michael was departing and was able to take over his role. He lost no time in denouncing Michael at every opportunity and in January 1870 he became editor of *L'Égalité*. By March 1870 he was sufficiently well established to suggest certain changes to the manifesto of the Alliance which, with Becker's influence, were taken up. Utin's next moves were to found the first Russian section of the International in Geneva and to suggest to Marx that he should become Russian Secretary in the General Council. He craftily pointed out that the new section would determinedly attack pan-Slavism and destroy Michael Bakunin.

This manoeuvre of Utin's supplied the decisive factor which seriously undermined Michael's influence in Switzerland. Marx, pleased at having the opportunity of attacking Michael, accepted the secretaryship, at the same time circularizing the German sections of the International with a general denunciation of Michael.

At the April 1870 Congress of the Fédération Romande in the Jura Utin took the battle a step further by moving that the application for the Alliance's membership of the Fédération should be put off for reconsideration. Once again he took the opportunity of the public platform of the meeting to launch into a venomous personal attack on Michael, citing the disastrous wording of Nechayev's 'Revolutionary Catechism', but Guillaume's vigorous defence carried the day and the Alliance scraped into the Fédération. The

Genevese refused to accept the decision, however, and the Congress split in two, both sections claiming to be the Fédération.

By this stage Michael was not unaware that his position was being seriously undermined, but absorbed as he was in Nechayev he pretended to ignore the situation and even sent some copies of the new *Bell* to Marx.

Encouraged by Michael's indifference, Utin then proposed that all members of the Alliance should be expelled from the central Geneva Section of the International. Twice the committee wrote to Michael, giving him the opportunity to defend himself in person, but he delayed so long that in early August 1870 Michael, Zhukovsky, Henry Sutherland and Perron were expelled.

Meanwhile Marx, although uneasily aware that as there had been a majority vote for the Alliance at the Jura Congress of the complete Fédération Romande the Bakuninists were basically in the right, did not let this factor deter him from telling the majority section of the Fédération which had voted in the Alliance to change its name to something else. As a sop they were told that they could still remain members of the International, but now the International was effectively divided in Switzerland, with the Jura divisions supporting Michael and the Geneva divisions supporting Marx.

II

On 16 July 1870 the Franco-Prussian War broke out. It was Napoleon III, in fact, who declared war, but within about six weeks most of the French armies had been defeated and Napoleon was a prisoner. On 4 September a provisional republican government was appointed in Paris but it was unlikely that the radicals would be satisfied to see the reins of government pass into bourgeois hands. A few months earlier, in March 1870, Eugène Verlin, an active member of the French branch of the International, accurately summarized the pre-war situation in a newspaper article:

At present our statesmen are trying to substitute a liberal-parliamentary Government (Orleans style) for the regime of personal rule, and hope thereby to divert the advancing revolution that threatens their privileges. We socialists know from experience that all the old political forms are incapable of satisfying the demands of the people. Taking advantage of the mistakes and blunders of our adversaries, we must hasten the arrival of the hour of deliverance by actively preparing the bases for the future organization of society. This will make easier and more certain the task of social transformation which must be carried out by the revolution . . .

Society can no longer permit the arbitrary distribution of the public wealth on the basis of birth or success. Since this results from the collective sum of all productive labour, it should be employed only for the benefit of the collective. In other words, all members of human society have an equal right to the advantages stemming from that wealth.

However, this social wealth cannot provide for the well-being of humanity unless it is put to use by labour.

Consequently, if the industrial capitalist or businessman is no longer to dispose of arbitrarily or collectively produced capital, who, then, can place this capital at the disposal of all? Who is to organize the production and distribution of goods?

Short of placing everything in the hands of a highly centralized, authoritarian State which would set up a hierarchic structure from top to bottom of the labour process . . . we must admit that the only alternative is for the workers themselves to have the free disposition and possession of the tools of production . . . through co-operative associations in various forms . . .

Newly formed labour groupings must join with the older ones, for it is only through the solidarity of workers in all occupations and in all countries that we will definitely achieve the abolition of all privileges, and equality for all.[1]

The revolutionary potential of the war was balm to the wounds inflicted on Michael by Nechayev. At first he was overjoyed that the Prussians were defeating Napoleon, but he soon became a staunch supporter of the French, giving his anti-Teutonic bias a free rein.

Cut off from the scene of activity, Michael became more and more excited. He felt that once again there was hope of widespread revolution – not only in France but in Italy also, for his Italian lieutenants had reported a certain amount of 'restiveness'. Above all he was anxious that this golden opportunity should not be wasted and that the revolution should not fall into bourgeois hands as it had in 1848. Shortly before the outbreak of the Franco-Prussian War Michael had already written to Albert Richard, clearly expressing the need for an anti-authoritarian revolution.

You keep on telling me that we both agree on fundamental points. Alas! my friend, I am very much afraid that we find ourselves in absolute disagreement . . . I must, more than ever, consider you as a believer in centralization, and in the revolutionary State, while I am more than ever opposed to it, and have faith only in revolutionary anarchy, which will everywhere be accompanied by an invisible collective power, the only dictatorship I will accept, because it alone is compatible with the aspirations of the people and the full dynamic thrust of the revolutionary movement! . . .

There must be anarchy, there must be – if the revolution is to become and remain alive, real, and powerful – the greatest possible awakening of all the local passions and aspirations; a tremendous awakening of spontaneous life everywhere. After the initial revolutionary victory the political revolutionaries, those advocates of brazen dictatorship, will try to squelch the popular passions. They appeal for *order*, for trust in, for submission to those who, in the course and in the name of the Revolution, seized and legalized their own dictatorial powers; this is how such political revolutionaries reconstitute the State. We, on the contrary, must awaken and foment all the dynamic passions of the people. We must bring forth anarchy, and in the midst of the popular tempest, we must be the invisible pilots guiding the Revolution, not by any kind of overt power but by the collective dictatorship of all our allies, a dictatorship without tricks, without official titles, without official rights, and therefore all the more powerful, as it does not carry the trappings of power. This is the only dictatorship I will accept, but in order to act, it must first be created, it must be prepared and organized in advance, for it will not come into being by itself, neither by discussions, nor by theoretical disputations, nor by mass propaganda meetings . . .

If you will build this collective and invisible power you will triumph; the well-directed revolution will succeed. Otherwise, it will not!! If you will play around with welfare committees, with official dictatorship, then the reaction which you yourself have built will engulf you . . . who are already talking yourselves into becoming the Dantons, the Robespierres and the Saint-Justs of revolutionary socialism, and you are already preparing your beautiful speeches, your brilliant 'coups d'états', which you will suddenly foist on an astonished world . . .[2]

As the war progressed it was only too clear that France was going to be heavily defeated by Prussia. The Provisional Republican Government was at a total disadvantage, for the Prussian troops were already near Paris. As Sam Dolgoff points out,

It was in the midst of this crisis that Bakunin developed ideas which have since become the watchwords of libertarian revolutionary movements and to which even the authoritarians still pay lip-service – ideas such as turning the wars between States into civil wars for the Social Revolution; the people-in-arms fighting a guerrilla war to repulse a foreign army and simultaneously defending the revolution against its domestic enemies; all power to the grass-roots organizations spontaneously created by the revolution; a federalist alternative to centralized statist revolution-by-decree, among others.[3]

Michael expressed these ideas in his essay *Letters to a Frenchman on the Present Crisis*, which was edited and printed by James Guillaume, who was careful to remove any passages that resembled Nechayev's views too closely. It is one of the most important of Michael's writings and while it reiterates his condemnation of the bourgeoisie it pays particular attention to the relationship between the anarchists themselves and the people.

... Faced with mortal danger from within and without, *France can be saved only by a spontaneous, uncompromising, passionate, anarchic and destructive uprising of the masses of the people all over France.*

I believe that the only two classes now capable of so mighty an insurrection are *the workers and the peasants.* Do not be surprised that I include the peasants. The peasants, like other Frenchmen, do wrong, not because they are by nature evil but because they are ignorant. Unspoiled by the over-indulgence and indolence, and only slightly affected by the pernicious influence of bourgeois society, the peasants still retain their native energy and simple unsophisticated folk ways. It is true that the peasants, being petty landlords, are to a considerable extent egoistic and reactionary, but this has not affected their instinctive hatred of the 'fine gentlemen' [country squires], and they hate the bourgeois landlords, who enjoy the bounty of the earth without cultivating it with their own hands. On the other hand, the peasant is intensely patriotic, i.e., he is passionately attached to his land, and I think that nothing would be easier than to turn him against the foreign invader.

It is clear that in order to win over the peasants to the side of the Revolution, it is necessary to use great prudence; for ideas and propaganda which are enthusiastically accepted by the city workers will have the opposite effect on the peasants. It is essential to talk to the peasants in simple language suitable to their sentiments, their level of understanding, and mindful of the nature of their prejudices, inculcated by the big landlords, the priests and the State functionaries. Where the Emperor is loved, almost worshipped, by the peasants, one should not arouse antagonism by attacking him. It is necessary to *undermine in fact* and not in words the authority of the State and the Emperor, by undermining the establishment through which they wield their influence. To the greatest possible extent, the functionaries of the Emperor – the mayors, justices of the peace, priests, rural police and similar officials – should be discredited.

It is necessary to tell the peasants that the Prussians must be ousted from France (which they probably know without being told) and that they must arm themselves and organize volunteer guerrilla units and attack the Prussians. But they must first follow the example set by the cities, which is to get rid of all the parasites and counter-revolutionary civil guards; turn the defence of the towns over to the armed people's militias; confiscate State and Church lands and the holdings of the big landowners for re-distribution by the peasants; suspend all public and private debts . . . Moreover, before marching against the Prussians, the peasants, like the industrial city workers, should unite by federating the fighting battalions, district by district, thus assuring a common co-ordinated defence against internal and external enemies.

This, in my opinion, is the most effective way of dealing with the peasant problem; for while they are defending the land they are, at the same time, unconsciously but effectively destroying the State institutions rooted in the rural communes, and therefore making the Social Revolution.[4]

Michael continues with a passionate and characteristic call for action:

Let us *talk less* about revolution and *do* a great deal *more*. Let others concern themselves with the theoretical development of the principles of the Social Revolution, while we content ourselves with spreading these principles everywhere, *incarnating them into facts.*

My intimate friends and allies will probably be surprised that I speak this way – I, who have been so concerned with the theory, who have at all times been a jealous and vigilant guardian of revolutionary principles. Ah! How times have changed! *Then,* not quite a year ago, we were only preparing for a revolution, which some expected sooner and others later; but now even the blind can tell that we are in the midst of a revolution. *Then*, it was absolutely necessary to stress theoretical principles, to expound these principles clearly and in all their purity, and thus to build a party which, though small in number, would be composed of sincere men, fully and passionately dedicated to these principles, so that in time of crisis each could count on the solidarity of all the others.

But it is now too late to concentrate on the enrolment of new men into such an organization. We have for better or worse built a small party: small, in the number of men who joined it with full knowledge of what we stand for; immense, if we take into account those who instinctively relate to us, if we take into account the popular masses, whose needs and aspirations we reflect more truly than does any other group. All of us must now embark on stormy revolutionary seas, and from this very moment we must spread our principles, not with words *but with deeds, for this is the most popular, the most potent and the most irresistible form of propaganda* . . .[5]

As the French armies were gradually defeated Michael became feverish with impatience in Locarno. He saw voluntary federated communes arising phoenix-like from the ashes of the French Empire and looked towards the loyal Bakuninists in Marseilles and Lyons to organize the revolution. Unable to stand aloof any longer, on 6 September Michael begged some money from Adolf Vogt and on 9 September he set out for France.

On the way he met a Russian friend, Colonel Postnikov, who by chance was travelling to Locarno to see him. Michael had first met General Postnikov at Ogarev's house in April 1870. Posing as a retired Russian Colonel with revolutionary leanings, Postnikov had in fact been one of the most successful of the Russian agents in Geneva for some time and was at that moment trying to trace Nechayev. Curiously enough, Michael made a very favourable impression on Postnikov and Michael for his part liked the Colonel's revolutionary spirit. Consequently, in July Michael called on Postnikov and immediately suggested to him that he should return to Russia, find out what was happening on the revolutionary front and report back, as Michael wanted to start a magazine (to replace *The Bell*) tentatively called *Russian Commune*. He also wanted Postnikov to visit Premukhino, convey Michael's compliments to his family and see if he could find out whether there was any chance of Michael receiving his share of his father's estate. After a slight delay (while Postnikov checked with his superiors) he departed with a sad letter from Michael to his brothers at Premukhino. An extract reads as follows:

My faith in your fraternal love struggled long against the most evident facts; I carried it to the point of stupidity. At length you have killed it. Crushed by fearful need, I wrote you a number of letters and know that they all reached you. At first you used to answer with mystifying arguments and nebulous calculations, the conclusion of which was that $+1 = -1$. In recent years you have answered with systematic and profound silence. Silence is a convenient means of getting rid of a man who lives a long way off, and is rendered impotent by his political position. Sometimes silence is the mark of injured self-esteem, but when it is combined with the retention of another man's property it requires another interpretation.[6]

Postnikov returned from Russia in September 1870, having extracted a loan of 70 roubles from Michael's brothers, and as he travelled towards Michael's home he met Michael in Lucerne. They travelled together as far as Berne, and en route Michael extracted the promise of a loan of 250 roubles from Postnikov. It was an ironic situation and Michael little realized that not only had a Russian agent acquired the Premukhino loan for him but that he had also lent him further sums that would no doubt be put down on his expense sheet and debited to the Russian Government.

After meeting Guillaume at Neuchâtel, and leaving in his hands the editing and publication of *Letters to a Frenchman*, Michael arrived in Lyons on 15 September 1870. By that time a moderate republican municipal council had replaced the radical Committee of Public Safety and as Albert Richard was away in Paris talking to the new republican Government Michael had ample opportunity to dominate the situation.

He began by creating a Central Committee for the Salvation of France, for which a public inaugural meeting was held on 17 September, but overjoyed to be in action once more he ignored the fact that few of his French associates were anarchists, not all were revolutionaries, and the majority were definitely not extremists. The French were logical and failed to understand Michael's deep belief in the natural goodness of humanity and his violent theories on how to bring about the Social Revolution.

However, although some of the factories had been turned into national workshops the municipal council had foolishly reduced the workers' wages. On 24 September, therefore, a public meeting was called and resolutions were passed demanding that army officers should be appointed by free election and that a levy should be imposed on the rich. Michael and some of his chief supporters then put their names to a proclamation in the name of the Federated Committees for the Salvation of France.

THE REVOLUTIONARY FEDERATION OF COMMUNES

The disastrous plight of the country, the incapacity of official powers and the indifference of the privileged classes have placed the French nation on the verge of destruction.

If the People do not hasten to organize and act in a revolutionary manner, their future is doomed; the revolution will have been lost. Recognizing the seriousness of the danger and considering that urgent action by the People must not be delayed for a moment, the delegates of the Federated Committees for the Salvation of France and its Central Committee propose the immediate adoption of the following resolutions:

Article 1 – The administrative and governmental machinery of the State, having become impotent, is abolished.

Article 2 – All criminal and civil courts are hereby suspended and replaced by the People's justice.

Article 3 – Payment of taxes and mortgages is suspended. Taxes are to be replaced by contributions that the federated communes will have collected by levies upon the wealthy classes, according to what is needed for the salvation of France.

Article 4 – Since the State has been abolished, it can no longer intervene to secure the payment of private debts.

Article 5 – All existing municipal administrative bodies are hereby abolished. They will be replaced in each commune by committees for the salvation of France. All governmental powers will be exercised by these committees under the direct supervision of the People.

Article 6 – The committee in the principal town of each of the Nation's Departments will send two delegates to a revolutionary convention for the salvation of France.

Article 7 – This convention will meet immediately at the town hall of Lyons, since it is the second city of France and best able to deal energetically with the country's defence. Since it will be supported by the People, this convention will save France. TO ARMS!!![7]

Marx, on the other hand, foreseeing that any immediate uprising would, owing to the presence of the occupying Prussian army, end in total and bloody defeat, considered that it would be better to profit by the current increase in democratic liberties in order to strengthen the organization of the working classes. Unfortunately, however, the following address of the General Council of the International was not received by many members in France at the time and really only appeared there some years after the fall of the Paris Commune of 1871.

TO THE MEMBERS OF THE INTERNATIONAL WORKING MEN'S ASSOCIATION IN EUROPE AND THE UNITED STATES

. . . Like them [German working men], we hail the advent of the Republic in France, but at the same time we labour under misgivings which we hope will prove groundless. That Republic has not subverted the throne, but only taken its place become vacant. It has been proclaimed, not as a social conquest, but as a national measure of defence. It is in the hands of a Provisional Government composed partly of notorious Orléanists [monarchists], partly of middle-class Republicans, upon some of whom the insurrection of June 1848 has left its indelible stigma. The division of labour among the members of that Government looks awkward. The Orléanists have seized the strongholds of the army and the police, while to the professed Republicans have fallen the propaganda departments. Some of their first acts go far to show that they have inherited from the Empire, not only ruins, but also its dread of the working class. If eventual impossibilities are in wild phraseology demanded from the Republic, is it not with a view to prepare the cry for a 'possible' government? Is the Republic, by some of its middle-class managers, not intended to serve as a mere stop-gap and bridge over an Orléanist Restoration?

The French working class moves, therefore, under circumstances of extreme difficulty. Any attempt at upsetting the new Government in the present crisis, when the enemy is almost knocking at the doors of Paris, would be a desperate folly. The French workmen must perform their duties as citizens; but, at the same time, they must not allow themselves to be deluded by the national *souvenirs* of 1792, as the French peasants allowed themselves to be deluded by the national *souvenirs* of the First Empire. They have not to recapitulate the past, but to build up the future. Let them calmly and resolutely improve the opportunities of Republican liberty, for the work of their own class organization. It will gift them with fresh Herculean powers for the regeneration of France, and our common task – the emancipation of labour. Upon their energies and wisdom hinges the fate of the Republic . . .

Let the sections of the *International Working Men's Association* in every country stir the working classes to action. If they forsake their duty, if they remain passive, the present tremendous war will be but the harbinger of still deadlier international feuds, and lead in every nation to a renewed triumph over the workman by the lords of the sword, of the soil, and of capital.

Vive la République![8]

Meanwhile Michael took three courses of action, but they had little revolutionary effect, owing to the cautiousness of his French associates. He wrote to Postnikov asking him to persuade Tchorzewski to send some funds, he wrote (in code) to Guillaume asking him to send from Switzerland copies of the newly printed *Letters to a Frenchman*, and he tried in vain to organize a coup.

On 28 September Michael's main revolutionary chance came. A demonstration was planned by the employees of the national workshops against the reduction in their wages and Michael's Committee for the Salvation of France held a meeting on the preceding evening with Michael in a highly militant mood advocating revolution. But, once again, the French were not prepared to take any really militant action, and a decision was made only to be re-presented at the next day's meeting at the Hôtel de Ville.

Discovering a singular absence of councillors, Michael and his Committee forced their way in and the large crowd that had gathered outside were told that the Municipal Council would be asked either to accept the September 25th proclamation or to resign. Shortly afterwards the National Guard appeared, and entered the Hôtel de Ville. In retaliation, the crowd outside broke in and disarmed the National Guard. As a result, for a brief period Michael and his Committee were in power and he ordered the arrest of a number of civil and military officials. Before any attempts had been made to carry out these instructions fresh battalions of the National Guard appeared, the Municipal Council reassembled at the Hôtel de Ville and Michael's Committee fled. Only Michael himself remained and he was thrown into a cellar by the returning mayor and his bodyguards, only to be released later by some friends.

Michael then went into hiding – hiding that was so effective that even Postnikov, armed as he was with a supply of *Letters to a Frenchman* which he had brought over from Switzerland, was unable to find him. On 29 September 1870 Michael slipped out of Lyons on a train bound for Marseilles and for the next three weeks Michael hid himself at an associate's house there. Once again he was completely insolvent and wrote a number of letters desperately begging for funds but he refused to be totally downcast by the failure at Lyons. Searching for the weak links Michael soundly condemned Cluseret, the Committee's military commander, who had suddenly got cold feet and had tried to make peace with the other side while Michael and the others were in the Hôtel de Ville. He also denounced Richard for allegedly collaborating with the provisional Government.

Having regained his incorrigible optimism, Michael determined on a second attempt to stir up revolution in Lyons. However, this second attempt ended in total disaster, as Lankiewicz, a Pole whom Michael sent back to Lyons, was arrested while carrying letters in one of Michael's famous codes. As a result the International and Alliance divisions, in fear of their lives, dispersed and Michael himself was in imminent danger of arrest. On 24 October 1870, therefore, disguised and with a false passport and a hundred franc loan, he returned to Locarno.

III

Extremely depressed, Michael started work on his pamphlet *The Knouto-Germanic Empire and the Social Revolution*, in which he saw the disaster in France as a direct result of Prussian and Russian imperialism. But he wrote miserably and desperately, conscious of his isolation and his insolvency, and in Part One indulged himself by bitterly attacking the German bourgeoisie. On a more optimistic note, however, Michael expressed confidence in the German proletariat.

> The German workers are daily becoming more and more revolutionary . . . Bismarck will no longer be able to fool them. His flirtation with 'socialism' is over . . . from now on Bismarck, in league with the German bourgeoisie . . . the nobility and the military will marshal all its power to crush the proletariat, and by fire and sword purge the proletariat of its socialist heresy. A battle to the death not only against the German workers, but also against the European working class. Although I am acutely aware of this danger, I await this war, confident that it will arouse in the masses the demon of revolt . . . that passion, without which victory is impossible . . .

No sooner did reports of the victory of the German army at the decisive battle of Sedan and the fall of Napoleon III reach Germany; no sooner did it become clear that France was no longer a threat to Germany, and that the war for national defence had been turned into a war of conquest; than the German proletariat at once reversed itself, and voiced its deepest sympathy with the French workers and demanded an immediate end to the war . . . And I hasten to compliment the German Socialist Workers' Party, its administrative committee, Bebel, Liebknecht, and so many others, who in the midst of the howls of the pro-war German bourgeoisie, courageously defied the whole bloody tribe and proclaimed their solidarity with the French people . . .[9]

The Lyons uprising, short and abortive as it was, and ridiculed as it was by Marx, was not by any means the demoralizing episode it seemed to be. Franz Mehring, the official biographer of Marx, pointed out that

> The ridiculing of this unsuccessful attempt might reasonably have been left to the reaction, and an opponent of Bakunin whose opposition to anarchism did not rob him of all capacity to form an objective judgment wrote: 'Unfortunately mocking voices have been raised even in the social democratic press, although Bakunin's attempt certainly does not deserve this. Naturally, those who do not share the anarchist opinions of Bakunin and his followers must adopt a critical attitude towards his baseless hopes, but apart from that, his action in Lyons was a courageous attempt to awaken the sleeping energies of the French proletariat and to direct them simultaneously against the foreign enemy and the capitalist system. Later the Paris Commune attempted something of the sort also and was warmly praised by Marx.'[10]

In January 1871 Postnikov, having been unable to discover Nechayev's whereabouts, was recalled to Russia. Michael came to say goodbye to him at Berne and Postnikov was horrified at Michael's appearance.

The old man's health had been sapped by the discomfiture at Lyons and by the hardships of his flight. He breathed heavily, complained of swellings and pains in his legs, and ate and drank little. But his spirits had recovered somewhat, and, averting his eyes from France, he talked cheerfully of the break-up of the Austrian Empire – his dream for thirty years – and of the general European war which would make propaganda possible in Russia itself. War, he felt, was imminent; and he begged particularly that Postnikov would, on his arrival in Russia, study ways and means of propaganda on the Volga and in the Urals, which he considered the most promising fields for this missionary enterprise. He invited Postnikov to visit his brothers at Premukhino; and finally he asked for a last loan of 60 francs.[11]

Michael was never to discover Postnikov's true identity.

Antonia later records that he spent the first few months of 1871 in a highly depressed state and the following financial budget for January 1871 shows how poverty-stricken the couple were:

January 2. Purse empty. Gave Antonia 5 fr. 3. No money. Borrowed 45 fr. from Marie. 5. Gave Antonia 20 fr. 9. Gave Antonia 3 fr. 11. No money. 13. No money. 14. Borrowed 40 fr. from Marie. 16. Received 200 fr. from Gambuzzi. 18. Paid 60 fr. to the butcher, and 17 fr. to [undecipherable]. 19. Paid 30 fr. to the baker. In hand 67 frs. 21. In hand 53 fr.70. 24. 20 fr. in pocket. 25. No tea. 28. Letter to Mme Franzoni; answer probably tomorrow. What answer? Nothing? 200? 300? 400? 29. Received 300 fr. from Mme Franzoni. Paris surrendered on the 28th. Bourbaki entered Switzerland. Paid 25 fr. to Nina [the *femme de ménage*] (balance due by Feb. 1st. 20 frs.), 40 fr. to Marie (balance due by Feb. 4th 208 fr.), 55 fr. to Bettoli (balance due 25 fr.) for wood 41 fr.50; in hand 88 fr.[12]

However, later in the spring Michael cheered up, having spent some time with a Russian friend in Florence, and he was further encouraged by two factors that improved their precarious financial position. Gambuzzi, concerned about the fate of his children, gave Michael a loan of 1000 francs and Antonia's family gave her a monthly allowance of 50 roubles. Now Michael could rely on Antonia's income and a little of his old optimism and energy returned.

During February and March 1871 Michael was engaged in writing the second part of his essay *The Knouto-Germanic Empire*. This second part was never finished, but an important fragment of it was published separately six years after Michael's death under the title *God and the State*. In his introduction to the Dover Edition of *God and the State* Paul Avrich comments that 'several of its themes – notably the idea that government and religion have always worked together to keep men in chains – can be traced to Bakunin's then unpublished essay, *Federalism, Socialism and Antitheologism* (written in 1867), and were to crop up again in his polemics with Giuseppe Mazzini after the fall of the Commune in May 1871'.

In March 1871, inspired largely by Michael's ideas, the Paris Commune was formed. The Government had attempted to disarm the Paris National Guard, 'a volunteer citizen force which showed signs of radical sympathies', but the latter had reacted by over-throwing the Government and electing a revolutionary committee in its place. This Commune was composed of seventy-eight members and was based on Proudhon's ideal of the federation of communes which Michael had adopted so enthusiastically. Its existence ended in great bloodshed and defeat in May 1871. The International had not been involved in its inception at all – Engels even stated that 'the International did not raise a finger to make the Commune' – but despite the fact that its anti-authoritarian principles were directly opposed to his own views on the State, Marx in fact gave public approval to the Commune in an address to the General Council. Isaiah Berlin suggests that this was a tactical move.

> The Commune was not directly inspired by Marx. He regarded it, indeed, as a political blunder: his adversaries the Blanquists and Proudhonists predominated in it to the end; and yet its significance in his eyes was immense. Before it there had indeed been many scattered streams of socialist thought and action; but this rising, with its world repercussions, the great effect which it was found to have upon the workers of all lands, was the first event of the new era. The men who had died in it and for it were the first martyrs of international socialism, their blood would be the seed of the new proletarian faith: whatever the tragic faults and short-comings of the Communards, they were as nothing before the magnitude of the historical role which these men had played, the position which they were destined to occupy in the tradition of proletarian revolution.
>
> By coming forward to pay them open homage he achieved what he intended to achieve: he helped to create a heroic legend of socialism.[13]

Michael of course was able to be more sincerely in favour of the Paris Commune, although he was fully aware of its mistakes. In the introduction to the second part of his essay *The Knouto-Germanic Empire and the Social Revolution* he analyses it in some detail but while he is critical of some points he is able to say quite truthfully, 'I am a supporter of the Paris Commune, which, for all the bloodletting it suffered at the hands of monarchical and clerical reaction, has nonetheless grown more enduring and more powerful in the hearts and minds of Europe's proletariat. I am its supporter, above all, because it was a bold, clearly formulated negation of the State.'[14]

Indirectly, the Paris Commune led to a considerable increase in Michael's influence in Italy. Already he had violently disagreed with Mazzini's concepts of religion and nationalism, but as yet he had not publicly attacked him, nor had Mazzini attacked Michael. But the Commune crystallized their differences of opinion and when Mazzini denounced the Commune in his paper *Roma del Popolo* as anti-religious and anti-nationalistic, and in July 1871 also attacked the International on the same grounds, Michael sprang to the defence of both the Commune and the International and published in a Milan paper 'The Reply of an Internationalist to Giuseppe Mazzini'. An extract reads as follows:

Where did we find the other day the materialists and atheists? In the Paris Commune. And where the idealists, the believers in God? In the Versailles National Assembly. What did the men of Paris want? The emancipation of labour and thereby the emancipation of mankind. What does the triumphant Assembly of Versailles now want? The final degradation of mankind beneath the double yoke of the spiritual and temporal power . . .

At the moment when the heroic population of Paris, more noble than ever before, was being massacred by tens of thousands, women and children among them, defending the most human, the most just, the most exalted cause ever known in history – *the emancipation of the workers of the whole world* – at the moment when the detestable coalition of every form of unclean reaction was pouring on their heads every calumny which unbounded infamy alone can invent – at that moment Mazzini, the great, the unspotted democrat Mazzini, turning his back on the cause of the proletariat and remembering only his mission of prophet and priest, begins to launch against them his insults.[15]

Michael followed this with a work entitled *Mazzini's Political Theology and the International* which was published at the end of 1871 by Guillaume. And in November 1871 Michael distributed a *Circular to my Italian Friends* to the delegates of the conference the Mazzinists had organized in Rome and in this way won over three delegates (one of which was Cafiero, who became a faithful follower of Michael's). Outright conflict broke out between the Bakuninists and the Mazzinists, but Michael's influence was in the ascendant, especially when Garibaldi supported the International.

Meanwhile the antagonism between the Alliance and the International had erupted once more. Utin, having already engineered the expulsion of Michael and his friends from the Geneva branch of the International, was now anxious to expel them from the entire structure of the International. He had tried to secure this in March 1871 by stating that the admittance of the Alliance (Geneva section) had never been properly confirmed by the General Council. The General Council infuriated Michael by taking three months to make the required confirmation and because of this Michael suspected that Marx was implicated. It was fast becoming clear to Michael that his power struggle with Marx, which had been smouldering for so many years, was soon going to come to a head.

At first events looked particularly bleak for Michael. An ominous private conference of the International had been summoned to meet in London in September 1871. Michael, although still prepared to fight, was weakened by physical deterioration and the Alliance, itself weak and lacking in morale, chose this inopportune moment to decide to disband. Michael was furious, and they hastily reconstituted the organization under the title 'Section For Propaganda and Social-Revolutionary Action'. Michael, now working on a second version of his history of the Alliance, tried to be optimistic, but the dwindling of the troops and the reconstitution of the Alliance under a different name which had *not* been recognized by the International hardly served as a morale-booster.

Marx himself summed up the International's dealings with Michael and the Alliance in a private circular, entitled 'Fictitious Splits in the International', from the General Council drawn up early in 1872. The following extracts from this document show the hardening of Marx's attitude towards Michael and reveal the subtle inaccuracies which he used to support his own actions.

The denunciations in the bourgeois press, like the lamentations of the international police, found a sympathetic echo even in our Association. Some intrigues, directed ostensibly against the General Council but in reality against the Association, were hatched in its midst. At the bottom of these intrigues was the inevitable *International Alliance of Socialist Democracy*, fathered by the Russian Mikhail Bakunin. On his return from Siberia, the latter began to write in Herzen's *Kolokol* preaching the ideas of Pan-Slavism and racial war, conceived out of his long experience. Later, during his stay in Switzerland, he was nominated to head the steering Committee of the League of Peace and Freedom founded in opposition to the International. When this bourgeois society's affairs went from bad to worse, its president, Mr G. Vogt, acting on Bakunin's advice, proposed to the International's Congress which met at Brussels in September 1868 to conclude an alliance with the League. The Congress unanimously proposed two alternatives: either the League should follow the same goal as the International, in which case it would have no reason for existing; or else its goal should be different, in which case an alliance would be impossible. At the League's Congress held in Berne a few days after, Bakunin made an about face. He proposed a makeshift programme whose scientific value may be judged by this single phrase: '*economic and social equalization of classes*'. Backed by an insignificant minority, he broke with the League in order to join the International, determined to replace the International's General Rules by the makeshift programme, which had been rejected by the League, and to replace the General Council by his personal dictatorship. To this end, he created a special instrument, the *International Alliance of Socialist Democracy*, intended to become an International within the International.

Bakunin found the necessary elements for the formation of this society in the relationships he had formed during his stay in Italy, and in a small group of Russian emigrants, serving him as emissaries and recruiting officers among members of the International in Switzerland, France and Spain. Yet it was only after repeated refusals of the Belgian and Paris Federal Councils to recognize the *Alliance* that he decided to submit for the General Council's approval his new society's rules, which were nothing but a faithful reproduction of the 'misunderstood' Berne programme. The Council replied [in the] circular dated December 22, 1868 . . .

Having accepted [certain] conditions, the Alliance was admitted to the International by the General Council, misled by certain signatures affixed to Bakunin's programme and supposing it recognized by the Romance Federal Committee in Geneva which, on the contrary, had always refused to have any dealings with it. Thus, it had achieved its immediate goal: to be represented at the Basle Congress. Despite the dishonest means employed by his supporters, means used on this and solely on this occasion, in an International Congress, Bakunin was deceived in his expectation of seeing the Congress transfer the seat of the General Council to Geneva and give an official sanction to the old Saint-Simon rubbish, to the immediate abolition of hereditary rights which he had made the practical point of departure of socialism. This was the signal for the open and incessant war which the Alliance waged not only against the General Council but also against all International sections which refused to adopt this sectarian clique's programme and particularly the doctrine of total abstention from politics.

Even before the Basle Congress, when Nechayev came to Geneva, Bakunin got together with him and founded, in Russia, a secret society among students. Always hiding his true identity under the name of various 'revolutionary committees', he sought autocratic powers based on all the tricks and mystifications of the time of Cagliostro. The main means of propaganda used by this society consisted in compromising innocent people in the eyes of the Russian police by sending them communications from Geneva in yellow envelopes stamped in Russian on the outside 'secret revolutionary committee'. The published accounts of the Nechayev trial bear witness to the famous abuse of the *International*'s name...

It goes without saying that none of the conditions accepted by the Alliance have ever been fulfilled. Its sham sections have remained a mystery to the General Council. Bakunin sought to retain under his personal direction the few groups scattered in Spain and Italy and the Naples section which he had detached from the International. In the other Italian towns he corresponded with small cliques composed not of workers but of lawyers, journalists and other bourgeois doctrinaires. At Barcelona some of his friends maintained his influence. In some towns in the South of France the Alliance made an effort to found separatist sections under the direction of Albert Richard and Gaspard Blanc, of Lyons, about whom we shall have more to say later. In a word, the international society within the International continued to operate.

The big blow – the attempt to take over the leadership of French Switzerland – was to have been executed by the Alliance at the Chaux-de-Fonds Congress, opened on April 4, 1870.

The battle began over the right to admit the Alliance delegates, which was contested by the delegates of the Geneva Federation and the Chaux-de-Fonds sections.

Although, on their own calculation, the Alliance supporters represented no more than a fifth of the Federation members, they succeeded, thanks to repetition of the Basle manœuvres, in procuring a fictitious majority of one or two votes, a majority which in the words of their own organ represented no more than *fifteen* sections, while in Geneva alone there were thirty! On this vote, the French–Switzerland Congress split into two groups which continued their meetings independently. The Alliance supporters, considering themselves the legal representatives of the whole of the Federation, transferred the Federal Committee's seat to Chaux-de-Fonds and founded at Neuchâtel their official organ, the *Solidarité*, edited by Citizen Guillaume . . .

On their return, the Geneva delegates convened their sections in a general assembly which, despite opposition from Bakunin and his friends, approved their actions at the Chaux-de-Fonds Congress. A little later, Bakunin and the more active of his accomplices were expelled from the old Romance Federation.

Hardly had the Congress closed when the new Chaux-de-Fonds Committee called for the intervention of the General Council in a letter signed by F. Robert, secretary, and by Henri Chevalley, president, who was denounced two months later as a *thief* by the Committee's organ the *Solidarité* of July 9. After having examined the case of both sides, the General Council decided on June 28, 1870 to keep the Geneva Federal Committee in its old functions and invite the new Chaux-de-Fonds Federal Committee to take a local name. In the face of this decision which foiled its plans, the Chaux-de-Fonds Committee denounced the General Council's *authoritarianism*, forgetting that it had been the first to ask for its intervention. The trouble that the persistent attempts of the Chaux-de-Fonds Committee to usurp the name of the Romance Federal Committee caused the Swiss Federation obliged the General Council to suspend all official relations with the former . . .[16]

At the London Conference Michael and his friends were fiercely attacked in their absence. Utin and another anti-Bakuninist represented Geneva whilst the Jura sections, having refused to obey the General Council's instructions to drop the title Fédération Romande, were not invited and were only able to make their points by post. The main attacks on Michael at the Conference centred around the following points:

1 Having re-established the fact that the International would at all times politically activate revolution, it forbade its branches to call themselves under a sectarian name or to form separate divisions of any kind for any purpose.
2 The Chaux-de-Fonds minority and its Geneva Committee were recognized as the Fédération Romande and the majority section was told to take the name Fédération Jurassiene.
3 Utin was asked to prepare a report on Nechayev and the General Council publicly disassociated themselves from the latter's activities.

The Bakuninists had no intention of letting the matter rest there, so in November 1871 a Bakuninist conference was organized in Sonvillier. Although not attended by Michael this conference, apart from tactfully agreeing with the first two points the London Conference had made, insisted that the London Conference itself was improperly constituted and the General Council far too autocratic. The Bakuninists then produced the Sonvillier Circular which demanded an immediate Congress of the International to debate its structure. They felt that the International should be composed of a free federation of autonomous groups instead of being governed by the General Council. The Circular received considerable support in Italy, Spain and Belgium and as a result the General Council was obliged to announce a Congress at The Hague in September 1872.

In the meantime Marx and Michael both prepared new campaigns, but the deterioration of Michael's private life made maximum concentration on the forthcoming struggle impossible. Despite his improved financial position in the summer of 1871, by the autumn the Bakunins were again reduced to poverty. In addition Antonia's brother died and she was attacked by a serious wave of homesickness. In June 1872 she could bear it no longer and, leaving Michael, she and the children returned to Russia on a visit to her family.

In May 1872 Marx countered the Sonvillier Circular by publishing *Fictitious Splits in the International* as a pamphlet and sending it to all branches of the International. In the following extracts Marx put forward his own interpretation of the events which lead to the convening of the Hague Congress:

The men of the Alliance, hidden behind the Neuchâtel Federal Committee and determined to make another effort on a vaster scale to disorganize the International, convened a Congress of their sections at Sonvillier on November 12, 1871. Back in July two letters from *maître* Guillaume to his friend Robin had threatened the General Council with an identical campaign if it did not agree to recognize them to be in the right '*vis-à-vis* the Geneva bandits'.

The Sonvillier Congress was composed of sixteen delegates claiming to represent nine sections in all, including the new 'Socialist Revolutionary Propaganda and Action Section' of Geneva.

The sixteen made their début by publishing the anarchist decree declaring the Romance Federation dissolved, and the latter retaliated by restoring to the Alliance members their 'autonomy' by driving them out of all sections. However, the

Council had to recognize that a stroke of good sense brought them to accept the name of the Jura Federation that the London Conference had given them.

The Congress of Sixteen then proceeded to 'reorganize' the International by attacking the Conference and the General Council in a 'Circular to All Federations of the International Working Men's Association' . . .

After having challenged the convocation of the Conference and, later, its composition and its allegedly secret character, the Sixteen's circular challenged the Conference resolutions.

Stating first that the Basle Congress had surrendered its rights, 'having authorized the General Council to grant or refuse admission to, or to suspend, the sections of the International', it accuses the Conference, farther on, of the following sin:

> 'This Conference has . . . taken resolutions . . . which tend to turn the International, which is a free federation of autonomous sections, into a hierarchical and authoritarian organization of disciplined sections placed entirely under the control of a General Council which may, at will, refuse their admission or suspend their activity!'

Still farther on, the circular once more takes up the question of the Basle Congress which had allegedly 'distorted the nature of the General Council's functions'.

The contradictions contained in the circular of the Sixteen may be summed up as follows: the 1871 Conference is responsible for the resolutions of the 1869 Basle Congress, and the General Council is guilty of having observed the Rules which require it to carry out Congress resolutions.

Actually, however, the real reason for all these attacks against the Conference is of a more profound nature. In the first place, it thwarted, by its resolutions, the intrigues of the *Alliance* men in Switzerland. In the second place, the promoters of the Alliance had, in Italy, Spain and part of Switzerland and Belgium, created and upheld with amazing persistence a calculated confusion between *the programme of the International Working Men's Association and Bakunin's makeshift programme.*

The Conference drew attention to this deliberate misunderstanding in its two resolutions on proletarian policy and sectarian sections. The motivation of the first resolution, which makes short work of the political abstention preached by Bakunin's programme, is given fully in its recitals, which are based on the General

Rules, the Lausanne Congress resolution and other precedents.[17]

Michael, amongst other epithets, described the pamphlet as a heap of filth, and saw it as a patent manifestation of Marx's domination over the General Council.

Marx, who was preparing for the ensuing confrontation very seriously indeed, had two main objectives: to ensure that Michael was defeated by weight of numbers and also that his reputation was destroyed. To this end he canvassed Germany and the U.S.A. to discover which candidates were unlikely to attend the Conference from various divisions of the International. All he wanted was blank mandates from these delegates which he could give to his own supporters, thus adding to the number of votes under his own control. Furthermore he despatched his son-in-law Paul Lafargue to Spain disguised as a Spaniard to report back on the strength of Michael's influence there. Lafargue proved a worthy disciple. Not only did he found and become appointed as delegate for a Marxist branch of the International in Madrid but he managed to obtain copies of the rules of the Spanish Secret Alliance and an instructional letter from Michael himself to one of his Spanish associates.

This information of course was extremely valuable to Marx if he wished to prove that Michael was a disruptive influence within the International and was not adhering to its rules, but in addition to this he had managed to acquire even more damning evidence against Michael in the form of Nechayev's letter to the Petersburg publisher threatening him with violence if he held Michael to his contract to translate *Das Kapital*.

Michael, on the other hand, was not entirely without support. There had been a most sympathetic reaction to the Sonvillier Circular from the Italian, Spanish, Dutch, Belgian, French and United States sections and even the British trade unions felt that the General Council had become too powerful and should be checked. Unfortunately, however, the new Italian sections in their zeal broke off relations with the General Council and refused to attend the Congress, thus depriving Michael of their valuable support.

Meanwhile in June 1872, Antonia and her two children having departed for Russia, Michael, desperately lonely, settled in Zurich where a number of young Russians escaping from persecution in Russia had congregated. The most important of these was Michael Sazhin (better known under his pseudonym of 'Armand Ross'), a young and dominating revolutionary, but there were also Holstein and Oelsnitz who, as students, had been expelled from the University of Petersburg, and Ralli, a former associate of Nechayev. These three had first met Michael in Locarno and had enrolled in a new anarchistic group that Michael suddenly decided to form. Enthusiastically he drafted a constitution and codes all over again – life was being kind to Michael once more.

In the midst of the heavily increasing young Russian colony Michael moved around like an amiable, eccentric *éminence grise*. As always he loved young people, seeing them as potential revolutionaries, and for his part the old revolutionary met great acclaim from the young Russian exiles. A young Russian girl describes the impact he made on her contemporaries at this time.

> The door opened wide, and there appeared the enormous form of Michael Alexandrovich Bakunin. All at once fell silent. The eyes of all were involuntarily riveted on Bakunin. It was so much a matter of habit for him to attract notice that he was not embarrassed by these challenging looks, and advanced the length of the room to his seat with an easy, measured, free gait. The attention of all present were fixed on him; and nobody noticed the numerous suite of Frenchmen, Spaniards, Russians and Serbs who followed in his wake . . .
>
> Turning first to one, then to another, he would speak without the least embarrassment, now in German, now in Italian, now in French, now in Spanish. But in the long run Russian got the upper hand . . . He was in good form today and was recalling his youth, Moscow, his friendship with Belinsky. Everyone listened to his easy, graceful utterance. Not only at his table was there a solemn, rather obsequious, silence; those sitting at our table also remained dumb, though inwardly annoyed with themselves for not having the courage to open their mouths.[18]

Surrounded by these young admirers, Michael plotted happily – and ineffectively – away. He founded a Slav 'section', which numbered half-a-dozen followers, amidst much imaginative fervour on Michael's part. He had an equally abortive involvement with the Polish colony when he attempted to turn the Polish Social Democratic Society into a branch of the Fédération Jurassienne and the International and failed, as did his attempted publication of a new Polish journal because of the Poles' aristocratic and class-conscious nationalism.

In August 1872 Nechayev was arrested in Switzerland and Michael was surprisingly merciful. Later, when Nechayev had been handed over to the Russians, Michael wrote to Ogarev, 'Nobody has done me, and deliberately done me, so much harm as he, and yet I am sorry for him. He was a man of rare energy; and when you and I first met him, there burned in him a clear flame of love for our poor down-trodden people, he had a genuine ache for the people's age-long suffering . . . Well, he's done for.'[19]

The all-important Congress at The Hague was due to open on 2 September 1872, and Marx was leaving nothing to chance. On receipt of Lafargue's information about the Alliance activities in Spain the Executive Committee of the General Council discussed the situation at a meeting on 24 July 1872, and as a result Engels submitted a draft address for the General Council's approval. This address laid out in painstaking detail all the 'evidence' against Michael and the Alliance, and ended as follows:

> . . . it is time once and for all to put a stop to those internal quarrels provoked every day afresh within our Association, by the presence of this parasite body [the Alliance]. These quarrels only serve to squander forces which ought to be employed in fighting the present middle-class *régime*. The Alliance, in so far as it paralyses the action of the International against the enemies of the working class, served admirably the middle class and the governments.
>
> For these reasons, the General Council will call upon the Congress of The Hague to expel from the International all and every member of the Alliance and to give the Council such powers as shall enable it effectually to prevent the recurrence of similar conspiracies.[20]

Engels also wrote letters along the same lines to a number of influential people such as Carlo Cafiero, originally an adherent of Marx's but now an enthusiastic follower of Michael's. The point he returned to again and again, both in his correspondence and draft speeches for the Congress, was the question of authoritarianism. It was the main point of departure between Marxism and Bakuninism and Engels must have felt that he and Marx were on weak ground, for he was continuously 'proving' that the Bakuninists were hypocritical and thoroughly impractical over this point.

The Hague Congress opened on 2 September, the delegates coming from most European countries, excluding Italy and Russia, the most enthusiastic being those from France and Germany. Forty of the delegates were strong Marxists and only four delegates from Spain and two from the Jura – Guillaume and a colleague – were committed Bakuninists. The other members of the minority group were against Marx's autocracy but showed little interest in Bakunin.

However, despite this solid majority at the Congress Marx was aware that it was not significant of the movement as a whole. The fact that the Congress was being held in Holland prevented many delegates from attending – Michael himself could not come, owing to his poverty and the impossibility of crossing French or German territory – whereas it was quite convenient for Marx's chief supporters. By now extremely worried about the tide of Bakuninism that was slowly spreading throughout Europe, Marx was already evolving a plan which was to amaze even his own close colleagues.

Meanwhile the Congress, after stressing how vital it was that the proletariat should take political action and after totally rejecting the Bakuninist proposal that the General Council should become a mere piece of administrative machinery, appointed a committee to look into the activities of the Alliance.

Marx then surprised everyone by suggesting that the General Council should be removed from London to New York, a city where there was no Bakuninist influence or danger. By doing this, Marx effectively killed the International, for he gave concern to his followers and caused confusion. The six Bakuninists at the Conference did not vote, but the motion was passed by a slim majority. At least Marx could reflect that he had saved the International from the influence of Bakunin – even if he had killed it in the process.

The committee investigating the Alliance heard the Bakuninist side of the question and also heard from other members of the General Council. Engels submitted the following detailed report which he had written at the request of the General Council:

REPORT ON THE ALLIANCE OF SOCIALIST DEMOCRACY PRESENTED IN THE NAME OF THE GENERAL COUNCIL TO THE CONGRESS AT THE HAGUE

The Alliance of Socialist Democracy was founded by M. Bakunin towards the end of 1868. It was an international society claiming to function, at the same time, both within and without the International Working Men's Association. Composed of members of the Association, who demanded the right to take part in all meetings of the International's members, this society, nevertheless, wished to retain the right to organize its own local groups, national federations and congresses alongside and in addition to the Congresses of the International. Thus, right from the onset, the Alliance claimed to form a kind of aristocracy within our Association, or élite with its own programme and possessing special privileges . . .

The General Council refused to admit the Alliance as long as it retained its distinct international character; it promised to admit the Alliance only on the condition that the latter would dissolve its special international organization, that its sections would become ordinary sections of our Association, and that the Council should be informed of the seat and numerical strength of each new section formed.

The following is the reply dated June 22, 1869, to these demands received from the Central Committee of the Alliance, which has henceforth become known as the 'Geneva Section of the Alliance of Socialist Democracy' in its relations with the General Council.

'As agreed between your Council and the Central Committee of the Alliance of Socialist Democracy, we have consulted the various groups of the Alliance on the question of its dissolution as an organization outside the International Working Men's Association . . . We are pleased to inform you that a great majority of the groups share the views of the Central Committee which intends to announce the dissolution of the International Alliance of Socialist Democracy. *The question of dissolution has today been decided.* In communicating this decision to the various groups of the Alliance, we have invited them to follow our example and constitute themselves into sections of the International Working Men's Association, and seek recognition as such either from you or from the Federal Councils of the Association in their respective countries. Confirming receipt of your letter addressed to the former Central Committee of the Alliance, we are sending today for your perusal the rules of our section, and hereby request your official recognition of it as a section of the International Working Men's Association . . . (Signed) Acting Secretary, C. Perron . . .'

The Geneva section proved to be the only one to request admission to the International. Nothing was heard about other allegedly existing sections of the Alliance. Nevertheless, in spite of the constant intrigues of the Alliancists who sought to impose their special programme on the entire International and gain control of our Association, one was bound to accept that the Alliance had kept its word and disbanded itself. The General Council, however, has received fairly clear indications which forced it to conclude that the Alliance was not even contemplating dissolution and that, in spite of its solemn undertaking, it existed and was continuing to function as a secret society, using this underground organization to realize its original aim – the securing of complete control. Its existence, particularly in Spain, became increasingly apparent as a result of discord within the Alliance itself, an account of which is given below. For the moment, suffice it to say that a circular drawn up by members of the old Spanish Federal Council, who were at the same time members of the Central Committee of the Alliance in Spain, exposed the existence of the Alliance. [Earlier] the circular, dated June 2, 1872, and published in *Emancipación*, informed all the sections of the Alliance in Spain that the signatories had dissolved themselves as a section of the Alliance and invited other sections to follow their example.

The publication of this circular caused the Alliance newspaper, the Barcelona *Federación*, to publish the rules of the Alliance, thus putting the existence of this society beyond question . . .

Clearly no one would wish to hold it against the Alliancists for propagating their own programme. The International is composed of socialists of the most various shades of opinion. Its programme is sufficiently broad to accommodate all of them; the Bakunin sect was admitted on the same conditions as all the others. The charge levelled against it is precisely its violation of these conditions.

The secret nature of the Alliance, however, is an entirely different matter. The International cannot ignore the fact that in many countries, Poland, France and Ireland among them, secret organizations are a legitimate means of defence against government persecution. However, at its London Conference the International stated that it wished to remain completely dissociated from these societies and would not, consequently, recognize them as sections. Moreover, and this is the crucial point, we are dealing here with a secret society created for the purpose of combating not a government, but the International itself . . .

Let it be said right from the start that the activities of the Alliance fall into two distinct phases. The first is characterized by the assumption that it would be successful in gaining control of the General Council and thereby securing supreme direction of our Association. It was at this stage that the Alliance urged its adherents to uphold the 'strong organization' of the International and, above all, 'the *authority* of the General Council and of the Federal Councils and Central Committees'; and it was at this stage that gentlemen of the Alliance demanded at the Basle Congress that the General Council be invested with those wide powers which they later rejected with such horror as being *authoritarian*.

The Basle Congress destroyed, for the time being at least, the hopes nourished by the Alliance. Since that time it has carried on the intrigues referred to in the *'Fictitious Splits'*; in the Jura district of Switzerland, in Italy and in Spain it has not ceased to push forward its special programme in place of that of the International. The London Conference put an end to this misunderstanding with its resolutions on working-class policy and sectarian sections. The Alliance immediately went into action again. The Jura Federation, the stronghold of the Alliance in Switzerland, issued its Sonvillier circular against the General Council, in which the strong organization, the authority of the General Council and the Basle resolutions, both proposed and voted for by the very people who were signatories to the circular, were denounced as *authoritarian* – a definition that, apparently, sufficed to condemn them out of hand; in which mention was made of 'war, the open war that has broken out in our ranks'; in which it was demanded that the International should assume the form of an organization adapted, not to the struggle in hand, but to some vague ideal of a future society, etc. From this point onwards tactics changed. An order was issued. Wherever the Alliance had its branches, in Italy and particularly in Spain the authoritarian resolutions of the Basle Congress and the London Conference, as also the authoritarianism of the General Council, were subjected to the most violent attacks. Now there was nothing but talk of the autonomy of sections, free federated groups, anarchy, etc. This is quite understandable. The influence of the secret society within the International would naturally increase as the public organization of the International weakened. The most serious obstacle in the path of the Alliance was the General Council, and this was consequently the body which came in for the most bitter attacks . . .

Considering:

1   That the Alliance (the main organ of which is the Central Committee of the Jura Federation), founded and led by M. Bakunin, is a society hostile to the International, insofar as it aims at dominating or disorganizing the latter;

2   That as a consequence of the foregoing the International and the Alliance are incompatible.

The Congress resolves:

1   That M. Bakunin and all the present members of the Alliance of Socialist Democracy be expelled from the International Working Men's Association and be granted readmission to it only after a public renunciation of all connections with this secret society;

2 That the Jura Federation be expelled as such from the International.[21]

However, this carefully worked-out case was not helped by the Spanish delegates themselves, who said that although the secret Alliance had existed they were no longer members. Eventually the committee's report stated that the secret Alliance had existed and that Michael had himself been implicated in founding it. More seriously it added that 'Bakunin has used fraudulent means for the purpose of appropriating all or part of another man's wealth – which constitutes fraud – and further, in order to avoid fulfilling his engagements, has by himself or through his agents had recourse to menaces.'[22]

There is no doubt that this third resolution came about as a result of Marx's acquisition of Nechayev's letter and his presentation of this incriminating piece of evidence to the committee. As a result the committee recommended that Michael, Guillaume and Schweitzguébel should be expelled from the International, the last two on the basis that they were still members of a society called the Alliance, despite the fact that there was practically no evidence to show that this society existed.

Marx had in fact appeared before the committee at a very late stage of its sitting and had produced the Nechayev letter. Had he not done so it is quite possible that the committee would have come to no serious conclusion and Michael would have remained within the International, but Marx was determined to remove Michael at any cost – even if he had to stoop to such underhand methods to achieve his objective.

With commendable resilience the Bakuninists refused to be daunted by this undoubted blow. On 15 September 1872 a Bakuninist conference was held at Saint-Imier in the Jura and was attended by the four Spanish delegates, five Italians, three French refugees, Guillaume, Schweitzguébel and of course Bakunin. Immediately the Hague decision was rejected and the Bakuninists formed themselves into a free union of federations within the International which would be controlled by friendship and mutuality rather than the autocratic General Council. The 'Anarchist' International then pledged themselves to the destruction of all political power by the proletariat. Michael, however, had little involvement with this new group. He was in fact mostly concerned with the serious slur that had been cast upon his reputation. There had been many attempts in the past to tarnish his image, but this attempt was the most serious because it carried with it the added weight of being 'official'. On 4 October Michael's Russian friends sent the following letter to the journal *Liberté* in Brussels (which had published the Hague Congress resolutions) and to the organ of the Fédération Jurassienne:

4 October 1872   Geneva and Zurich

They have dared to accuse our friend Michael Bakunin of fraud and blackmail. We do not deem it necessary or opportune to discuss the alleged facts on which these strange accusations against our friend and compatriot are based. The facts are well known in all details and we will make it our duty to establish the truth as soon as possible. Now we are prevented from so doing by the unfortunate situation of another compatriot [Nechayev] who is not our friend, but whose persecution at this very moment by the Russian Government renders him sacred to us. Mr Marx, whose cleverness we do not, like others, question, has this time at least shown very bad judgment. Honest hearts in all lands will doubtless beat with indignation and disgust at so shameful a conspiracy and so flagrant a violation of the most elementary principles of justice. As to Russia, we can assure Mr Marx that all his manœuvres will inevitably end in failure. Bakunin is too well esteemed and known there for calumny to touch him.

Signed: Nicholas Ogarev, Bartholomy Zaitsev, Vladimir Ozerov, Armand Ross, Vladimir Holstein, Zemphiri Ralli, Alexander Oelsnitz, Valerian Smirnov.[23]

Not content to let the matter rest there, Michael then proceeded to deal with the charge that he had used the Bahkmetiev fund for his own purposes. He wrote to Ogarev, begging him to sign an enclosed draft statement to the effect that he, Ogarev, had given the fund directly to Nechayev, that Michael had not been there when it was handed over (which was totally untrue) and that no part of the fund had come into Michael's possession. But Ogarev was now extremely ill, and at his death Michael's draft document was found, signed, amongst his papers.

IV

Between October 1872 and September 1873 Michael made a last stand as a perpetrator of revolutionary activity. Unfortunately none of the projects with which he involved himself were successful and he achieved nothing but the sapping of his already failing strength. In November 1872 he became involved with the liberal Russian exile Peter Lavrov, who was anxious to start a similar journal to Herzen's *The Bell*. Lavrov tried to pay lip-service to radicalism as he and his supporters negotiated with Michael for contributors, but negotiations broke down as a compromise could not be reached. In April 1873, however, Lavrov did manage to publish the first number of his journal without any help from the Bakuninists. Rival groups of Bakuninists and Lavrovists developed in Zurich; and while Michael looked on from Locarno and attacked the Lavrovists in correspondence, a young Bakuninist physically attacked Lavrov's secretary, and the whole affair became a scandal. Eventually Michael held a summit conference with Lavrov and despite recriminations there was an uneasy truce.

In the spring of 1873 two of Michael's lieutenants, Armand Ross and Ralli, fell out and the unity of the Bakuninists slowly collapsed. In March 1873 Michael made a desperate attempt to close the breach by reorganizing what he chose to call 'The Russian branch of the International Brotherhood' but he was unable to reclaim Ralli's loyalty. In August 1873 Oelsnitz and Ralli asked Michael to choose between them and Ross, and when Michael refused to disown Ross, Ralli formed a separate but ideologically identical revolutionary group called the Revolutionary Commune of Russian Anarchists. Michael was furious at being cut out and further bitter debate took place, but to no avail. Most of Michael's Russian supporters in Zurich joined the new group and, having been so sweepingly superseded, Michael's revolutionary career was finished.

Michael was now sixty, physically broken and suffering from a severe persecution-complex. Vogt, who had unsuccessfully been trying to help him medically for some years, now found himself trying to assist him psychiatrically. Michael was gripped by the old terror of being handed over to the Russians by the Swiss and was desperately anxious to gain Swiss nationality as a protection against this eventuality. Despite the fact that he still retained a strong following in Spain and Italy, he therefore decided to remain in Locarno and to set up a new and uncharacteristic policy of non-involvement.

In September 1873 Michael's new-found retirement was shattered by Engels and Lafargue, who anonymously issued a pamphlet entitled *L'Alliance de la démocratie socialiste et l'association internationale de travailleurs*. In it they defended their decision to expel Michael from the International. The pamphlet was published by the *Journal de Genève* on 19 September, along with some highly damaging extracts from *How the Revolutionary Question Presents Itself* – a pamphlet written by Michael in the disastrous Nechayev era. On 26 September Michael wrote a reply, attacking Marx for his constant and slanderous persecution. He concluded on a weary, wistful note, citing his age and infirmities as his reason for abandoning all further revolutionary activity: 'Let other and younger men take up the work. For myself, I feel neither the strength nor, perhaps, the confidence which are required to go on rolling Sisyphus's stone against the triumphant forces of reaction . . . Henceforth I shall trouble no man's repose; and I ask, in my turn, to be left in peace.'[24]

Most of his friends and enemies in Switzerland, however, took this to be a cover for further revolutionary activities. It was impossible for anyone to believe that at last Michael Bakunin had laid down arms. In order to underline his retirement, therefore, Michael wrote a letter of resignation to the Fédération Jurassienne.

Michael's career was at an end, but it is an ironic fact that Marx's manœuvres had reverberated against him and in the same year the International was destined to change its form to the one advocated by Michael. Early in 1873 the Italian, French, Belgian, Spanish and American sections had endorsed the resolutions of the Saint-Imier Congress as had the Jura Federation, and the English Federation refused to accept the resolutions of the Hague Congress. However, the final disaster for Marx occurred at the Geneva Congress of the International in September 1873, for the Congress proceeded to revise the statutes and dissolve the General Council. Article 3 of the new statutes stated, 'The federations and sections comprising the International each reclaims its complete autonomy, the right to organize itself as it sees fit, to administer its own affairs without any outside interference, and to determine the best and most efficient means for the emancipation of labour.'[25]

V

In October 1873 Michael began a campaign on a more domestic level as he attempted to buy a house, mainly in order to acquire Swiss citizenship. By a fortunate chance Carlo Cafiero had recently inherited a large amount of money from his rich merchant father and he agreed to provide the capital required and register the house under Michael's name. The house would also serve as a clandestine meeting-place for revolutionaries.

Michael therefore proceeded to purchase a property near Locarno named Baronata, but as the building was not ideal for their purpose Michael and Cafiero decided to build a new house in the grounds. Nabruzzi, an Italian revolutionary, was put in charge of the construction and lost no time in moving in with his family and friends. Nabruzzi and Michael then settled down to spend Cafiero's fortune on Baronata. They tried to turn it into a self-supporting commune and spent thousands of francs on the most amazingly unpractical purchases, but at this stage even Cafiero was quite happy, believing his resources to be limitless.

To complete the family atmosphere, Michael wanted Antonia and her three children (she had recently given birth to another in Siberia) to join him. Using more of Cafiero's money and implying to Antonia that the money was his own share of the family estates, Michael persuaded her to return to Italy. She set out in the spring of 1874, together with her children, her parents and her married sister.

Cafiero, meanwhile, had also married and he and his wife arrived at Baronata at the beginning of July 1874, Antonia and her entourage following later in the month. Ross also arrived and Baronata became a crowded and very expensive operation indeed. Unfortunately rumours were beginning to circulate over the way Michael was bleeding his disciple, and they soon reached Antonia's ears. Michael asked Cafiero to tell Antonia that the rumours were unfounded but unfortunately Cafiero had just discovered that his resources were not limitless after all and that he had wasted his entire fortune. He turned on Michael bitterly and Michael was forced to sign over Baronata to him.

Desperately Michael decided that he could not face telling Antonia the truth, so he resolved to join an uprising in Bologna as a way of dying nobly. Once again he deceived Antonia, telling her he was visiting friends in Zurich, and set off for Italy with Ross. Pausing at Splügen he wrote down the true story of Baronata for Antonia, and posted it to a friend who was to pass the information to Antonia via Cafiero. Preparing for a noble death with great panache, Michael then wrote to Guillaume and told him that he did not expect to leave the insurrection alive.

On 30 July 1874 Michael and Ross reached Bologna, where they quarrelled and split up. Michael spent a week in lodgings under the pseudonym 'Tamburini' and was soon involved in the plans for the insurrection, which was to begin on the night of 7 August. The revolutionaries were to meet at two points outside the city walls, where they would be joined by other Italian revolutionaries and together would march on Bologna and capture the city.

Unfortunately, owing to the arrest of one of the chief revolutionaries and a shortage of numbers, the revolutionaries took fright and went home. Michael contemplated suicide, but was dissuaded and smuggled out disguised as an ancient country priest with a basket of eggs. In this undignified way he turned his back on an honourable death and returned to Splügen. Meanwhile at Baronata Cafiero had decided not to give Antonia Michael's letter. Unfortunately, however, Antonia was disliked by Michael's revolutionary associates at Baronata because of her noninvolvement with revolution and cold personality, and eventually Ross took it upon himself to tell her the unpalatable truth. She was at first unbelieving and then deeply shocked and hurt. A few days later she left Baronata and moved down to Arona in Italy.

Michael, meanwhile, was stranded at Splügen without any money and his desperate appeals to Baronata went unheeded. Eventually Antonia, still anxious about her husband's welfare in spite of his irresponsibility and their unorthodox relationship, sent some friends to find him, but he seemed befuddled, was totally unable to take decisions, and could only concentrate on the hope that Cafiero would send him some money.

On 25 August 1874 Ross condescendingly sent him two hundred francs and also included a message from Cafiero agreeing to meet him at Sierre in Valais. Michael took a long time to reach Sierre and pathetically waited for them at the nearby spa of Saxon-les-Bains, whiling away his time by gambling at the casino. Meanwhile Cafiero and Ross had broken their journey to acquaint Guillaume with Michael's scandalous behaviour over Baronata and Antonia. Their meeting was successful, for Guillaume also condemned Michael. Eventually they arrived at Sierre, and frigidly offered to lend him money which had to be paid back with interest and be backed by a guarantor.

Antonia had now moved to Lugano. She had already received countless letters from Michael, but she was very unsure about living with him again. However, in September 1874 she relented and asked him to join her. Broken, his mind wandering, sometimes filled with feverish plans and sometimes with despair, Michael gratefully returned to his much neglected wife.

On the way he saw Cafiero, Ross and Guillaume at Neuchâtel. Cold, unfriendly and censorious, they offered him three hundred francs a month, but although it was extremely humiliating money was money, and Michael was loath to refuse it. He would rather have accepted Cafiero's original offer of a loan, but already his sister-in-law had refused to act as guarantor. They parted without any warmth and Michael realized that he had even lost the friendship of one of his most ardent supporters, Guillaume. Pausing only to pick up a deaf-aid from Adolf Vogt in Berne, Michael arrived in Lugano on 7 October 1874. He had come home to die, and the warmth of his reception convinced him that Antonia was ready to minister over the final years of his life.

VI

Once Michael was back with Antonia in Lugano he began to relax and a vestige of his sense of humour and optimism returned, though they were pale shadows of their former selves. He dismissed Cafiero and Ross from his mind, trying to draw a veil over his humiliation. However, Antonia, although kind, was far from stimulating, and so Michael encouraged a new circle of friends of whom the most important was Arthur Arnoud, who had fled from the Paris Commune. He also found disciples in a group of Italian working men who admired him and also cared for his welfare. The way in which he spent his time is described by Arnoud as follows:

> He would rise soon after eight and betake himself to a café on the principal square of the town. Here he would spend the morning breakfasting, reading the newspapers, writing letters and meeting his friends. When he had no money he would obtain what he needed on credit, or even borrow from the proprietress, though when his debts rose too high, he would sometimes be obliged to transfer his patronage to another café. At two o'clock he returned home to lunch, bringing with him, if he had money or could obtain credit, cakes or sweetmeats for the children. From four to eight o'clock he slept. Then he would appear in Antonia's drawing room and regale her guests with stories of his past exploits. At midnight he retired, and would write or read half the night, ready to begin the same programme again on the morrow. He normally slept, fully dressed, on a plank or camp bed; and it was rumoured that the famous grey cap, in which he always appeared in public, never left his head.[26]

Despite the reminiscences of his revolutionary past Michael had no appetite for plunging himself once again into the active political scene, although Garibaldi became more reactionary day by day in Italy and the monarchy was re-established in Spain. However, he did develop an obsessive hatred towards the Church which even overtook his hatred of the State.

Money continued to be a pressing problem. Michael was still convinced that Cafiero would extend a loan somehow, reasoning that this would be a marginally honourable transaction, but as usual his chief hope was that he would receive his inheritance from Premukhino. By the end of 1874 Michael became more and more optimistic over his share of the estates and this example of eternal optimism proved that despite old age and broken health he was still very much his old self. In fact, he was so certain that he would soon receive his portion of the estates that in February 1875 he purchased a large and splendid villa near Lugano called the Villa Bresso.

In March 1875 he wrote a letter to his brothers urging them not just to release the money but also to visit him. An extract from his letter reads as follows:

> Many, many memories would come to life if we met – are we never to meet again? Yes, I want to see you all, to embrace you all with warm, brotherly love – only come . . . I invite not only all of you, but my unknown nephews and nieces – all who come will be welcome. But most of all, *you* must come, Paul and Alexis and Nicholas, you can advise me about the arrangement of the house and garden. I want to make here a little kingdom of heaven – the soil and climate, everything is favourable. There will be a mass of fruit and vegetables and flowers, and we will revive the memory of our father's house.[27]

Michael intended to cultivate and administer the Villa Bresso in the same way as Baronata, but unfortunately the inheritance was slow in coming and when at last he did hear from Premukhino it turned out to be much less than he expected and payable only in instalments over the next two years.

In December 1875 Michael moved into the Villa Bresso. His health had deteriorated still further. He suffered from loss of memory, dropsy, incontinence, deafness, asthma and heart trouble. Local doctors and even specialists could do little to help him, and he had to be dressed and undressed by two of his working-men friends. Nevertheless he retained a certain vigour of mind and speech and there were even reconciliations with Ross and Cafiero. In the spring of 1876 he acquired a last disciple – a young Russian student named Alexandra Weber. It was she who gave him the necessary companionship and stimulation during his last months, for Antonia was distant and uninterested. He played with the children, but received his guests alone in his room, where

> on a long table by the door there would be a samovar and tea service, continually in use; a little heap of tobacco to be rolled into cigarettes; an inkpot standing on an open newspaper; fragments of children's toys and pieces of chocolate. Two other tables and many parts of the floor were piled high with newspapers of many countries and in many languages, manuscripts, and papers of every kind; and medicine bottles were scattered and half buried among them. The newspapers often overflowed on to the bed – a plain iron frame covered with a woollen rug and scarcely broad enough to accommodate the veteran's massive form, under which it creaked and trembled as he moved. Alexandra Weber noticed with indignation that in the room reserved for Gambuzzi, there was a bed with a soft mattress, linen sheets and a silk counterpane.[28]

Michael suggested to his young disciple Alexandra that he would dictate his memoirs to her, but little came of it. In the main he reminisced about the past and Alexandra Weber was able to remind him of the Russian countryside which was so dear to his heart.

Suddenly his peace was rudely shattered by the return of his sister-in-law from Premukhino with a balance of 7,000 roubles which was all his family would allow him in respect of his share of the estates, taking into account that they had already sent him 1,000 roubles a few months before. As a result the villa was seized by Michael's debtors and arrangements were made to move to Gambuzzi in Naples. In order to receive formal permission for the old revolutionary to live in Italy, Michael had to write to the Minister of the Interior of the Italian Government, assuring him that he would not engage in any revolutionary activity. In June 1876 Antonia left for Italy to present this petition, and a few days later Michael went to Berne to see Adolf Vogt about his medical condition. Vogt immediately had him admitted to hospital, where the Reichels visited him and gave him considerable comfort.

There could have been little doubt in his own mind and in the minds of his friends that he would not recover, and as he lay dying it is probable that his thoughts were with Premukhino. Not with the recent Premukhino out of which he had only hoped to gain money, or with the bleak and unfamiliar Premukhino that he had visited on his way to Siberian exile, but the Premukhino of his youth with the portrait of Catherine the Great, the old grandfather clock in the dining-room, the tapestry upholstery on the chairs, the beloved landscape outside, the hedgerows, the cranes, Mytnits wood, the fire that was lit in that wood and the way the dying Lyubov had come in a carriage to watch it, the river to which Alexander had written his poem. 'Everything around us breathed a happiness such as is difficult to find on earth,' Paul had written of the Bakunin childhood, and Michael had never found such a profound happiness again. A flash of that kind of happiness may have returned in his triumphs, during revolutionary action, in some of his most emotive relationships – especially perhaps with Nechayev – but in the main Michael had sought for but never found the old Premukhino happiness that, in his loneliness, he had built into a sacred memory that was not entirely faithful to reality. No matter how vital a role he had played in the revolutionary movement and no matter how great his importance as the mainspring of anarchism, Michael Bakunin was broken, lonely and disillusioned. All that remained to those around him were dwindling flashes of the old fire, and all that remained inside him was jumbled memory.

On 1 July 1876 at midday Michael Bakunin died. The funeral was held on Monday, 3 July. It was comparatively small and was attended by representatives of some divisions of the Swiss International and other friends. Guillaume, who was also there despite his latter-day censoriousness, burst into tears during his formal speech. Antonia came to Berne a few days after the funeral and with the exception of Reichel's wife Maria was ostracized by Michael's friends. Their ostracism was unfair, for she had tried first as a wife and then as a housekeeper to see to Michael's well-being. It was only when it became increasingly obvious that he had never cared – and never would care – for her that she began to give up. Perhaps even Antonia, in her naive and withdrawn way, had begun to realize that Michael was totally absorbed in the struggle to make the unobtainable obtainable. To him what was there was not important – or was to be demolished – for in Michael's view it was only when the demolition of what existed was complete that true anarchism could really take place.

PART NINE

Bakuninism: 1876–1974

I

It is an ironic fact that as Michael's colourful life was drawing to a close in a welter of ill-health and failure, the ideas which he had defended so vigorously were at last taking a more concrete shape and finding a considerably wider following.

In the same year that Michael died James Guillaume published an essay entitled *On Building the New Social Order* in which he out-lined proposals for the reorganization of society after the revolution had taken place. Michael himself had been too involved in the practical problems of organizing the overthrow of the existing order to write fully on this subject himself, but there is little doubt that Guillaume was expressing Michael's known feelings when he wrote this essay.

Taken as a whole, *On Building the New Social Order* is a curious mixture of impractical idealism and constructive ideas that were far in advance of their time. Above all it proves that the anarchists did have a positive policy of administration and did not intend to substitute total chaos for total authoritarianism. Initially, the revolu-tion, as seen by the Bakuninists, would be a destructive force. The existing institutions would not be modified but would be completely demolished. The Government, the Church, the courts, the army, the banks and the schools would all immediately disappear and the workers would take over all capital and production. Land would be taken from the Church, from the aristocracy and from the bour-geoisie and given to landless peasants, while landowning peasants would have their holdings left untouched, untaxed and unmortgaged.

No new central administration would take up the reins of government. Common ownership and co-operative cultivation of land, communal selling of produce and elected commune administration would characterize agricultural communities, whilst the industrial communities would be divided into three categories:

1 Small and individual industries such as tailoring or shoe-making where private ownership was permissible;
2 Small-scale industries such as foundries, workshops and printing-plants where collective ownership was essential;
3 Large industries where big-scale production was in progress and where collective ownership was equally essential.

Society would be composed of federated communes and within these the public services would be administered as follows:

Housing would be the property of the commune and would be apportioned according to need. Housing construction would be a post-revolutionary priority and would be carried out at the commune's expense. Guillaume somewhat idealistically points out that

> while awaiting new construction people will have to be patient and do the best they can with the existing facilities. The commune will, as we have said, attend to the most pressing needs of the poorest families, relocating them in the vast palaces of the rich; and as to the rest of the people, we believe that revolutionary enthusiasm will stimulate and inspire them with the spirit of generosity and self-sacrifice, and that they will be glad to endure for a little longer the discomforts of poor housing; nor will they be inclined to quarrel with a neighbour who happens to have acquired a new apartment a little sooner. In a reasonably short time, thanks to the prodigious efforts of the building workers powerfully stimulated by the demand for new housing, there will be plenty of housing for all and everyone will be sure to find satisfactory accommodation.[1]

Each commune would begin a Bank of Exchange in which spare commodities would be placed. These would then be exchanged throughout the federations at a previously established exchange rate. Communal markets would be set up for vital and perishable foods and goods, a general commune warehouse would cater for the export market, and the Bank of Exchange would issue vouchers of the same value as goods received. Demand would be carefully studied (so the Bank of Exchange did not itself risk facing bankruptcy), non-exchangeable goods would still be valued by voucher and priced in advance, and a steady export-import scheme would be devised in exchanging goods, food and materials with other communes.

Free distribution of essentials such as bread, meat and dairy products would be immediately instigated (Guillaume listed wine as another essential commodity), and a statistical commission would take over the recording of births and deaths from the now demolished State departments. Marriage would be a personal union and would not require official sanction, medical services would be free of charge, and material well-being, it was believed, would eliminate social crime. A communal police force would, however, be established and every able-bodied man or woman would staff it in shifts, to ensure all-encompassing security and personal protection. Criminals, rare as they were hoped to be in the anarchist society, would be treated 'like the sick and the deranged; the problem of crime which today gives so many jobs to judges, jailers and police will lose its social importance and become simply a chapter in medical history.'[2]

Education was analysed in some detail. Essentially it was society and not the child's parents who were responsible for his or her welfare, and members of the commune (not specifically designated teachers) would teach the child their own abilities and skills. There would be two stages in development.

1   *Five to eleven*   Development of the physical faculties.
2   *Twelve to sixteen*   Development of the intellect and acquiring of a craft or trade.

The classroom would be abolished and the work and play of a child's life would be organized by the child. They might well themselves choose a lay teacher, the number of lay teachers would increase in the second educational division, and working productivity would be developed hand-in-hand with intellectual learning.

Guillaume states that

We do not claim that the child should be treated as an adult, that all his caprices should be respected, that when his childish will stubbornly flouts the elementary rules of science and common sense we should avoid making him feel that he is wrong. We say, on the contrary, that the child must be trained and guided, but that the direction of his first years must not be exclusively exercised by his parents, who are all too often incompetent and who generally abuse their authority. The aim of education is to develop the latent capacities of the child to the fullest possible extent and enable him to take care of himself as quickly as possible. It is painfully evident that authoritarianism is incompatible with an enlightened system of education. If the relations of father to son are no longer those of master to slave but those of teacher to student, of an older to a much younger friend, do you think that the reciprocal affection of parents and children would thereby be impaired? On the contrary, when intimate relations of these sorts cease, do not the discords so characteristic of modern families begin? Is not the family disintegrating into bitter frictions largely because of the tyranny exercised by parents over their children?

No one can therefore justly claim that a free and regenerated society will destroy the family. In such a society the father, the mother and the children will learn to love each other and to respect their mutual rights; at the same time their love will be enriched as it transcends the narrow limits of family affection, thereby achieving a wider and nobler love: the love of the great human family.[3]

It was hoped that eventually the anarchistic society would broaden into regional corporative federations and that a federated network of producers and consumers would cover the country in question. A general congress of the corporative federations would be initiated and a congress-elected bureau would link the federations. Needless to say, none of this administrative machinery would be allowed to develop along authoritarian lines.

Guillaume concludes his essay by pointing out that

It goes without saying that artificial frontiers created by the present governments will be swept away by the Revolution. The communes will freely unite and organize themselves in accordance with their economic interests, their language affinities and their geographic circumstances. And in certain countries like Italy and Spain, too vast for a single agglomeration of communes and divided by nature into many distinct regions, there will probably be established not one but many federations of communes. This will not be a rupture of unity, a return to the old fragmentation of petty, isolated and warring political states. These diverse federations of communes, while maintaining their identity, will not be isolated. United by their intertwining interests, they will conclude a pact of solidarity, and this voluntary unity founded on common aims and common needs, on a constant exchange of informal, friendly contacts, will be much more intimate and much stronger than the artificial political centralization imposed by violence and having no other motive than the exploitation of peoples for the profit of privileged classes.[4]

II

As has been mentioned previously, Michael's anti-authoritarian views as opposed to Marx's statism had been endorsed by many sections of the International before his death and for some years afterwards his influence was very clearly at work, particularly in Spain, Italy and Switzerland.

The anarchist movement in Spain was not only the most persistent anarchist movement in the world but, owing to the fact that the economy was particularly backward, had the most favourable social environment for its growth. It was, of course, Michael's follower Giuseppe Fanelli who had done much to organize Spanish anarchism. Despite the doubts of many historians it is certainly possible that some of Michael's beloved secret societies had, in fact, emerged in Spain. Either way, however, it was Fanelli who had started the first Spanish group of the International in 1868 and by the Congress of Cordoba in 1872 it had a membership of over 25,000. By 1874 the membership had swelled to 50,000, but on 9 January 1874 the International was outlawed in Spain, although it continued to exist underground for the next seven years. During the earlier part of this period Michael's views were fully accepted by the Spanish anarchists, but at the 1870 Anarchist Conference in Barcelona it was decided that Spanish anarchism should be organized in the same way as labour groups and therefore the local craft unions should be used as the central anarchist core. These unions in turn would unite into local federations, headed by the Spanish Federal Committee. The Bakuninists saw this body as the main destructive weapon against the State, but as a result of the bureaucratic insecurity following the Paris Commune the Federation was made illegal and revolutionary anarchistic activities went underground. When the Federation was eventually allowed to reopen membership was 3000 – a number that grew to 60,000 by 1882, with anarchism now being strongly centred in both the north-east and the south of Spain. But despite a promising second start the Federation split over the peasant uprising of 1882 and southern leaders then adopted the anarcho-communism which was advocated by Kropotkin. Anarcho-communism attacked Michael's views on anti-governmentalism and decentralization as unimaginative and egocentric and it was at this point that direct

Bakuninism began to wane. But anarchism persisted in various forms and during the Spanish Civil War Catalonia was briefly controlled by the anarchists from July to October 1936 when all factories and public services were controlled by the workers of Barcelona. George Orwell describes the atmosphere as follows:

The Anarchists were still in virtual control of Catalonia and the revolution was still in full swing. To anyone who had been there since the beginning it probably seemed even in December or January that the revolutionary period was ending; but when one came straight from England the aspect of Barcelona was something startling and overwhelming. It was the first time that I had ever been in a town where the working class was in the saddle. Practically every building of any size had been seized by the workers and was draped with red flags or with the red and black flag of the Anarchists; every wall was scrawled with the hammer and sickle and with the initials of the revolutionary parties; almost every church had been gutted and its images burnt. Churches here and there were being systematically demolished by gangs of workmen. Every shop and café had an inscription saying that it had been collectivized; even the bootblacks had been collectivized and their boxes painted red and black. Waiters and shopwalkers looked you in the face and treated you as an equal. Servile and even cere-monial forms of speech had temporarily disappeared. Nobody said 'Señor' or 'Don' or even 'Usted'; everyone called everyone else 'Comrade' and 'Thou', and said 'Salud!' instead of 'Buenos dias'. Tipping was forbidden by law; almost my first experience was receiving a lecture from a hotel manager for trying to tip a lift-boy. There were no private motor-cars, they had all been com-mandeered, and all the trams and taxis and much of the other transport were painted red and black. The revolutionary posters were everywhere, flaming from the walls in clean reds and blues that made the few remaining advertisements look like daubs of mud. Down the Ramblas, the wide central artery of the town where crowds of people streamed constantly to and fro, the loudspeakers were bellowing revolutionary songs all day and far into the night. And it was the aspect of the crowds that was the queerest thing of all. In outward appearance it was a town in which the wealthy classes had practically ceased to exist. Except for a small number of women and foreigners there were no 'well-dressed' people at all. Practically everyone wore rough working-class clothes, or blue overalls, or some variant of the militia uniform. All this was queer and moving. There was much in it that I did not understand, in some ways I did not even like it, but I recognized it immediately as a state of affairs worth fighting for. Also I believed that things were as they appeared, that this was really a workers' State and that the entire bourgeoisie had either fled, been killed, or voluntarily come over to the workers' side; I did not realize that great numbers of well-to-do bourgeois were simply lying low and disguising themselves as proletarians for the time being.[5]

The experiment, however, ended abruptly when the Communists (the Anarchists' former allies) and the Republican Government terminated the Anarchists' activities even before Franco emerged victorious. Nevertheless urban guerrilla groups continued to function, and in 1951 the Barcelona general strike typified a new, if halting wave of resistance to fascism. This was crushed, however, by the *Brigada Politico-Social*, though such libertarian activists as Francisco Sabate tenaciously and courageously kept alive the spirit of the Spanish Resistance. Sabate was eventually killed in 1960 during a gun battle with a large force of the *Guardia Civil*.

The anarchistic movement in Italy flourished for many years after Michael's death. Malatesta, of course, was a vital influence on Italian anarchism, but eventually revolutionary dictatorship triumphed largely because of the strong individualism that was so marked a factor of Italian revolutionary theory. In Switzerland, on the other hand, Michael's influence remained extremely strong, particularly among the faithful Jura watchmakers. Kropotkin was converted to anarchism by the watchmakers of the Jura and in his memoirs he makes the following assessment of Michael's influence in Switzerland:

Bakúnin was at that time in Locarno. I did not see him, and now regret it very much, because he was dead when I returned four years later to Switzerland. It was he who had helped the Jura friends to clear up their ideas and to formulate their aspirations; he who had inspired them with his powerful, burning, irresistible revolutionary enthusiasm. As soon as he saw that a small newspaper, which Guillaume began to edit in the Jura hills (at Locle) was sounding a new note of independent thought in the socialist movement, he came to Locle, talked for whole days and whole nights also to his new friends about the historical necessity of a new move in the direction of anarchy; he wrote for that paper a series of profound and brilliant articles on the historical progress of mankind towards freedom; he infused enthusiasm into his new friends, and he created that centre of propaganda, from which anarchism spread later on to other parts of Europe.

After he had moved to Locarno, – whence he started a similar movement in Italy, and, through his sympathetic and gifted emissary, Fanelli, also in Spain, – the work that he had begun in the Jura hills was continued independently by the Jurassiens themselves. The name of 'Michel' often recurred in their conversations, – not, however, as that of an absent chief whose opinions were law, but as that of a personal friend of whom every one spoke with love, in a spirit of comradeship. What struck me most was that Bakúnin's influence was felt much less as the influence of an intellectual authority than as the influence of a moral personality. In conversations about anarchism, or about the attitude of the federation, I never heard it said, 'Bakúnin says so', or 'Bakúnin thinks so', as if it settled the question. His writings and his sayings were not regarded as laws, – as is unfortunately often the case in political parties. In all such matters, in which intellect is the supreme judge, every one in discussion used his own arguments. Their general drift and tenor might have been suggested by Bakúnin, or Bakúnin might have borrowed them from his Jura friends; at any rate, in each individual the arguments retained their own individual character. I only once heard Bakúnin's name invoked as an authority in itself, and that impressed me so deeply that I even now remember the spot where the conversation took place and all the surroundings. Some young men were indulging in talk that was not very respectful towards the other sex, when one of the women who were present put a sudden stop to it by exclaiming: 'Pity that Michel is not here: he would put you in your place!' The colossal figure of the revolutionist who had given up everything for the sake of the revolution, and lived for it alone, borrowing from his conception of it the highest and the purest views of life, continued to inspire them.[6]

In France, however, despite the Paris Commune and the spread of syndicalism which was based on Michael's collectivist anarchism, the mutualist theories of Proudhon had predominance.

Curiously enough it was the Russian Revolution which gave anarchism a further burst of energy. Daniel Guérin comments that

This statement may at first surprise the reader, accustomed to think of the great revolutionary movement of October 1917 as the work and domain of the Bolsheviks alone. The Russian Revolution was, in fact, a great mass movement, a wave rising from the people which passed over and submerged ideological formations. It belonged to no one, unless to the people. In so far as it was an authentic revolution, taking its impulse from the bottom upward and spontaneously producing the organs of direct democracy, it presented all the characteristics of a social revolution with libertarian tendencies. However, the relative weakness of the Russian anarchists prevented them from exploiting situations which were exceptionally favourable to the triumph of their ideas.[7]

Up until 1917 only a few copies of some of Michael's writings had been secretly available in Russia and there was little interest in anarchism in revolutionary circles. The anarchist movement was therefore very small indeed, yet between 1918 and 1921 the anarchists came briefly into their own with the uprising of the Southern Ukrainian peasants led by the anarchist leader Nestor Makhno. Faced with both White and Red threats, his army was, however, completely dispersed by Trotsky in 1921.

The main value of the anarchist contribution to the February and October revolutions in Russia was that

(a) They contributed heavily towards housing socialization when the Bolsheviks were holding back on the issue;

(b) the Anarcho-Syndicalists were partly responsible for bringing about the workers' factory take-overs, often in pre-revolutionary months;

(c) they opposed the Constituent Assembly well before the Bolsheviks did.

'All power to the Soviets' was a cry that sprang from anarchist lips well before it sprang from Lenin's, and during the revolution each major city had an anarchist or anarcho-syndicalist group. There was massive distribution of anarchist literature, anarchist newspapers appeared in Moscow and Petrograd, and indeed so great did the danger of their influence become that the Bolsheviks, extremely uneasy, rapidly began to curtail all anarchist activities.

Their eventual defeat was made easier by a philosophical division in the anarchist ranks; one of the two main anarchist factions was driven underground while the other temporarily acceded to the regime by regarding its dictatorial attitude as one of 'historical necessity'.

Anarchist ideas migrated to America when the labour movement was at its weak period between the 1880s and the 1890s. For instance, the militant union, the Wobblies (the Industrial Workers of the

World), was heavily influenced by anarcho-syndicalism. However, Michael's influence was mainly felt in Mexico, in Cuba and in Argentina, where his theories were first transported in the 1870s. The Buenos Aires branch of the International was founded in 1872 but Nettlau describes it as 'good socialism, rather general, neither anarchistic nor . . . political nor authoritarian'.[8] In 1876, however, the Bakuninists founded the Centre for Workers' Propaganda and an anarchist newspaper, *El Descamisado*, begun publication. In 1897 *La Protesta Humana* was first published (by Dr John Creaghe from Sheffield, England) – a newspaper that still survives today, though in a rather different form. Over the years the Workers' Federation continued to be orientated towards anarchism, not on a national scale but rather in a few individual anarchistic groups. However, during General Perón's regime anarchism went underground, all trade unions were closed and the newspaper *La Protesta* was banned; after the fall of Perón the anarchist movement had withered away to a few small groups.

Anarchism in Uruguay was an extremely dynamic movement in the first quarter of the twentieth century and the Uruguayan Workers' Regional Federation originally adopted a Bakuninist collectivist policy. A leaflet, published by the F.A.U. (Federación Anarquista Uruguay), now defunct, which was anarcho-communist and essentially Bakuninist in policy, described Bakunin in the following terms:

> Bakunin correctly foresaw the risks of State centralism, but he did not outline clearly any intermediate or genuinely transitory solution for the suppression of all power once the period of construction of socialism-communism was complete. His choice between the despotic State and spontaneous freedom has not provided a practicable model in concrete historical situations. The solution to the problem of power during the post-insurrectional period must be looked for in concrete historical events.[9]

Today, when the centenary of Michael's death will be celebrated in less than three years' time, anarchism has again assumed importance. In 1959 Daniel Guérin published a collection of essays entitled 'Jeunesse du Socialisme Libertaire' which he dedicated to the 'youth of today'.

> I know that you turn your back on ideologies and 'isms', which have been made hollow by the failures of your elders. I know that you are deeply suspicious (and alas with much justification) about

everything connected with 'politics'. I know that the grand old men who thought about the problem of society in the nineteenth century seem old bores to you. I know that you are justly sceptical of 'socialism', which has been so often betrayed, so brazenly botched up by its supporters. In replies made to an inquiry by the magazine *Nouvelle Vague* you gave the answer: 'A socialist future is not desirable because of the absolute subordination of the individual to a political idea, to the State.'

You tell us that what puts you off about socialism is not the perspective of ending the oppression of man by man, it is 'the bureaucrats and the purges'.

In other words you would desire socialism if it were authentic. The majority of you have a very strong feeling against social injustice and there are many among you who are aware that 'capitalism is condemned'. Moreover, you are passionately attached to liberty and one of your spokesmen writes that 'French youth is more and more anarchist'. You are libertarian socialists without knowing it. In contrast to the out-of-date, bankrupt, authoritarian and totalitarian nature of Jacobin socialism, libertarian socialism bears the sign of youth. Not only because it is the secret of the future, the only possible rational and human substitute for an economic regime condemned by history, but also because it corresponds to the deepest, though often confused, aspirations of the youth of today. And without your agreement and participation it would be vain to try to reconstruct the world.

One of these young people wrote 'I think I shall see this civilization collapse in my lifetime'. It is my modest wish to live long enough to witness and take part in this gigantic clean-up with you, youth. I hope that the case against false socialism presented in this work may suggest to you a few of the materials with which you will build a more just and free society with a new enthusiasm from which scepticism has disappeared.[10]

In May 1968 Daniel Guérin had his wish and revolution broke out in France. It was a revolution after Michael Bakunin's own heart, because its direct action, its meeting of force by force and its policy of collectivity were all well within the framework of his philosophy. The leading spirit, of course, was the Franco-German Jewish anarchist, twenty-three-year-old Daniel Cohn-Bendit. Like Michael he was a remarkable orator and a distinctive libertarian. Unlike Michael he did not wish to be the actual leader and although he did in fact emerge as such he preferred to try and remain simply one of a revolutionary group. All authority was attacked and the theme of self-management was inspired by the example of the 1936 Spanish collectivization, although there was no opportunity to put this into practice.

In 1971, writing in *Anarchism Today*, Michael Lerner in his attack on 'Anarchism and the American Counter-Culture' pointed out that 'many of the young are moving ever closer to Bakunin's view than to the love tactics espoused a few years ago. For the espousal of a neo-anarchist world view by intelligent young people in the historical situation of the 1960s seemed *prima facie* even less likely than the emergence of the youth culture itself.' He went on to say that 'it remains true that historical anarchists such as Bakunin saw something akin to the sacred in the violent response of individuals to governmental oppression or dispossession, and this vision has returned in the counter-culture today'. In the same work James Joll expressed the opinion that

the acceptance of violence is characteristic of the 'counter-culture'; and there is no aspect of the revolutionary movement among the young which separates it more clearly from that of the liberal radicals of the previous generation. In philosophical terms, they are obsessed by what Herbert Marcuse calls 'the liberating function of negation'; and this is very easily transferred from the philosophical to the practical plane. This is perhaps why it is Bakunin among the classical anarchist thinkers who has most strongly captured the imagination of the contemporary revolutionaries.[11]

III

Whether he was behind the barricades of Dresden in 1848, deeply involved in the revolutionary conspiracies of Naples in the 1860s, or at the hoped-for initiation point of revolution in Lyons in 1870, Michael Bakunin was inevitably in the forefront of events. He was a universal revolutionist and a personal contradiction to his own philosophical creed. He loved to organize, to lead, to plot clandestinely and to have ultimate authority over his followers, yet he preached fraternalism and equality in a commune-like society. No one who came into contact with him could fail to react forcibly one way or the other, and the result had to be either love or hate.

In Michael's own words, religion was 'an evil necessary to the State'.[12] Both establishments were an unpalatable autocracy that interfered with the essential freedom of man. Yet inevitably, Michael's great mistake was his genuine belief in the essential goodness of mankind and man's ability to live compatibly with each other.

Stuart Christie, who with Albert Meltzer wrote *The Floodgate of Anarchy*, says that without Bakunin 'anarchism would have existed, but perhaps not an anarchist movement as such. Without such a movement Kropotkin would inevitably have identified with the whole working-class movement; nobody else was capable of making a clear-cut break to distinguish between Marxism, social democracy and anarchism.'[13]

Michael once confided in a letter to Herzen that he did not have the 'talent of the literary architect'. After he had built the house, someone was required to 'arrange the windows and doors in a proper manner'. No one would dispute this, but it is his example of personal involvement as well as his writings that have won him and his ideas increasing popularity and influence among contemporary revolutionaries.

Moreover, his frequently expressed opinion that the result of Marx's authoritarian revolution would be a highly authoritarian society is freely endorsed by today's revolutionaries who are looking carefully at Michael's blueprint for revolution and a new structure for society. As a result, therefore, at the philosophical head of this new movement stands Michael Bakunin: contradictory, erratic, given to wild enthusiasms, insolvent, lonely, unpredictable, creatively destructive – and essentially the father of Anarchism.

Notes

PREFACE

 1. Florence Elliott, *A Dictionary of Politics*.
 2. Peter A. Kropotkin, 'Anarchism', *Encyclopaedia Britannica*, 11th Edition (New York, 1910), I, p. 914.
 3. *Anarchism Today*, ed. Apter and Joll, pp. 1–2.
 4. Bert F. Hoselitz in his Introduction to *The Political Philosophy of Bakunin* by G. P. Maximoff.

PART ONE: PREMUKHINO 1814–40

 1. P. 28.
 2. A Nikitenko, *Zapiski i Dnevnik, 1804–1877* (Notes and Diary, 1804–1877).
 3. Guy A. Aldred, *Bakunin*, p. 10.
 4. E. Lampert, *Studies in Rebellion*, p. 5.
 5. E. H. Carr, *Michael Bakunin*, p. 18.
 6. Lampert, *Studies in Rebellion*, p. 38.
 7. A. Herzen, *My Past and Thoughts*, pp. 398–400.
 8. Turgenev, *Vestnik Europy*, January 1899.
 9. Herzen, *My Past and Thoughts*, II, p. 397.
 10. Carr, *Michael Bakunin*, p. 25.
 11. Op. cit., pp. 25–6.
 12. Op. cit., p. 26.
 13. Op. cit., p. 29.
 14. P. Annenkov, 'Reminiscences and Critical Essays'.
 15. Lampert, *Studies in Rebellion*, p. 65.
 16. Ibid.
 17. Carr, *Michael Bakunin*, p. 46.
 18. Lampert, *Studies in Rebellion*, p. 69.
 19. Op. cit., p. 70.
 20. Op. cit., p. 72.
 21. Ibid.
 22. Ibid.
 23. In the *Polar Star*, 1855.

24. Carr, *Michael Bakunin*, pp. 81–2.

PART TWO: ACADEMY OF UNREST 1840–8

1. Bakunin, *Oeuvres*, vol. III, pp. 389–90.
2. *Roots of Revolution. A History of the Populist and Socialist Movements in Nineteenth-Century Russia*, p. 43.
3. Carr, *Michael Bakunin*, p. 105.
4. Karl Löwith, *From Hegel to Nietzsche*, p. 115.
5. Op. cit., pp. 118–19.
6. Lampert, *Studies in Rebellion*, pp. 121–2.
7. Turgenev, *Collected Works*, vol. xi, p. 49.
8. Lampert, *Studies in Rebellion*, pp. 122–3.
9.
10. Löwith, *From Hegel to Nietzsche*, pp. 85–6.
11. Op. cit., p. 86.
12. *Bakunin on Anarchy*, ed. Sam Dolgoff, pp. 56–7.
13. Op. cit., p. 57.
14. Carr, *Michael Bakunin*, p. 116.
15. Bakunin, *Works*, ed. Steklov, III, p. 227.
16. Isaiah Berlin, *Karl Marx*, pp. 85–6.
17. Op. cit., p. 113.
18. *Bakunin on Anarchy*, ed. Dolgoff, p. 26.
19. Ibid.
20. Op. cit., p. 25.
21. *My Past and Thoughts*, vol. II, p. 961.
22. Op. cit., p. 958.
23. Lampert, *Studies in Rebellion*, p. 95.
24. Ibid.
25. Op. cit., p. 96.
26. Op. cit., p. 97.
27. *Bakunin on Anarchy*, ed. Dolgoff, p. 59.
28. Op. cit., pp. 59–60.
29. Op. cit., p. 60.
30. Wermer Blumenberg, *Karl Marx*, pp. 72–3.
31. *Bakunin on Anarchy*, ed. Dolgoff, p. 27.
32. J. Hampden Jackson, *Marx, Proudhon and European Socialism*, pp. 73–4.
33. Herzen, *My Past and Thoughts*, II, pp. 678–80.
34. George Woodcock, *Anarchism*, p. 142.
35. Carr, *Michael Bakunin*, p. 150.

PART THREE: SEEDS OF REVOLUTION 1848–51

1. *The Doctrine of Anarchism of Michael A. Bakunin*, p. 1.
2. Bakunin, *Works*, ed. Steklov, III, p. 151.
3. Aldred, *Bakunin*, p. 28.

4. Ibid.
5. *The Political Philosophy of Bakunin*, ed. Maximoff, p. 39.
6. Carr, *Michael Bakunin*, pp. 170–1.
7. *Bakunin on Anarchy*, ed. Dolgoff, p. 63.
8. Woodcock, *Anarchism*, p. 143.
9. *Bakunin on Anarchy*, ed. Dolgoff, p. 68.
10. Berlin, *Karl Marx*, p. 176.
11. Carr, *Michael Bakunin*, p. 184.
12. Aldred, *Bakunin*, pp. 31–2.
13. Carr, *Michael Bakunin*, p. 187.
14. Aldred, *Bakunin*, p. 33.
15. *Bakunin on Anarchy*, ed. Dolgoff, p. 31.

PART FOUR: PRISON AND EXILE 1851–61

1. Peter Kropotkin, *In Russian and French Prisons*, pp. 84–6.
2. Reproduced from Kropotkin, op. cit., p. 87.
3. Op. cit., pp. 92–6.
4. *Bakunin on Anarchy*, ed. Dolgoff, p. 70.
5. Op. cit., p. 69.
6. Aldred, *Bakunin*, p. 38.
7. Carr, *Michael Bakunin*, p. 220.
8. Op. cit., pp. 220–1
9. Carr, *Michael Bakunin*, p. 223.
10. *Michael Bakunin*, p. 234.
11. Herzen, *My Past and Thoughts*, III, p. 1351.

PART FIVE: SECOND WIND 1861–3

1. Herzen, *My Past and Thoughts*, III, pp. 1351–3.
2. Carr, *Michael Bakunin*, p. 239.
3. Herzen, *My Past and Thoughts*, III, pp. 1357–9.
4. *Bakunin on Anarchy*, ed. Dolgoff, p. 388.
5. Woodcock, *Anarchism*, p. 147.
6. Herzen, *My Past and Thoughts*, III, pp. 1309–10.
7. Carr, *Michael Bakunin*, p. 254.
8. Op. cit., p. 265.
9. Herzen, *My Past and Thoughts*, III, p. 1368.
10. Op. cit., pp. 1370–71.
11. Op. cit., p. 1373.
12. Op. cit., pp. 1382–3.
13. Carr, *Michael Bakunin*, p. 297.

PART SIX: INTERNATIONAL REVOLUTION 1863–9

1. Woodcock, *Anarchism*, p. 148.
2. Aldred, *Bakunin*, p. 52.

3. Ibid.
4. Carr, *Michael Bakunin*, p. 309.
5. *Bakunin on Anarchy*, ed. Dolgoff, p. 74.
6. Op. cit., pp. 76–8.
7. Op. cit., pp. 78–9.
8. Op. cit., pp. 80–81.
9. Op. cit., pp. 81–2.
10. Op. cit., p. 98.
11. Op. cit., p. 101.
12. Vyrubov, *Vestnik Evropy*, p. 54.
13. Carr, *Michael Bakunin*, p. 331.
14. *Bakunin on Anarchy*, ed. Dolgoff, p. 106.
15. Op. cit., pp. 106–7.
16. Carr, *Michael Bakunin*, p. 336.
17. Op. cit., p. 340.
18. Aldred, *Bakunin*, p. 45.
19. From an unpublished translation by Sam Dolgoff.
20. Ibid.
21. Woodcock, *Anarchism*, p. 154.
22. Carr, *Michael Bakunin*, p. 350.
23. Aldred, *Bakunin*, p. 54.
24. Ibid.
25. Op. cit., p. 55.

PART SEVEN: THE BATTLE WITH MARX 1869–70

1. *Bakunin on Anarchy*, ed. Dolgoff, pp. 163–4.
2. Nechayev, *The Catechism of the Revolutionist*, pp. 1–4.
3. From an unpublished translation by Sam Dolgoff.
4. Woodcock, *Anarchism*, pp. 158–9.
5. Carr, *Michael Bakunin*, pp. 364–5.
6. Aldred, *Bakunin*, p. 56.
7. Prawdin, *The Unmentionable Nechaev*, p. 44.
8. 'The Diary of Natalie Herzen', tr. Lydia Bott, *Encounter* (May 1970), p. 3.
9. Op. cit., p. 9.
10. Op. cit., p. 16.
11. Op. cit., p. 18.
12. From an unpublished translation by Sam Dolgoff.
13. 'Bakunin and Nechayev', *Encounter* (July 1972), p. 81.
14. Op. cit., p. 82.
15. Op. cit., p. 84.
16. Op. cit., p. 86.
17. 'Bakunin to Nechayev', *Encounter* (August 1972), p. 89.
18. Op. cit., p. 90.
19. Op. cit., p. 91.
20. Op. cit., p. 93.

21. Ibid.
22. Prawdin, *The Unmentionable Nechaev*, p. 54.
23. Op. cit., p. 81.
24. Op. cit., pp. 98–100.
25. Carr, *Michael Bakunin*, p. 393.

PART EIGHT: THE FINAL DISILLUSIONMENT 1870–6

1. *The Paris Commune of 1871*, ed. Eugene Schulkind, pp. 63–4.
2. *Bakunin on Anarchy*, ed. Dolgoff, pp. 178, 180–1.
3. Op. cit., pp. 183–4.
4. Op. cit., pp. 188–90.
5. Op. cit., pp. 195–6.
6. Carr, *Michael Bakunin*, p. 398.
7. *The Paris Commune of 1871*, ed. Schulkind, pp. 73–4.
8. Op. cit., pp. 70–2.
9. From an unpublished translation by Sam Dolgoff.
10. *Karl Marx, The Story of His Life*, p. 467.
11. Carr, *Michael Bakunin*, p. 408.
12. Op. cit., p. 409.
13. Berlin, *Karl Marx*, pp. 258–9.
14. *Bakunin on Anarchy*, ed. Dolgoff, pp. 263–4.
15. Carr, *Michael Bakunin*, p. 417.
16. *Documents of the First International*, V, pp. 360–1, 366–7, 368–70.
17. *Documents of the First International*, V, pp. 382, 385–7.
18. Carr, *Michael Bakunin*, p. 447.
19. Op. cit., p. 450.
20. *Documents of the First International*, V, p. 445.
21. *Documents of the First International*, V, pp. 505–7, 510, 512–13, 518.
22. Woodcock, *Anarchism*, p. 167.
23. *Bakunin on Anarchy*, ed. Dolgoff, p. 48.
24. Woodcock, *Anarchism*, p. 169.
25. *Bakunin on Anarchy*, ed. Dolgoff, p. 49.
26. Carr, *Michael Bakunin*, pp. 477–8.
27. Op. cit., p. 481.
28. Op. cit., p. 484.

PART NINE: BAKUNINISM 1876–1974

1. *Bakunin on Anarchy*, ed. Dolgoff, p. 365.
2. Op. cit., p. 372.
3. Op. cit., p. 375.
4. Op. cit., p. 379.
5. George Orwell, *Homage to Catalonia*, pp. 8–9.
6. Kropotkin, *Memoirs of a Revolutionist*, pp. 288–9.
7. Guérin, *Anarchism*, p. 82.

8. Max Nettlau, *Contribución a la Bibliografía Anarquista en América Latina hasta 1914*, ed. La Protesta, Buenos Aires.

9. *Anarchism Today*, ed. Apter and Joll, p. 208.

10. Guérin, *Anarchism*, pp. 155–6.

11. *Anarchism Today*, ed. Apter and Joll, p. 215.

12. God and the State.

13. In a letter to the author.

Bibliography

Aldred, Guy A.: *Bakunin* (Glasgow, 1940)

Annenkov, Paul: *Vospominanya i Kriticheskie Ocherki* ('Reminiscences and Critical Essays') (Petersburg, 1881)

Apter, David E. and Joll, James, eds: *Anarchism Today* (Macmillan, 1971)

Avrich, Paul: *The Russian Anarchists* (Princeton University Press, 1967)

Baldelli, Giovanni: *Social Anarchism* (Penguin, 1972)

Baldwin, Roger N., ed.: *Essential Writings of Karl Marx* (Panther, 1967)

Berkman, Alexander: *A.B.C. of Anarchism* (Freedom Press, 1942)

Berlin, Isaiah: *Karl Marx* (Oxford University Press, 1939)

Blumenberg, Werner: *Karl Marx* (N.L.B., 1972)

Braunthal, Julius: *History of the International 1864–1914* (Nelson, 1966)

Carr, E. H.: *The Bolshevik Revolution, 1917–1923* (Macmillan, 1953)

Carr, E. H.: *Michael Bakunin* (Macmillan, 1937)

Carr, E. H., ed.: *Bukharin and Preobrazhensky: The ABC of Communism* (Penguin, 1969)

Carr, E. H.: *The Romantic Exiles* (Penguin, 1949 and 1968)

Carr, E. H.: *Socialism in One Country, 1924–1926* (Macmillan, 1959)

Carter, April: *The Political Theory of Anarchism* (Routledge & Kegan Paul, 1971)

Caute, David, ed.: *Essential Writings of Karl Marx* (Panther, 1967)

Caute, David: *The Left in Europe* (World University Library, 1966)

Christie, Stuart and Meltzer, Albert: *The Floodgate of Anarchy* (Kahn and Averill, 1970)

Cleaver, Eldridge: *Post-Prison Writings and Speeches*, with an introduction by Robert Scheer (Cape, 1969)

Conquest, Robert: *Lenin* (Fontana, 1972)

Cranston, Maurice: 'A Dialogue on Anarchy' (B.B.C. Broadcast, October 1962)

Documents of the First International, Volume IV, 1870–1871 (Lawrence & Wishart)

Documents of the First International, Volume V, 1871–1872 (Lawrence & Wishart)

Dolgoff, Sam, ed.: *Bakunin on Anarchy*, with an introduction and commentary by Sam Dolgoff; preface by Paul Avrich (Alfred A. Knopf, New York, 1972)

Dostoyevsky, Fyodor: *The Possessed* (Penguin, 1953)

Elliott, Florence: *A Dictionary of Politics* (Penguin, 1957)

Engels, Frederick: *The Condition of the Working Class in England in 1844*, translated by Florence Kelley Wischnewetzky (London, 1892

Engels, Frederick: *Selected Writings*, edited with an introduction by W. O. Henderson (Penguin, 1967)

Feuer, Lewis S.: *Marx and Engels. Basic Writings on Politics and Philosophy* (Fontana, 1969)

Freedman, Robert, ed.: *Marx on Economics* (Pelican, 1962)

Gerassi, John, ed.: *Venceremos! The Speeches and Writings of Che Guevara* (Weidenfeld & Nicolson, 1968)

Gogol, Nikolai: *Dead Souls* (Penguin, 1961)

Guérin, Daniel: *Anarchism* (Monthly Review Press, 1972)

Hampden Jackson, J.: *Marx, Proudhon and European Socialism* (English Universities Press, 1967)

Herzen, Alexander: *My Past and Thoughts*, vols I–IV (Chatto & Windus, 1968)

Hook, Sidney: *From Hegel to Marx* (University of Michigan Press, 1962)

Horowitz, David: *Imperialism and Revolution* (Allen Lane, The Penguin Press, 1969)

Hyde, H. Montgomery: *Stalin* (Rupert Hart-Davis, 1971)

Jellinek, Frank: *The Paris Commune of 1871* (Victor Gollancz, 1937)

Joll, James: *The Anarchists* (Eyre and Spottiswoode, 1964)

Joll, James: *The Second International 1839–1914* (Weidenfeld & Nicolson, 1955)

Karol, K. S.: *Guerrillas in Power* (Cape, 1971)

Kedward, Roderick: *The Anarchists* (British Publishing Corporation, 1971)

Kropotkin, Peter: *In Russian and French Prisons* (Schocken Books, 1971)

Kropotkin, Peter: *Memoirs of a Revolutionist* (Dover Publications, 1971)

Lampert, E.: *Studies in Rebellion* (Routledge & Kegan Paul, 1957)

Lehning, Arthur: *Anarchisme et Marxisme dans la Révolution Russe* (Spartacus)

Lichtheim, George: *Marxism* (Routledge & Kegan Paul, 1961)

Lichtheim, George: *A Short History of Socialism* (Weidenfeld & Nicolson, 1970)

Löwith, Karl: *From Hegel to Nietzsche: the Revolution in Nineteenth-Century Thought*, translated by David E. Green (Constable, 1965)

MacIntyre, Alasdair: *Marxism and Christianity* (Duckworth, 1969)

Malcolm, X, written with the assistance of Alex Halley: *The Autobiography of Malcolm X* (Hutchinson, 1966)

Marcuse, Herbert: *An Essay on Liberation* (Allen Lane, The Penguin Press, 1969)

Marcuse, Herbert: *One Dimensional Man* (Routledge & Kegan Paul, 1964)

Marcuse, Herbert: *Soviet Marxism: A Critical Analysis* (Routledge & Kegan Paul, 1958)

Marx, Karl: *Selected Writings in Sociology and Social Philosophy* (Pelican, 1963)

Marx, Karl and Engels, Friedrich: *The Communist Manifesto* (1888)

Marx, Karl, Engels, Friedrich and Lenin, Vladimir: *Anarchism and Anarcho-Syndicalism* (Progress Publishers, Moscow, 1972)

Matthews, Herbert L.: *Castro* (Allen Lane, The Penguin Press, 1969)

Maximoff, G. P., ed.: *The Political Philosophy of Bakunin: Scientific Anarchism* (Collier-Macmillan, 1953)

Maximoff, G. P.: *Syndicalists in the Russian Revolution* (Direct Action Pamphlets No. 11)

McLellan, David: *Marx Before Marxism* (Macmillan, 1970)

Mills, C. Wright: *The Marxists* (Dell, 1962)

Nechayev, Sergei: *The Catechism of the Revolutionist* (Kropotkin's Light-house Publications, 1971)

Nettlau, Max: *Bakunin e l'Internazionale in Italia 1864–1872* (Geneva, 1928)

Orwell, George: *Homage to Catalonia* (Secker & Warburg, 1938)

Parkinson, C. Northcote: *Left Luggage* (John Murray, 1967)

Prawdin, Michael: *The Unmentionable Nechaev* (George Allen & Unwin, 1961)

Proudhon, P. J.: *What is Property?* (Dover Publications, 1970)

Pyziur, Eugene: *The Doctrine of Anarchism of Michael A. Bakunin* (Gateway, 1968)

Rahv, Philip: *The Other Dostoevsky* (The New York Review of Books, 20 April 1972)

Reznek, Samuel, ed.: *The Political and Social Theory of Michael Bakunin* (reprinted from *The American Political Science Review*, vol. XXI, no. 2, May 1927)

Schulkind, Eugene (ed.): *The Paris Commune of 1871* (Cape, 1972)

Shatz, Marshall S.: *The Essential Works of Anarchism* (Bantam, 1971)

Shub, David: *Lenin* (Pelican, 1966)

Tolstoy, Leo: *Anna Karenina* (New American Library, 1961)

Tolstoy, Leo: *Childhood, Boyhood, Youth* (Penguin, 1964)

Tolstoy, Leo: *The Death of Ivan Ilych and Other Stories* (Oxford University Press, 1935 and 1971)

Toryat, Henri: *Tolstoy* (Pelican Books, 1970)

Venturi, Franco: *Roots of Revolution. A History of the Populist and Socialist Movements in Nineteenth-Century Russia* (Groset, 1966)

Walter, Nicolas: *About Anarchism* (Freedom Press, 1969)

Woodcock, George: *Anarchism* (Pelican, 1963)

Index